WARS AND BATTLES OF
THE ROMAN REPUBLIC

WARS AND BATTLES OF
THE ROMAN REPUBLIC

753 BC–100 BC
The Bloody Road to Empire

PAUL CHRYSTAL

FONTHILL

For no one is so mad that they prefer war to peace:
in the one sons bury fathers; in the other fathers bury sons.

Herodotus 1, 87, 4

Fonthill Media Limited
Fonthill Media LLC
www.fonthillmedia.com
office@fonthillmedia.com

First published in the United Kingdom
and the United States of America 2015

British Library Cataloguing in Publication Data:
A catalogue record for this book is available from the British Library

ISBN 978-1-78155-305-3

Typeset in 10pt on 13pt Minion Pro
Printed and bound in England

CONTENTS

	About the Author	6
	Preface	7
1	War Before Rome	9
2	The Roman Way of War	18
3	Legal, Religious, and Social Aspects of Roman War	25
4	Early Roman Conflicts: Etruscans, Latins, and Sabines	30
5	Battles for Early Italy	40
6	War With the Gauls	48
7	The Conquest of Italy	54
8	The War Against Pyrrhus	66
9	The First Punic War	72
10	The Gauls and Illyria	84
11	The Second Punic War	87
12	Gaul, Macedonia, Greece, and Spain	110
13	The Third Punic War	123
14	Transalpine Gaul and the War Against Jugurtha	127
15	The Invasion from the North	131
	Epilogue	133
	Endnotes	139
	Maps	148
	Chronological List of Wars and Battles	154
	Glossary of Greek and Latin Terms	158
	Appendix 1: Typical Cursus Honorum *in the Second Century BC*	162
	Appendix 2: Roman Assemblies	163
	Appendix 3: The Seven Kings of Rome	164
	Illustrations and Credits	165
	Bibliography	167
	Index	173

About the Author

Paul Chrystal was educated at the Universities of Hull and Southampton, where he took degrees in Classics. He has been in medical publishing for thirty-five years, but now combines this with writing features for national newspapers and appearing regularly on BBC local radio and on the BBC World Service. He is the author of forty or so books on a wide range of subjects, including histories of York and other places in northern Britain, the Rowntree family, the social history of chocolate, the British infatuation with the cup of tea, classical literature, and classical social history. He is married, with three children, and lives in the Roman city of York.

E-mail: paul.chrystal@btinternet.com

Preface

Warfare in classical Rome is one of the most popular and published areas of ancient history. There are countless books and journal articles on every imaginable aspect of war in ancient Rome. So why add to the pile? What is so different about this book? *Wars and Battles of the Roman Republic* is no arid list of wars and battles, with endless exaggerated casualty figures and repetitive tactics. Each of the one hundred or so battles covered here is placed in its historical, political and social context: why was the battle fought, how was it fought, what was the outcome, and what happened next?

These victorious battles and wars are not described in isolation, but instead form part of an historical narrative that takes us from the foundation of Rome in 753 BC to the birth of Julius Caesar in 100 BC. I will describe the early wars leading to the conquest of the Italian peninsula, war with the Gauls, the war against Pyrrhus, the three wars against Carthage and the rise of the Roman navy, conflicts with Illyria, Gaul, Macedonia, Greece, Spain, Portugal, Jugurtha, and the invasion from the north. Along the way I will place each campaign in its military, social, and political context. No war or battle was ever fought in isolation—there is always a *casus belli* and a set of consequences.

This book opens with four detailed chapters covering topics fundamental to the study of war in classical antiquity: warfare in civilisations and cultures before Rome; the Roman war machine; legal, religious, and social aspects of Roman war; and early Roman conflicts against Etruscans, Latins, and Sabines. Roman battles were most often fought to defend Rome and Roman territory; this in turn triggered expansionism and imperialism. There was always an undercurrent of social unrest at home, related to the power of the plebeians, the Conflict of the Orders, or to land ownership, distribution, and settlement.

In each battle I also try to bring out individual points of military interest, highlighting the first or last appearance or use of one thing or another, or describing the significance of a certain action and its consequences. I will cover the use of the elephant as a weapon of war; the deployment of incendiaries; psychological warfare; 'friendly fire'; the rise of the Roman navy; the suicidal but valiant *devotio*; the honorific *spolia opima*; single combat, fought to the death; booty; ethnic cleansing; war rape; siege machinery; weaponry; and tactical strategies.

Wars and Battles of the Roman Republic is the dynamic story of Rome's inexorable and endless battle to win control of the Italian peninsula, and the lands surrounding the

Mediterranean Sea, as she pushed deeper into parts of Asia and Gaul. It covers 100 or so Roman victories, between the traditional foundation of Rome in 753 BC to the birth of Julius Caesar in 100 BC. For most of the 650 years covered in this book, the doors of the Temple of Janus in Rome—traditionally closed during times of peace—remained resolutely open. This book tells the fascinating story of Rome's wars and battles, her expansionism, and her imperialism. It is the story of Rome's progress from agrarian hill-dwellers to one of the world's most powerful empires.

The book focuses on Roman military victories in the Republic, describing as it does the inexorable and bloody march towards Empire. Obviously, the Romans suffered reverses along the way, not least Lake Trasimene and Cannae, and the ramifications of and reasons for these are just as important in the history of Rome's warfare and battling. Roman defeats and disasters are covered separately and in detail in my book, *Roman Military Disasters*.

War Before Rome

Warfare and battles were an inextricable and constant part of Roman life, from the foundation of the state in 753 BC to the eventual fall of the Roman Empire some 1,200 years later. The belligerence of the state was always integral to Roman political life; Roman bellicosity shaped their economy and defined their society. Josephus, writing in the AD first century, stated that the Roman people emerged from the womb carrying weapons. Centuries later, F. E. Adcock echoed these words when he said 'a Roman was half a soldier from the start, and he would endure a discipline which soon produced the other half'.[1]

Rome's obsession with war stretched over her 1,200 years of history and saw Roman armies fighting in and garrisoning the full extent of her territories, from Parthia in the east (modern-day Iran), to Africa (Tunisia) and Aegyptus in the south (Egypt), and to Britannia in the cold north-west. The constitution and equipment of the Roman war machine evolved throughout its long history, from its early days as a citizen militia to its later status as a professional army. There were few years in which there was no conflict: each summer, when the campaigning season began, an army was levied, consuls or dictators took command, and battles were fought, before the army was disbanded at the close of the fighting year.

Of course warfare was nothing new in ancient societies. Territorial defence or expansion, mineral deposits, naked aggression, trade protectionism, and despotism all played their part in fuelling wars, conflict, and confrontation before the Roman era. Ovid, in his *Metamorphoses* (written at the dawn of Empire), would have us believe that once upon a time men were ever true to their word, and that they inhabited a righteous, peaceful world in which laws, punishment, armies, and fortifications were superfluous.[2] This golden age, the *aurea aetas*, had of course never existed; violence, wars, and the battles that constitute them have been as constant and ubiquitous as taxes and death. In The Bible Cain slays his brother, Abel, soon after the cataclysm in the Garden of Eden.[3] War has existed for as long as man has had land—and a food supply—to protect. It seems probable that the trouble all started around 6500 BC, when the nomadic hunter-gather settled down from a life of wandering in his search for food and began living in a settlement. From here he emerged daily to hunt before returning home each evening to eat, procreate, and protect. Later, population growth and the quest for *lebensraum* on fertile land would have caused additional conflict, as mountain people—for example—came down to occupy lands already settled and cultivated by other tribes. In

Mesopotamia, in around 3500 BC, the defensive ditches developed into walled defences and citadels to defend the new cities and their more complex societies, and to assert power and control over neighbouring, weaker settlements.

Early descriptions of war date from around 3200 BC with the Sumerians of Mesopotamia; the city states of Ur, Lagash, Uruk, and Kish squabbled internally with each other while they struggled externally with the nearby Elamite kingdom. Early depictions of war include the Standard of Ur wall panel (2500 BC), and the Stele of the Vultures of Lagash (2330 BC) which show kings leading orderly and disciplined formations of men into battle. The Standard depicts two-man war chariots drawn by four mules, and close formation spearmen; the Stele commemorates the long-running conflict between Umma and Lagash over a tract of agricultural land on their borders—it shows soldiers in an even-closer formation, not seen again for some 1,800 years in the shape of the Greek hoplite phalanx. The British Museum describes the Standard as follows, illustrating the importance of war in Sumerian society:

> The main panels are known as 'War' and 'Peace'. 'War' shows one of the earliest representations of a Sumerian army. Chariots, each pulled by four donkeys, trample enemies; infantry with cloaks carry spears; enemy soldiers are killed with axes, others are paraded naked and presented to the king who holds a spear.
>
> The 'Peace' panel depicts animals, fish and other goods brought in procession to a banquet. Seated figures, wearing woollen fleeces or fringed skirts, drink to the accompaniment of a musician playing a lyre. Banquet scenes such as this are common on cylinder seals of the period, such as on the seal of the 'Queen' Pu-abi, also in the British Museum.

The limestone stele is typical of a victory stele at the time, and displays a mythological and historical side. The historical side is divided into four: the top register shows Eannatum (the King of Lagash) leading soldiers into battle, with their enemies trampled underfoot. The vultures, after whom the stele gets its name, fly above, carrying the decapitated heads of the enemy in their beaks. The next register depicts soldiers marching with their spears behind the king, who is in a chariot and also holds a spear. In the third register a cow is shown tethered to a pole while a naked priest, standing on a pile of animal carcasses, performs a libation; to the left is a pile of naked bodies, surrounded by skirted workers carrying baskets on their heads. The damaged fourth register shows a hand holding a spear touching the head of an enemy. The land dispute ended in a battle, after which the leader of Umma swore that he would not trespass into the territory of the Lagash again, or he would have the gods to answer to.

A famous slate palette from Egypt in 3000 BC graphically depicts King Narmer slaying his foes.[4] In Mesopotamia, in around 2500 BC, Naram-Sim desecrated the temple of Enlil and devastated Nippur, Enlil's city. In mindless retaliation Enlil unleashed the ferocious Gutians— an uncontrollable people with the minds of dogs and the faces of apes. They swarmed all over the land like locusts, destroying everything—including Nippur. The Sumerian king, Shulgi (2029–1982 BC) later not only destroyed the Gutians in battle but also laid waste their lands, reducing it, and their economy and society, to a virtual desert; the Gutians were scattered far and wide.[5]

The gradual introduction of the bow and its archers had a significant impact on warfare. Its first serious exponent was the Akkadian army of Sargon. Sargon had moved south in search of fertile land, after the salinization of his own country. The victory steles of Sargon's son, Rimus (r. 2278–2270 BC), and of the Akkadian King Naram-Sin (r. *c.* 2254–2218 BC) both depict bows being deployed—their range was 250–300 yards.

Treaties and coalitions proliferated: Naram-Sin allied with Elam in south-west Iran. The Hittites were particularly accommodating (see, for example, King Shuppululiuma's concord with Niqmaddu, King of Ugarit in northern Syria, in the middle of the fourteenth century).[6] Dynastic marriages and the forging of alliances between families were widespread; one notable instance of this was the marriage of the daughter of Ashur-uballit of Assyria to the King of Babylonia in around 1500 BC. The protection of state boundaries, living space, and economic and mineral resources were a common cause of war and battles. Around the same time as the Ashur-uballit marriage Assyrians were attacked by the Mittannians, who were anxious to annex the rich agricultural lands along the Tigris. The Assyrians repelled them, and from then on made punitive raids on Mittannian tribesmen to prevent further incursions—thereby expanding their own territory. The Israelites theologised their reprisals when Yahweh decreed that the raiding Amalekites would be expunged from memory for all time—an early *damnatio memoriae*—for their attacks on and appropriation of Israelite settlements. This hateful curse endured into the time of Samuel and Saul (*c.* 1100 BC) when the former ordered the latter to exterminate the Amalekites down to the last woman and child, and to erase their agrarian economy.[7] The Assyrians were the champions of logistics—they laid down the rules for lines of supply, supply depots (*ekal masharti*), arsenals, barracks, and transport columns, and these rules are still followed to this day. Their expertise in maintaining an armed, watered, fuelled, and fed army allowed them a hitherto unheard of reach and penetration (up to 300 miles) at an awesome speed of up to thirty miles a day—on horses, using ancient highways. Naval warfare was launched by Sennacherib in the early seventh century. He brought in Syrian shipbuilders to build a fleet at Nineveh to oppose the Elamites; crewed by Phoenicians, this fleet sailed as far down the Tigris as far as it could and then followed a canal linked to the Euphrates. Through this they entered the Persian Gulf and then went on into Elamite territory with their horses and soldiers. The Assyrians were notorious for ransacking enemy lands once their armies had replenished and eaten their fill of the local grain, oil, wine, and dates. Sargon II and his son Sennacherib were seasoned devastators, with enemy irrigation systems, granaries, and fruit orchards falling victim to them.

Another way in which the belligerent Assyrians led the way was in their understanding of the value of loyalty—what the Romans later called *fides*. Any suspicious people they encountered were resettled far from home; those trusted to be loyal were integrated into the army, regardless of their ethnicity. The bonds between victor and vanquished were further strengthened by a policy of linguistic and religious tolerance; the Assyrian armies were further reinforced by allowing the defeated to form ancillary units which used their own armour and weapons. The Romans were to adopt a similarly constructive and diplomatic attitude to some of their vanquished. The Assyrians were devotees both of siege warfare and (like the Egyptians) the use of chariots. They boasted an impressive arsenal of siege equipment: metal tipped battering rams, mobile assault towers crammed with archers, miners tunnelling under walls, engineers chipping away at foundations and gates, and shock spearmen scaling walls. Chariots were to become largely obsolete over time and survived only in remote societies such as those of the Celts in Britannia. The first recorded engagement of chariots was at the Battle of Megiddo in northern Palestine, in 1469 BC, when they were deployed by the pharaoh Tuthmosis III. Megiddo is the world's first dateable battle for which we can trace location, outcome, and combatants. Under Sargon II (r. 721–705 BC) the charioteers moved forward onto the back of their horses, marking the evolution from charioteer to mounted archer and the introduction of cavalry. The key to Assyria's success probably lay in their willingness to learn from their enemies, and to blend progressive new ideas and strategies into their military thinking—a quality which would also benefit the Romans later. The use of propaganda to promote Assyria—both as a terror to be avoided and as an attractive ally—was equally successful.

Yahweh's sanction of the Amalekite genocide was indicative of the fact that a warring state's actions could be justified and mitigated by the will of God. Divine approval has been necessary before the opening of hostilities in many theatres of war throughout the ages; omens in the ancient world were interpreted and had to be favourable before battle, and failure to observe them could be costly. An imprudent and impious Naram-Sin lost 250,000 men when he chose to ignore ill omens before one battle. Divine sanction was also useful in justifying and mitigating atrocities. The Assyrians had a shocking reputation, as did some Egyptians—not least Amenophis II (1439–1413 BC), who massacred all surviving opposition at Ugarit. The Egyptians were also notorious for mutilating the defeated; for example, the Battle of Megiddo yielded eighty-three severed hands. The walls of the temple at Medinet Habu show piles of phalluses and hands, which were hacked from Libyan invaders and their allies by Ramesses III (1193–1162 BC). Ashurbanipal, the Assyrian king who reigned from 668–627 BC, rejoiced in the violence, stating: 'I will hack up the flesh [of the defeated] and then carry it with me, to show off in other countries'. His ostentatious brutality is widely depicted—one picture shows him implanting a dog chain through the cheek and jaw of a vanquished Bedouin king, Yatha, and then reducing him to a life in a dog kennel, where he guards the gate of Ninevah or pulls the royal chariot.[8] Babylon was a particular threat; when Ashurbanipal destroyed the city he tore out the Babylonians' tongues, smashed them to death with the statuary, and then fed their corpses—cut into little pieces—to the dogs, pigs, zibu birds, vultures, and fish. Ashur-etil-ilani (627–623 BC), Ashurbanipal's heir, had a predilection for cutting open the bellies of his opponents 'as though they were young rams'. In The Bible we read of the children of the defeated being dashed to death, and pregnant women being ripped open.[9] War rape was constant; again in The Bible, the prophet Zechariah announces, 'I will gather all the nations against Jerusalem to battle, and the city shall be taken and the houses plundered and the women raped'. Isaiah's vision was equally apocalyptic when he states: 'Their little children will be dashed to death before their eyes. Their homes will be sacked, and their wives will be raped'. In *Lamentations* it is written that 'women have been violated in Zion, and virgins in the towns of Judah'.[10]

Throughout its long history, Egypt consistently justified its many military conflicts as defence against the violation of its borders—for example by the Hittites or the Hyksos (Rulers of Desert Uplands)—or as safeguarding threatened trade. The Middle Kingdom Egyptians of around 1900 BC were one of the first exponents of the battering ram, depicted with its metal tip and protective hut on the Beni-Hasan wall painting. Scorched-earth attacks and the erasing of nations, as well as the mass deportation of conquered peoples, were routine practice. The horse-drawn chariot, the bow, bronze weapons, scale armour, and state-of-the-art daggers and swords had come into play by 1600 BC. *The Papyrus Lansing* gives a fascinating (if biased) account of the life of an Egyptian soldier. It dates from the reign of Senusret III (1878–1839 BC) and was written by the scribe Nebmare-nakht to his apprentice Wenemdiamun, persuading him that the profession of a scribe is the best—decrying other trades such as farmer, merchant, or soldier. And what a wretched life the soldier had: dirty, salty water every three days; relentless uphill marching; no rest; no clothes or sandals; a body racked with disease; desertion punished by the extermination of the whole family; and an anonymous, unremembered death at the end of an unremembered life.

Given the Nile, the Delta, and the Mediterranean, it is not surprising that naval warfare played a major role in Egyptian conflict. The Theban Kamose saw action in the revolt against the Hyksos, delighting in his victory and the resulting booty. Having sailed upstream from Thebes he—'happy in heart'—encountered the fortress of a collaborator: 'I was on him [like] a hawk ... I razed his wall, I slew his people, I caused his wife to go down to the river bank [presumably a euphemism for rape]. My soldiers were like lions with their prey, with serfs, cattle milk, fat and honey, dividing up their possessions'. The Hyksos capital of Avaris was eventually taken after a naval victory by Amosis (r. 1552–1524 BC).

In the New Kingdom, one of the rites of passage for new kings was a successful first military campaign; Nubia was often the unfortunate target for this, not because she posed a threat but rather because she was weak, and already subdued.

Nearer home in place and time, the Athenians, Persians, Macedonians, Spartans, and Etruscans all engaged in serial warfare. The city state *(polis)* of the Greeks has its origin in the Mycenaean Greeks based around Athens, who established twelve fortified cities in the tenth century, along the Aegean coast, looking to Athens as their base. These were supplanted by the Dorians, barbaric invaders from the north who captured the cities, grabbed the lands, and enslaved the inhabitants. In Crete, in the period of 850–750 BC, political rights were granted only to those rich enough to bear arms, thus forging a society in which allegiance to the state far outweighed any domestic obligations. Military service began at seventeen, comprised of strict discipline, athletics, military exercises, hunting, and mock battles. By nineteen, cadets were assigned to mess halls which were paid for out of public funds. Marriage was permitted, but wives lived separately and family life was kept to a minimum. Later migrations to the Greek mainland saw the exportation of this way of life, notably to Sparta, where we can recognise many aspects of the Cretan military lifestyle. This was where the distinction between the franchised warrior and the serf—devoid of rights—was at its most pronounced.

The Greeks, like the Romans, were serial warmongers. As Finley points out: 'Athens ... was at war on average more than two years out of every three between the Persian wars and the defeat ... at Chaeronea in 338 BC, and ... it never enjoyed ten consecutive years of peace in all that period'. Thucydides tells us that early Greek wars were largely squabbles over territory;

one of the first, he says, was the Lelantine War between Chalkis and Eretrea, in Euboea, which took place between *c.* 710 and 650 BC.[11] The war was caused by a dispute over the fertile Lelantine Plain, but the conflict spread and took in many other city states. According to Thucydides it was the only war to take place in Greece between the time of the Trojan War (*c.* 1300 BC) and the Persian Wars (499–449 BC) in which a number of allied cities, rather than single ones, were involved. The Persian Wars themselves, in which the cities of Greece eventually repulsed the Persians, is famous for its battles of Marathon, Thermopylae, Salamis, and Plataea. The thirty-year-long war was pivotal in Greek history, leading to the Athens-led Delian League and a huge expansion of Athenian influence, as well as the establishment of Athenian democracy. Conflict with Sparta was inevitable, and took up much of the latter part of the fifth century; the Peloponnesian War from 431–404 BC was the most significant of these conflicts, and was fought against the Peloponnesian League under Sparta. Historians have traditionally divided the war into three phases: the first part, the Archidamian War, saw Sparta attacking Attica and Athens deploying its superior navy for raids on the coast of the Peloponnese. The Peace of Nicias, in 421 BC, brought this phase to an end, but the peace was short-lived. In 415 BC, Athens sent a huge expeditionary force to attack Syracuse; this was a disaster, and foreshadowed the destruction of the entire force in 413 BC. The Decelean (or Ionian) War followed, in which Sparta was joined by Persia. Ultimately Athens lost her naval supremacy at the catastrophic Battle of Aegospotami, leading to her surrender in the following year.

Until this time there was little in the way of strategy or tactics, with land armies on either side content to confront each other head-on. The Greek model of combat was based on the hoplite phalanx, supported by missile-hurling troops. The hoplites were infantry recruited from of the middle-classes—the *zeugites*—who could afford the required heavy armour. This comprised a breastplate (*linothorax*), greaves, a helmet, and a large, round, concave shield—the *aspis* or *hoplon*—made with wood and iron and measuring three feet in diameter. Close combat was the order of the day, with troops standing shoulder to shoulder in rows eight deep. Hoplites also carried long spears (the *dory*) and a sword (*xiphos*). The *psiloi*—lightly armed skirmishers—were also an element of Greek armies at this time.

Large-scale naval warfare and the maintenance of a standing fleet had a significant effect on Athenian politics, economics, and society. A large number of rowers were obviously required to crew the ships, and skilled craftsmen were needed to build, maintain, and repair the fleet. This caused a demographic shift from country villages to the *polis*, raising social issues and—to some extent—the politicisation of the workers as *thetes*. All of this contributed to the development of democracy in Athens.

As we have already seen, Greek naval warfare first came with the Peloponnesian War. Sparta, under the command of Lysander, eventually defeated the Athenians by cutting off their sea-borne supplies going into Piraeus, and by defeating the Athenian fleet at Aegospotami, where Lysander sank 168 ships and captured up to 4,000 Athenian sailors. In the meantime, Alcibiades had defected to Sparta. The Athenian army (5,000 infantry and light-armoured troops) and navy (100 or so ships) had been virtually wiped out at Syracuse, where a bad omen—a lunar eclipse—delayed their retreat; they were run down and killed or enslaved by the Spartan cavalry. The Spartans were joined by Persia and by disaffected Athenian allies. Athens was brought to its knees politically and economically, as well as militarily; Sparta, however, was on the rise.[12]

Philip II of Macedonia (382–336 BC) was probably the first Greek military strategist or tactician of any note. He made good use of the phalanx infantry—in rectangular formation—who were armed with the long spear (*sarissa*), and utilised the interplay between *hetairoi* (foot companions) and cavalry against the Illyrii. At the decisive Battle of Chaeronea, in 338 BC, he simulated retreat, allowing his cavalry full reign and emphatically defeating the Thebans and Athenians. This brought an end to the Fourth Sacred War and re-established peace to war-riven Greece. Philip was also a gifted military diplomat (not averse to bribery) and an astute judge of when to join battle and when to avoid it. Alexander the Great, his son, continued his expansionism, defeating the Persians at the battles of Issus and Gaugamela and conquering the Persian Empire. He died undefeated in battle, and military academies still teach his strategies and tactics today.[13]

Sparta was very much a militaristic society, but perhaps not to the extent that we are often led to believe. We have to exercise caution with the sources, as much of what we know about Sparta is given to us by Athenian writers—whose work is freighted with bias and hostility towards their enemy. Nevertheless, in the eighth century BC Lycurgus famously said that Sparta's walls were made of men, not bricks. Sparta was a well-oiled war machine, which required a ready and constant supply of warriors.[14] Men were preoccupied with their military careers, and although they married from their mid-twenties they saw very little of domestic life before the age of thirty. Even then they still dined in their mess and devoted most of their time to the military (*syssitia*). Their women had a crucial economic role in bringing up their children and running the household. They were responsible for raising sons until they were seven, when they left to join the junior army (*agoge*) and begin training. For that reason it was considered important for women (of the citizen class) to be physically and mentally equipped for conception and motherhood. Girls remained at home, were educated in the arts, and received training in athletics, dancing, and chariot racing; a strong, fit, and educated mother delivered strong babies and made a strong army. For boys, training included endurance exercises and competitive sports; combat training began at eighteen, incorporating what we might call special operations intelligence gathering against the serfs. At twenty the boys moved into barracks and, although permitted to marry, lived in the mess. At thirty they were eligible for full citizenship and, if selected, became an 'equal'—this entailed suppressing the serfs (helots) and being prepared for war. Those serfs deemed in any way unsuitable by the intelligence officers were winnowed out each year in a cull.

In the early fourth century, we have an example of the active, competitive Spartan woman in Cynisca, the daughter of the King of Sparta, Archidamus II. Xenophon records that her brother, Agesilaus II, encouraged her to compete in the four-horse chariot race at the Olympic Games, because he wanted to rubbish the sport and show that it could be won by a woman. Bravery and virtue were required for the other events, but only wealth was needed for the chariot race; Cynisca won the four-horse race in 396 BC and in 392 BC. It would be nice to think that Cynisca's victories were achieved with determination to prove her brother wrong. Whatever her motivation, the sport became fashionable, and she was honoured with a bronze statue of a chariot and horses, a charioteer, and a statue of herself in the Temple of Zeus in Olympia; an accompanying inscription stated that she was the only woman to win in the chariot events at the Olympic Games. Pausanias describes a shrine of Cynisca that was erected in Sparta—usually, only Spartan kings were honoured in this way.[15] Other Spartan and Greek female chariot-race winners included Euryleonis, Belistiche, Timareta, Theodota and Cassia. A Spartan, Euryleonis, also won the two-horse chariot races in the 368 BC games. Belistiche was a *hetaira* (courtesan), and she won the *tethrippon* and *synoris* (four and two-horse chariot) races in the 264 BC games; after this, Ptolemy II Philadelphus took her as his mistress and deified her as Aphrodite Bilistiche. According to Clement of Alexandria, she was buried beneath the shrine of Sarapis in Alexandria.

By around 473 BC Sparta had become the dominant power on the Peloponnesian Peninsula and was leader of the Peloponnesian League. She achieved this in three protracted wars, in which Messenia to the west (940–20 and 750–650 BC), Arcadia to the north (570–470 BC), and Argolis to the north-east (670–494 BC) were subdued. In the Greek wars against Persia, the Spartan forces were crucial in the Battles of Plataea and Thermopylae. The end of the hostilities, however, saw Sparta withdraw into relative isolation, deepened by the machinations of Pausanius, by a destructive earthquake, and by revolts by their allies. This allowed Athens to flourish and, eventually, led to the confrontation in the Peloponnesian wars.[16]

Land ownership was vital to the Greek citizen-soldier. He depended on his fifteen acres or less to grow his grain, olives, and wine—the livelihood which permitted him to sell off any surplus to pay for weapons and armour. This in turn enfranchised him and gave him an indirect role in politics and government. Any threat to this was obviously a serious affair, and goes some way to account for the spasmodic—rather than protracted—nature of Greek belligerence. Incursions needed a speedy outcome, because the undefended smallholding back home was itself vulnerable to attack. As a result, victors rarely pressed home their successes; if an enemy remained intractable, then they would simply be attacked again. A phalanx might lose up to fifteen per cent of its strength in an unsuccessful engagement, through death in the fray, in flight, or in post-battle wound infections, such as peritonitis. The fleeing hoplite was able to discard his hard-earned weapons, but he remained encumbered by armour as he fled for his life, stumbling away from the field of battle.

The Greeks did little without the sanction of the gods, and battle was no exception. Armies on the move were always accompanied by a flock of sheep for sacrifice—the rites of bloodletting, or *sphagia*—at every critical juncture, whether it was crossing a river, invading a border, striking camp, or even starting the battle. Often the sacrifices were preceded by a meal, washed down by generous amounts of alcohol—the meal could be their last, the alcohol gave courage and abandon.[17]

As we chart the wars and battles of the Roman Republic, it will soon become apparent that many of the more successful military policies, strategies, and tactics of their predecessors were adopted and developed by the Romans. This ability to integrate the military know-how of enemies and allies goes some way to explaining Rome's success on the battlefield over the next few centuries. Much of the military ingenuity of the Assyrians, early Greeks, and Spartans would resurface in the endless wars fought by the Romans.

A bronze statuette of an Etruscan warrior (left); a bronze statuette of an early-Empire Roman legionary soldier (right).

The Roman Way of War

Looking back on 800 years of Roman history, Josephus remarked that the Romans left the womb ready-equipped for battle. Warfare was a fact of life for many men during the monarchy and the early Republic; they would have seen service at one time or another unless they were of the lowest orders—freedmen or slaves. Women would have taken on the responsibility of running the farmstead and the household in their husbands' and older sons' increasingly frequent absences. Indeed, the doors of the Temple of Janus in Rome (traditionally closed during times of peace) remained firmly shut on only two occasions between the reign of Numa Pompilius (Rome's second king after Romulus, 715–673 BC) and the reign of Augustus some 600 years later. Livy tells us that the first occurred soon after the First Punic War, during the consulship of Titus Manlius Torquatus, in 235 BC; the second occurred after Augustus' victory in the Battle of Actium. The temple was a visible, eloquent sign of Rome's belligerence. It was ironic in that it had been constructed under one of Numa's first acts, when he re-established the city on peaceful, religious, and forensic grounds that were in direct contrast to its warlike origins. Almost entirely uniquely, Numa was able to keep the doors closed for the duration of his reign.[1] He clearly appreciated the civilizing benefits of protracted peace; however, his successors throughout the monarchy, republic, and empire were to civilize through force.

Roman warfare was inextricably linked with politics and economics, with land and the Conflict of the Orders being constant concerns during wars. Economic return on his land gave the soldier the wherewithal to qualify for service, and to pay for his armour and weapons. The Conflict ran from 494–287 BC and can be described as the 200-year struggle for the plebeians to win political equality; the *secessio plebis* was their powerful bargaining tool, where the plebeians refused to work and effectively closed down Rome, letting the patricians get on with it themselves. This was the Roman equivalent to a general strike. The first *secessio*, in 494 BC, saw the lower order withdrawing military support during the wars against the Aequi, Sabines, and Volsci.[2]

Servius Tullius, Rome's sixth king (578–535 BC), fought successful campaigns against the Veii and the Etruscans. He allegedly divided the citizenship into groups according to wealth—their status in the army was determined by which weapons and armour they could afford to buy, with the richest serving in the cavalry. He is often thought to have taken the first steps in militarizing Rome, but this is unlikely to be the case. Servius was, however, responsible for a far-reaching shift in the organisation of the Roman army: he moved the emphasis from cavalry to infantry, and this brought about an inevitable change in battlefield tactics which would serve Rome well for centuries to come. Before Servius the army was comprised of approximately 600 cavalry, supported by heavily-armed infantry and light-armed skirmishers. It seems likely that the Etruscans and the Romans were influenced by the Greeks, and adopted comprehensive body armour, the hoplite shield, and a thrusting spear (as opposed to the throwing version) which was essential for phalanx-style close-combat warfare. Men without property, assessed by headcount (*capite censi*), were excluded from the army, as were debtors, convicted criminals, women, and slaves—although slaves were recruited in exceptional circumstances (for example, after the Battle of Cannae). Servius is also credited with the organisation of the army into centuries and the concomitant formation of political assemblies, highlighting the inextricable link between Roman politics and the military. His ground-breaking census presumably had the purpose of establishing who was physically and economically fit enough to serve in the Roman army.[3] It is no accident that the census was held at the Campus Martius, the home of military training and the meeting place for the centuriate assembly. Eligibility extended from age seventeen to forty-six (*iuniores*) and forty-seven to sixty (*seniores*)—the latter usually forming a kind of home guard. By the second half of the second century BC there were between 380,000 and 480,000 men under arms—three quarters of whom were *iuniores*. The Second Punic War saw the army at its greatest strength, with twenty-two legions on hand comprising of (on average) 4,200 infantry and 200 cavalry.

Sixty centuries made up a legion (*legio*)—originally a militia of heavily armed landowner infantry wielding *pilum*, a shield, and a sword (*gladius*). The legions initially operated like Greek hoplites, in the time-honoured phalanx formation. These would be supported by the cavalry, with the wealthy *equites* initially in eighteen centuries—thirty-two centuries of slingers provided further back-up. The original *legio* was divided into two in the early Republic, each the responsibility of one of the two consuls. By 311 BC there were four legions, reinforced by troops provided by Rome's Italian allies and by mercenary archers. By the middle of the Republic the legions were generally divided into cavalry, light infantry, and heavy infantry. The heavy infantry were, in turn, subdivided into three further groups: the *hastati*—green, raw recruits; the *principes*—troops in their twenties and thirties; and the *triarii*—veterans deployed in crises or in support of the *hastati* and *principes*. The *triarii* wielded the long spear (the *hasta*) rather than the *pilum* and *gladius*. Each of these groups subdivided into ten units, or 'maniples', comprising two centuries and commanded by the senior of the two centurions. Each century of *hastati* and *principes* was made up of sixty men, while a century of *triarii* was thirty men. These 3,000 troops (twenty maniples of 120 men, and ten maniples of 60 men), along with 1,200 *velites* and 300 cavalry, added up to a legion about 4,500 men strong. Soldiers were required to serve in six consecutive campaigns and to be available for up to sixteen years; cavalrymen had to be on hand for ten years. The legions were raised and disbanded according to need, with the soldiers anxious to return to their land as frequently as possible.

Military service demonstrated patriotism, *pietas*, and responsibility; it was also prestigious, offering the *gens* and the family palpable opportunities for visible glory in decorations, citations, prizes, and—pinnacle of them all—a triumph processing through the streets of Rome. Moreover, military service allowed the proud and patriotic Roman to demonstrate his bravery and virtue (his *virtus*). Glory and kudos were boosted by the complex system of decorations (*dona militaria*) and rewards that was established to reflect military success. Discipline and loyalty were also strengthened by a tangible array of benefits, which included elevation to the rank of centurion—where, after the consulship of Marius, the pay was double that of the common soldier and the booty share was sizeably bigger. Gratuities, pay rises, better rations, and promotion all contributed, as did better social mobility for the common soldier and political success for the elite. However, the average pay for a soldier or sailor remained miserly; he could earn three times more doing manual labour at twelve asses per day. It took until 49 BC, during the time of Julius Caesar, before a soldier's remuneration was raised to ten asses per day. Pay was probably introduced in around 406 BC, after the wars with the Veii, but it was never meant to provide a living wage—it was more of a contribution to the cost of food, equipment, and clothing. Booty increasingly became the source of finance. In the empire symbolic spears (*hasta pura*), crowns and collars (*phalerae* and *phiale*), and standards (*vexilla*) were also there for all to see. The *spolia opima* was, of course, a highly prestigious and rare award.[4] The highest level of recognition for conspicuous military success came with the triumph, but both this and the *spolia opima* were largely restricted to commanders.

The origin of the triumph remains something of a mystery, but its roots are probably in an old Latin rite which absorbed various Etruscan and monarchical influences over time. The ceremony had three parts: the first was focused on the army and the commander, assembled on the Campus Martius, with praise heaped on the commander and individual soldiers who had shown conspicuous gallantry. Next came the procession along the traditional route, which took in the *Porta Triumphalis*, the *Circus Maximus*, the *Palatine*, *Forum* and the *Capitoline*, ending at the temple of Jupiter Optimus Maximus. The procession also had three parts: the booty and prisoners of war; the general, accompanied by magistrates; and the army. The general rode in a four-horse chariot—he was decked out in a purple and gold tunic and a purple toga, he carried a laurel branch and an ivory sceptre, and on his head was a laurel crown. His face was painted red.[5]

The Roman war machine needed to be constantly fuelled by new recruits, a fact which created something of a vicious circle. By the end of the third century approximately one third of Italians south of Rome had been subdued, and were Roman citizens; they were, therefore, eligible for military service.[6] These citizens were supported by troops supplied by allies, often as auxiliary forces. However, the casualties sustained in continuous bloody wars often meant that Rome had to keep on conquering if she was to maintain her steady supply of recruits, and thereby keep her forces up to strength. It was also commonly felt, amongst more conservative Romans, that the cessation of war encouraged laxity and moral decay amongst the menfolk of Rome. As a champion of tradition (*mos maiorum*) and a despiser of all things Greek, Cato the Elder (234–149 BC) had spoken out sternly against what he saw as a period of moral decline, and the erosion of the sturdy principles on which Rome had lain her foundations. The defeat of Hannibal at Zama, in 202 BC, the victory over the Macedonians at Pydna, in 168 BC, and the final extinguishing of the Carthaginian threat in 146 BC all allowed Rome to relax, and encouraged the unprecedented influx of Greek and eastern luxuries into a receptive Rome. The waging of war, then, was the answer to all manner of political and social issues.[7]

The navy took something of a back seat until the wars against Carthage, with the army undoubtedly the senior service. Carthage maintained a fleet because their extensive overseas trade demanded one. Egypt, Athens, and Rhodes all kept a standing navy at one time or another for the purposes of trade and warfare. In comparison, Rome up until now had a casual attitude towards overseas trade; their naval capability was similarly restricted. Foreign expansion, the conquest of Sicily, and the inescapable fact that the Carthaginians had a formidable fleet, a navy, dockyards, and harbours encouraged the expansion of the Roman navy. This paved the way for the eventual defeat of Carthage, and Octavian's victory at Actium. However, it remained the Roman way to raise a navy only when the situation demanded, and to lay it up when the crisis was over.

The Punic Wars changed everything. There were now serious manpower shortages, caused by heavy casualties and the poverty created by widespread depredation of Roman land and farms. It is estimated that over 120,000 Roman citizens perished during the three wars—a casualty rate that would have crippled most nations. Slaves were enlisted, as an emergency measure, to make up the losses. The lands acquired by the elite and the rich were worked by slaves—captured, in their droves, by conquest—meaning less land was left for the indigenous farmer and no work was left for the peasant workforce. Therefore peasants seeking work moved into the towns and cities. Land-owning soldiers found their lands devastated or confiscated on their return from the battlefield, or else they faced high taxation and growing debt; this meant that they too headed for the towns. State land distribution ceased in 170 BC, but demand for land did not. The inevitable result was that commanders were now able to raise armies independently, tempting recruits with their beneficence and distribution of private land.

Casualties notwithstanding, Rome was still to some extent able to absorb the wounded and dead, and fielded armies in various theatres through its policy of enfranchisement of overrun territories and a prudent policy of building a network of alliances. A condition of the former and an obligation of the latter was military service in the Roman army or navy. Between 225–200 BC the allies *(socii)* provided between one half and three quarters of Rome's total forces. Military campaigns were increasingly extensive and costly, taking men away from their land and families for long periods as Rome's expansionism continued apace; new far-away territories required permanent garrisons. Now that much of the Italian peninsula was under Roman control, booty and land from earlier conquests was less plentiful. The pressure to recruit was relentless.

In 107 BC Gaius Marius saw the need to accept volunteers *(proletarii)* without land or wealth qualification, and the need to have the state pay for their equipment and weaponry for the war against Jugurtha in Africa. Soldiers now lived and died for the army—they had no land to return to. The legion was their lives, and they developed an intense loyalty to their commanders. Hitherto these *proletarii* were only conscripted as a last resort, in times of crisis *(tumultus)*. Marius scrapped the maniples and replaced them with cohorts, which were comprised of six *centuriae* of approximately eighty men, commanded by a centurion.[8] The Social War of 91–87 BC also had an effect; defeated Italians (the *socii*) revolted when Rome refused them the vote. Rome eventually relented, citizenship was granted to inhabitants south of the Po, and with the vote came military service. This significantly increased the number of potential recruits available to the Romans. The allies were often deployed as auxiliary cavalrymen (*auxilia*). The extended franchise was to foment the civil wars of 88–82 BC.

It is unlikely that Marius anticipated one of the major consequences of his military reforms. As we have seen, the new non-land-owning class of soldiers had no lands to return to, so they grew dependent on their generals for support. At the same time, the state had no means of paying adequate discharge payments to its burgeoning armies. Commanders saw an opportunity here: they could recruit and retain armies with the promises of generous pay and pensions which, through long-term mutual loyalty, might well lead to prodigious military and political power for themselves. From now on the soldiery was in the pay of the consuls and generals—and not the state. Individual military leaders could exercise significant political power and influence through their armies, perhaps to effect revolutionary change in Rome. Sulla, in 88 BC, was the first to try this, but he was not the last.

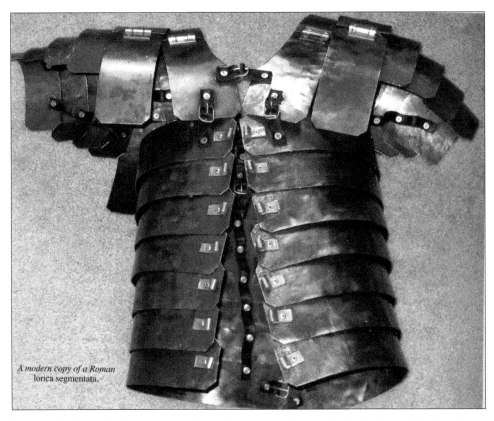

A modern copy of a Roman lorica segmentata.

A copy of a Roman *lorica segmentata*. It consisted of metal strips attached to internal leather straps. Originally published in 'Ancient Military Technology', Tracey Rihll, *Omnibus 62*.

A triumph processing down the Via Sacra in Rome, with prisoners of war behind the legionnaires.

A Mediterranean port scene, showing fully-armed battleships being re-supplied. From a German atlas, published in 1813.

Roman society was changing: the ten-year service stipulation was enforced increasingly less; alternative routes along the *cursus honorum* were increasingly popular, as law and politics replaced soldiering as careers of choice; dissenting voices emerged from 'bohemian' poets and their hangers-on, who enjoyed a life of leisure (*otium*) and fought the war of love as *milites amoris*, soldiers of love—languishing, locked out on the doorsteps, *exclusus amoris*, of their domineering *dominae*. All very un-Roman; the very antithesis to the *mos maiorum* and the traditional active military career where the centurion was very much the dominant force and the war was for the glory and survival of Rome.[9]

To finance his largesse, the ambitious Roman consul-commander needed money. Booty from foreign conquests was recognised as obvious, easy pickings, fuelling a scramble to overrun and despoil rich new territories—particularly in Greece and the eastern Mediterranean. Money from booty was also needed to support and finance the expanding urban economies that were generated by the influx of agricultural workers from surrounding lands. As increasing numbers of foreign territories fell under Rome's sway, the wealth, extravagance, opulence, tax revenues, and ostentatious military triumphs increased. It would all culminate in the bloody civil wars, in which the various triumvirates and their armies relentlessly battled and battered each other, until one general, Octavian, emerged as the victor at the Battle of Actium. By then the Republic was ancient history—the Empire was its future.

Legal, Religious, and Social Aspects of Roman War

In his De Officiis, Cicero provides the first surviving attempt of a Roman to give moral justification and rules of conduct to a just war (*iura belli*). Livy also details various criteria, which include keeping one's word (*fides*) with allies; retaliatory action when that *fides* is not reciprocated; and maintaining security (*salus*) when boundaries and territory are threatened by hostile forces. A three-stage procedure had to be performed before a war could be deemed legitimate: the war had to be declared (*denuntio*); a formal warning had to delivered (*indictio*); and reparations had to be sought (*rerum repetitio*) by a delegation of four *fetiales*, or *oratores*. Declarations of war were the responsibility of the *fetiales,* whose involvement introduced a religious element to the business of war. These twenty priests were responsible for establishing the rightness of any conflict (the *fas*), and for acting as ambassadors and diplomats before any hostilities began. The *fetiales* were devoted to the religious administration of international affairs of state and to apply the fetial law (*ius fetiale*), checking rigorously that *fides*, treaties (*foedera*), and oaths had been properly observed. The chief *fetial* invoked the god Iuppiter Lapis during the rite surrounding the treaty. Three *fetiales* and the chief *fetial* (*pater patratus*) were dispatched as envoys to the perpetrator of the crime committed against Rome, which might be anything from cattle theft to a full-scale incursion. Their task was to secure restitution (*ad res repetundas*), and enemy failure to comply after thirty days would lead to action (*denuntiatio* or *rerum repetitio*). If this happened, the *fetiales* returned and called the gods to witness that the case of the Romans was right and legitimate—the *testatio deorum*. Jupiter and Quirinus would be invoked as witnesses to any potential violation of the *ius*. The chief *fetial* was then empowered to declare war within thirty-three days; after ratification by the Senate and the people the two adversaries would officially be at war, as sanctioned by the gods. A sacred spear was then ceremoniously hurled into the enemy's territory to delimit their power (*indictio belli*). Over time, as Rome's reach extended further from the city, it became increasingly difficult and impractical to adhere to all of these traditions. The *fetiales* often needed longer than thirty days, and it was not always possible to find a suitable place to hurl the spear. In 270 BC a special location, near the Temple of Bellona, was reserved for the spear hurling. By the start of the Second Punic War the whole procedure was secularized after the *fetiales* were replaced with senatorial envoys (*legati*). The traditional three journeys were telescoped into one, without recourse to Rome.

In the *De Officiis* Cicero asserts that:

> The only excuse, therefore, for going to war is that we may live in peace unharmed; and when the victory is won, we should spare those who have not been blood-thirsty and barbarous in their warfare. For instance, our forefathers actually admitted to full rights of citizenship the Tusculans, Acquians, Volscians, Sabines, and Hernicians, but they razed Carthage and Numantia to the ground ... the rights of war must be strictly observed. For since there are two ways of settling a dispute: first, by discussion; second, by physical force (*unum per disceptationem alterum per vim*), and since the former is characteristic of man, the latter of the brute, we must resort to force only in case we may not avail ourselves of discussion ... (*illud proprium sit hominis, hoc beluarum*). We should always strive to secure a peace that shall not admit of guile...Not only must we show consideration for those whom we have conquered by force of arms but we must also ensure protection to those who lay down their arms and throw themselves upon the mercy of our generals, even though the battering-ram has hammered at their walls.[1]

Cicero could point to the magnanimity of the Romans when they defeated the Tuscans and other Italian cities. He deplored the sacking of Corinth, but saw this as necessary to avoid a future threat to Roman hegemony in the Mediterranean. Cicero's noble sentiments are echoed by Virgil a few decades later, when the ghost of Anchises prescribes to Aeneas the Roman way of civilising; a cornerstone of this was sparing the conquered and crushing the proud (*parcere subiectis et deballare superbos*). Horace took up the theme in the *Carmen Saeculare* with specific reference to Augustus. Before them all, the Greek historian Polybius attributed the following to Titus Quinctius Flamininus at the Congress of Nicaea in 197 BC, after he had defeated the Macedonian Philip V:

> For brave men, when actually at war, should be terrible and full of fire; when beaten, undaunted and courageous; when victorious, on the other hand, moderate, placable, and humane.[2]

Cicero, was also at pains to separate the men from the brutes. Plunder and booty were legitimate reasons for going to war, but fair play was important too. Fair play in the prosecution of war (*mores belli)*, however, was notably absent in Verres' sacking of Syracuse, where massacre and rape went hand in hand and the law of the victors (*ius victoriae*) was taken to extremes.

In the Jugurthine War the city of Capsa was razed to the ground by Marius—not for reasons of greed or brutality, but to avoid any future resurgence of the strategic city. Moreover, the people there were a duplicitous and fractious lot. The men were butchered, the women and children were sold into slavery, and the booty was divided up. To Sallust this was a breach of the *ius belli*: '*id facinus contra ius belli non avaritia neque scelere consulis admissum, sed quia locus Iugurthae opportunus*' ('as for the rules of war, the crime against the rules of war was not committed because of the greed or criminality of the consul, but because of the strategic advantage of the place to Jugurtha').[3]

Women came under the definition of property, as they legally were under the power of a man (*patria potestas*) or guardian. The rape of a woman was a property crime, committed against the man who owned the woman. The Greeks had considered the rape of women acceptable behaviour within the rules of warfare; vanquished women were booty, later to be redeployed as wives, concubines, slaves, or war trophies. The practice goes back at least to the *Iliad*, where Andromache speculates on what will happen to her if and when Troy loses the war. Recalling the destruction of Cilicia, she reminisces how Achilles took her 'mother, who ruled' and 'haled her ... with his other plunder'. The fact that she was a queen did not save Andromache's mother from slavery, nor did it save Andromache—she too was reduced to a spoil of war. As soon as Troy falls she will be forced from royalty into a life of domestic servitude, and will no doubt be raped on a regular basis.[4] Archaeological evidence from the thirteenth century BC supports this—ration lists for palace servants show the names of women from various towns and cities along the coast of Asia Minor, who were no doubt captured in war and enslaved.

The opening and closing of the Roman campaigning season were both marked by important rituals—the Roman religious calendar was replete with sacred preparations for warfare. In February and March the Salii performed their sacred dances, striking their holy shields, purifying the ordnance and horses in races at the feast of *Equirria*. Trumpets were sanctified on the day of the March *tubilustrium,* and weapons on the *armilustrium* in the autumn; the October horse (the one on the right in the winning team in the Field of Mars chariot race) was slain. Before an army left for war it was lustrated, with the commander shaking the Salian shields and holding up the lance of Mars. The doors of the Temple of Janus were opened (if they were ever shut). During a campaign omens were sought at every critical juncture, sacrifices were made, and auspices were taken.

Waging war was, of course, indicative of 'Roman-ness' (*Romanitas)*, that is, the essential qualities of a Roman and of how a Roman conducted himself in the world. He did so with virtue and bravery, both qualities being embodied in the same word (*virtus*) which has its root in *vir* (man). Although it was possible for a woman to exhibit *virtus*, it was essentially a badge and expression of masculinity. Indeed, *virtus* was often associated specifically with courage in war: Caesar, Sallust, and Horace all use it in this context.[5] Conversely, Rome's enemies were often portrayed as weak, lazy, and effeminate, devoid of *virtus*; both Greeks and Carthaginians felt the lash of this xenophobic Roman tongue.[6] The Romans stated that Carthaginians had no control over their sexual urges, that they were cowards, and that they ate dogs. Greeks, according to Tacitus, were also cowards; Lucan, through Julius Caesar, would have us believe that they were soft, lazy, and frightened by their own shouting.[7] This is perhaps understandable, as Rome excelled in war while her enemies did not—her catologue of victories proved that. Indeed, the sickening-to-some influx of things Greek during the late Republic, in a tide of Hellenization, was seen as a dangerous threat to the security of the Roman state. As we have seen, Cato the Elder, the champion of the good old days, spoke for many when he vilified all things Greek. At the end of the first century AD the malaise was still there. Juvenal, in his excoriating sixth satire, records his disgust at the trend of women speaking Greek: '*omnia Graece ... concumbunt Graece*' ('everything's gone Greek ... they even have sex in Greek').[8]

An essential ingredient of *Romanitas* was the *cursus honorum*, the path on which elite Romans typically progressed over their military and political careers, with a consulship as the glittering prize at the end of the road. However—as an apt metaphor for the erosion of *Romanitas* in the first century BC—a number of male poets were able to eschew the traditional *mos maiorum*, rejecting the *cursus honorum*, for a life of *otium* during which they would while away their time penning poetry and pursuing the objects of their affection. Horrified traditionalists regarded this otiose lifestyle as frivolous and decidedly un-Roman. The poets allowed themselves to be dominated by their women (their *dominae*), and even to be enslaved by them in *servitium amoris*; their *cursus honorum* and military career was *militia amoris*; they languished, locked-out and rejected, on the doorstep of a capricious woman, *exclusus amator*. Good Roman *militia* was being supplanted by weak, lovelorn 'soldiers', who were under the control of women rather than centurions.

There was, of course, plenty of advice to be had on strategy and tactics, and the proper way to prosecute a war. Apart from Julius Caesar expatiating on the conflict in Gaul and the Civil Wars, there was the *Strategikos* of Onasander, Polybius' work on camps, the *Strategemata* by Frontinus, the *De Re Militari* of Vegetius, and the work of Zosimus.[9] Taking siege warfare as an example, Onasander recommends restraint when it comes to plunder, and argues it is best not to threaten massacre, as both just lead to a more defiant and intractable enemy. He states prisoners of war should be spared—at least for the duration of the conflict—for the same reasons. Indeed, he writes that all prisoners should be shepherded into the besieged city to exacerbate food shortages and hasten starvation; Onasander is not averse to brutality when it is necessary.[10] Zosimus records how, at the siege of Cremna in AD 278, Lydius evicted all the prisoners, young and old. The Romans sent them back only for Lydius to hurl them into a ravine, to their deaths.[11] Frontinus advocated terrorising the besieged, and these terror tactics were strategies utilised by Gnaeus Julius Agricola during his first year in charge of Britannia.[12]

Sieges generally seem to have brought out some of the worst atrocities perpetrated by the Romans, particularly their aftermath. They also generated exceptions to the general *iures belli* and rules of fair play; retribution and exacting reparations for the time, trouble, and lives expended by the Romans seem to have provided good reasons to reject the rule book. Frontinus tells how Sulla broke the siege at Preaeneste (in 82 BC) by sticking the heads of the enemy generals on spears, displaying them to the remaining inhabitants to break their resolve to hold out.[13] Domitius Corbulo was especially brutal while besieging Tigranocerta in AD 60; he executed the noble Vadandus, whom he had captured, and shot his head out of a balista into the enemy camp. The human projectile landed in the middle of an enemy meeting, causing them to seek terms for surrender.[14] Scenes 24, 72, and 57 of Trajan's Column depict Dacian heads on poles, and scene 147 shows the severed head of Decebalus, King of the Dacians. Of course, such atrocities were not exclusive to the Romans—Frontinus also tells us how in AD 9 the Germans, under Arminiuson, fastened the heads of dead Romans on spears and brought them to the Roman camp.[15] The Germans did the same at Teutoburg Wald.

It seems that cities which surrendered, rather than being taken by storm, received a relative degree of clemency. Livy describes two such cases: Pometia in 502 BC and Phocaea in 190 BC.[16] At Cartagena in 209 BC, Scipio stopped the wholesale slaughter (which included slicing dogs and other animals in half) once Mago had surrendered.[17] The clear message from the Romans was that resistance was not worth the vicious reprisals that would inevitably follow; in that respect, holding out in a siege was no different from any other form of anti-Roman hostility. In 216 BC Capua induced retribution when the inhabitants locked a number of Roman citizens in a steaming, airless bath-house, where they died a terrible death.[18] At Uxellodunum in 51 BC, Julius Caesar had the enemies' hands cut off as a terrible and visible warning to anyone else contemplating resistance.[19] In AD 78 Agricola massacred the Ordovices because they had the temerity to attack one of his cavalry squadrons. He then took the island of Anglesey.[20]

Early Roman Conflicts:
Etruscans, Latins, and Sabines

The early Romans were an agricultural, pastoral society, made up of people who built their houses on hilltops and grazed their sheep in the pastures of the plains below. They had arrived in the hills above the Tiber in the second millennium BC and were one branch of the Italian peoples, derived from the Indo-European tribes who settled in Italy. However, the early Romans were heavily influenced by the Etruscans, who had come from Asia Minor in two waves of immigration during the tenth and eighth centuries; they brought with them expertise in city building, skills in metalworking, and ideas tinged with Phoenician and early Greek influences. The result was a series of Etruscan cities, extending from the Po valley to Rome. These urban dwellers traded enthusiastically with the Greek cities of Italy and they commanded important trade routes close to Rome, with crossings over the Tiber at Fidenae and Lucus Feroniae. Metalwork and pottery, in particular, were imported from and exported to Egypt, Phoenicia, and Greece. Rome was the last point at which the Tiber could be crossed before the sea, and the mouth of the Tiber was a vital source of salt—much coveted by Romans and Etruscans alike. From around 625 BC the relatively cosmopolitan Etruscans swamped pastoral Rome, bringing with them new ideas in architecture, town planning, commerce, science, medicine, and art. The Romans can thank the Etruscans for the Latin alphabet; the *fasces*, symbols of a magisterial power and jurisdiction; temple design; elements of their religion; and many aspects of their heritage.[1]

Rome was gradually transformed over the 200 years leading up to the end of the monarchy in 509 BC, turning from a society that lived in hill-top huts to a sophisticated, thriving conurbation, complete with a unique religion and history. Rome was now one of the biggest cities in Italy; she could boast a past with legends—Aeneas, Romulus and Remus—a socio-political system, a burgeoning culture, and a citizen army. The monarchy, dating from 753 BC, was unusual in that it was elective rather than hereditary. When the hill dwellers came down from the hills and populated the valleys, they built a central market there—the forum. The earliest evidence of the Sacra Via dates from around 575 BC, suggesting that Rome was already a *polis* by then. The king had absolute power (*imperium*) and the ability to consult the gods (*auspicium*). Very little was done without the sanction of the gods, including declarations of war and all manner of military activity.

The Etruscans were in conflict with the early Romans over land disputes in central Italy between 700 and 500 BC. However, Rome was initially but one of many settlements in

Latium, vying to defend and preserve their lands from un-neighbourly attacks; they just happened to be the largest. As we have seen, the early hostilities are shrouded in the mists of legend, as described by Livy in the opening books of his *Ab Urbe Condita,* and by Virgil in the *Aeneid*—both written some seven hundred years after the alleged events. In the beginning the Etruscans, under King Mezentius, formed an alliance with King Turnus of the Rutuli and attacked the Latins and Trojans, who were led by Latinus and Aeneas. The Latins and Trojans won, but Aeneas was killed in the battle.[2] Peace came with the agreement that the River Tiber would form the frontier between Latins and Etruscans. During the reign of Romulus, the Etruscan Fidenates saw Rome as a threat and accordingly attacked them; Romulus retaliated by marching on Fidenae, where he ambushed the Fidenate army and took the town. This unsettled the neighbouring Veientes, Etruscan allies of the Fidenates, who then invaded Roman territory only to be defeated by Romulus outside Veii. Romulus did not have the resources to besiege the city, so he devastated the land of the Veientes instead. The Veientes sued for peace, and a one-hundred-year treaty was signed which required the Veientes to cede parts of their territory to Rome.[3]

The Fidenates and Veientes would not lie down. During the reign of Rome's third king, the bellicose Tullus Hostilius (r. 673–642 BC), the Fidenates and the Veientes were secretly incited to war by Mettius Fufetius, the dictator of Alba Longa. Mettius was still smarting from an earlier defeat by the Romans and his ignominious new status as a vassal of Rome.[4] Tullus called on the Albans, and together the two armies marched on Fidenae, crossing the Anio and camping at the confluence of the Anio and the Tiber. The Fidenates and Veientes lined up against the Romans. Mettius and the Alban army toyed with the idea of deserting, and retreated to a hill top where they waited to see who would be victorious before committing themselves. But Tullus saw this and craftily encouraged his troops, telling them that the Alban army had moved exactly according to his plans. Crucially, the Fidenates believed that the Albans were about to attack from the rear and fled. The Romans then routed the Veientes. Tullus ordered Alba Longa to be destroyed and forced the Albans to Rome, where they became Roman citizens.[5] His neat assessment of the battle was that, since Mettius had been torn between two cities, so would his body. Accordingly, his arms were tied to two chariots which were driven off at speed in different directions—a graphic, gruesome warning to anyone who dared to betray Rome.[6] Livy was disgusted by the atrocity, pointing out that it was, apparently, never repeated in his lifetime.

However, despite his impressive victory Tullus was not quite as circumspect as he might have been. He routinely snubbed his gods and underestimated the importance of keeping them on side. Towards the end of his reign, Rome was beset by bad omens: a shower of stones fell on the Alban Mount, a voice boomed out complaining that the Albans had failed to show due devotion, and a plague struck Rome. Tullus fell ill, obsessed with superstition. Sacrifices, as recommended by Numa Pompilius to Jupiter Elicius, were ineffective because Tullus failed to perform them correctly. Jupiter was enraged and dispatched a thunder bolt which struck Tullus and his house, reducing both to ashes. Another warning—this time to successful commanders and kings, who were well-advised to show *pietas* to the gods at all times.[7]

On the expiry of an earlier truce, the sixth king of Rome, Servius Tullius (r. 578–535 BC) declared war on the Veientes and the Etruscans. His subsequent victory consolidated his tenuous position in Rome. According to the *Fasti Triumphales*, Servius celebrated three triumphs over the Etruscans, the first two of which were in 571 BC and 567 BC.[8]

In 509 BC the monarchy, under Lucius Tarquinius Superbus, was deposed and replaced by a republic. In an attempt to regain his throne, Tarquinius enlisted the support of the similarly disaffected cities of Veii and Tarquinii; they were defeated by the Romans at the Battle of Silva Arsia. The victorious consul, Publius Valerius Poplicola, returned to Rome freighted with Etruscan booty, celebrating a triumph in which he rode in a four-horse chariot; this set a precedent for subsequent triumphs.[9] The other consul, Lucius Junius Brutus, fought a duel with Arruns, the son of Tarquin; both combatants died. Brutus was awarded a lavish funeral, and the women of Rome mourned him for a year—a fitting tribute to the revenge he took on Sextus Tarquinius, after he had raped Lucretia, one of Rome's foremost *matronae* and a paragon of feminine virtue.[10]

The following year Poplicola did battle with Lars Porsenna, king of the powerful Etruscan city of Clusium, because Porsenna was in league with Tarquinius Superbus. The war with Clusium and Lars Porsenna spawned two famous legends. When Porsenna approached the Pons Sublicius, one of the Tiber bridges leading into Rome, Publius Horatius Cocles commandeered the bridge to hold off the enemy. This allowed the Romans, by then a quaking rabble (*trepidam turbam*) time to destroy it. While his comrades Titus Herminius Aquilinus and Spurius Lartius retreated from the bridge, Horatius held on until it had fallen to the enemy, then swam back across the river under fire—but not before a spear had hit him in the buttocks. Horatius' outstanding bravery was rewarded with a bronze statue set up in the *comitium*; now disabled and discharged from the army, he was given as much public land as he could plough in one day with a yoke of oxen, while every Roman citizen gave him one day's food.[11] The war continued; Porsenna besieged the city, establishing a garrison on the Janiculum, blocking supplies to the city via Tiber river transport, and sending raiding parties to plunder the surrounding countryside.

The Sublicius Bridge was later deemed so sacred that alterations or repairs could not be made until sacrifices were given by the chief priest, the *pontifex maximus*. Livy got his wish that the legend be read for years to come when Thomas Babington Macaulay wrote his poem *Horatius*, composed in 1842 as part of the *Lays of Ancient Rome*, which—if nothing else— captures the proud spirit of Livy's description:

> 'Hew down the bridge, Sir Consul, with all the speed ye may!
> I, with two more to help me, will hold the foe in play.
> In yon strait path, a thousand may well be stopped by three:
> Now, who will stand on either hand and keep the bridge with me? ...
> Oh Tiber, father Tiber, to whom the Romans pray,
> A Roman's life, a Roman's arms, take thou in charge this day!'
> So he spake and, speaking, sheathed the good sword by his side,
> And, with his harness on his back, plunged headlong in the tide.

The second legend involves a Roman boy, Gaius Mucius Scaevola, who was detailed to infiltrate the Etruscan camp and assassinate Porsenna. Unfortunately Mucius could not distinguish the king from his secretary, and so murdered the secretary in error. Mucius was captured and revealed his mission to Porsenna, after which Porsenna threatened to have him burned alive. Mucius was undaunted and boasted that he was but one of three hundred Roman youths who would volunteer to do the same:

> I am Gaius Mucius, a citizen of Rome. I came here an enemy to kill my enemy, and I am as ready to die as I am to kill. We Romans act bravely and, in adversity, we suffer bravely...Look, and see how cheap the body is to men who have an eye on great glory.

Mucius then thrust his right hand into a nearby fire to prove his courage; he showed no signs of pain, winning for himself and his descendants the cognomen *Scaevola* (which means 'left-handed'). Mucius was also rewarded with farming land on the right bank of the Tiber, later known as the *Mucia Prata*. As for Porsenna, he was taken aback by the boy's pride, valour, and initiative, and allowed him to return to Rome with the words 'Go home—you harm yourself more than me,' ringing in his ears. Porsenna then sent ambassadors to Rome to offer peace terms.[12] Poplicola negotiated a conclusive peace treaty with Porsenna in which he surrendered hostages, including his daughter Valeria, whom Porsenna protected from the Tarquinii.

The stories of Publius Horatius Cocles and Gaius Mucius are, of course, legendary; while variations exist in other literatures and cultures, they may well have their foundation in kernels of historical truth. Their purpose is not just to pose as reliable history, but also to demonstrate— to the Romans of Livy's day—the virtues of good old-fashioned values, at a time when Augustus was struggling to introduce a program of moral reform. The heroes here exemplify conspicuous bravery in the face of death, quick-wittedness in extreme situations, and unquestioned, unselfish loyalty to Rome (*pietas*). Furthermore, they clearly show that the Roman state was only too ready to publicly and financially reward such virtues and valour, and that enemies could be persuaded to act humanely and honourably (with *fides*) when faced with such deeds.

The Sabines were as much a problem to the early Romans as the Etruscans. The first significant contact between the two was the legendary incident from 750 BC: the 'rape' of the Sabine women.[13]

Titus Tatius (d. 748 BC) was the Sabine King of Cures, who attacked Rome and captured the Capitol—aided by the treacherous Tarpeia. The Sabine women managed to persuade Tatius and Romulus to bury their differences, leading to their joint rule over the Romans and Sabines. Livy gives us the details:

> [They] went boldly into the midst of the flying missiles with disheveled hair and rent garments. Running across the space between the two armies they tried to stop any further fighting and calm the excited passions, by appealing to their fathers in the one army, and their husbands in the other, not to bring upon themselves a curse by staining their hands with the blood of a father-in-law or a son-in-law, nor upon their posterity the taint of parricide. 'If,' they cried, 'you are weary of these ties of kindred, these marriage-bonds, then turn your anger upon us; it is we who are the cause of the war, it is we who have wounded and slain our husbands and fathers. Better for us to perish rather than live without one or the other of you, as widows or as orphans.'[14]

The words of brave, selfless and, despite appearances, rational women. Some time later, during the reign of Rome's third king Tullus Hostilius (r. 673–642 BC), the Sabines captured some Roman merchants at a market near the Temple of Feronia (a site which was special to the Sabines even though it was in Etruria). The Sabines, in their defence, claimed that a number of their citizens were being detained in Rome. They were aided by mercenary volunteers from Veii, but the government of Veii stayed neutral—in compliance with a peace treaty already made with Romulus. Tullus invaded and faced the Sabines at the forest of Malitiosa. The Roman force was superior; the cavalry had recently been strengthened by ten new *turmae* of *equites* (squadrons of cavalry) recruited from the Albans, who were by now citizens of Rome. The Romans won the battle with a successful cavalry charge, inflicting heavy losses on the Sabines.[15]

The *Fasti Triumphales* reveal a triumph for a victory over the Sabines and the Veientes for Rome's fourth king Ancus Marcius (r. 642–617 BC). Ancus is, however, more famous for his subjugation of the Latins, in the days before the Latin League accepted the leadership of Rome during the reign of Tarquinius Superbus (535–509 BC). The League was a confederation of about thirty towns and tribes in Latium, who came together in the seventh century for mutual defence. Rome's treaty with Carthage—dated by Polybius to 507 BC, in which Rome assumed Latin lands surrounding Rome to be part of their territory—was to become an enduring and festering source of enmity between Roman and Latin forces down the years.[16] The Latins had naively thought that Ancus would pursue a pacifist foreign policy—as his grandfather, Numa Pompilius, had done—and duly invaded Roman territory. A Roman embassy sought restitution for the war damage, but received nothing more than an insulting reply from the Latins. Ancus accordingly declared war. This declaration is important, because it was the first time that the Romans had declared war by means of the rites of the *fetiales*. Ancus Marcius took Politorium and relocated its inhabitants to the Aventine Hill, where they became Roman citizens. The ghost town that Politorium became was then occupied by other Latins, so Ancus took the town again—sacking and demolishing it, along with the Latin villages of Tellenae and Ficana. The war then moved to the garrison town of fortified Medullia, where the Romans were victorious. Much booty was returned to Rome, and more Latins were sent to Rome as citizens, settling at the foot of the Aventine. Ancus fortified the city: he annexed the Janiculum, strengthening it with a wall, and connected it with the city by the Pons Sublicis—this had vital implications for trade. He built the Fossa Quiritium, a ditch fortification, and opened Rome's first prison, the Mamertine; he established important salt mines at the mouth of the Tiber, on the south side, near the later port of Ostia; he also grabbed the Silva Maesia, a coastal forest north of the Tiber, from the Veientes.[17]

In 530 BC Tarquinius laid siege to Gabii, south of Collatia. Progress was slow, however, so he resorted to what Livy called 'decidedly un-Roman and shameful treachery and duplicity' (*postremo minime arte Romana, fraude ac dolo, adgressus est*). His youngest son Sextus Tarquinius—notorious violator of Lucretia—was planted as a fifth columnist amongst the Gabii, and gradually ingratiated himself with his hosts, who were taken in by Sextus' tales of abuse by his father. He finally won access to the councils of the Gabii and was particularly vocal in discussions regarding war with Rome, rekindling old grudges and animosities. War was declared, but the battles were minor and inclusive. Taking advice from his father, Sextus then embarked on a terror campaign in which all the leading men of Gabii were either murdered or exiled, their property confiscated and turned over to Tarquinius. Gabii was then taken by the Romans without a fight. Tarquinius was much more lenient, according to Dionysius, offering the Gabians equal rights with Rome. The peace treaty was written on an ox-hide shield cover, which was preserved in the Quirinal temple of Semo Sancus until the time of Augustus. Sextus eventually got his just desserts: he was murdered in Gabii, when he took refuge there after the monarchy was toppled.[18]

In 585 BC, during the reign of Rome's fifth king Lucius Tarquinius Priscus (r. 616–579 BC), the Sabines resumed hostilities with an assault on Rome. This interrupted Tarquinius' plans to fortify Rome with a stone wall around the city; the initial engagement led to much loss of life on both sides, but it was inconclusive. The Sabines withdrew, giving the Romans valuable time to raise more troops, in particular to bolster their inadequate cavalry. In the second battle the Romans shipped rafts of burning logs down the River Anio, in a bid to torch the bridge over the river. The Sabine infantry were winning the centre-ground, but the Roman cavalry flanked the Sabines, routed them, and blocked their flight from the battlefield—helped by the destruction of the bridge. The weapons of the Sabines who had drowned in the Anio drifted downstream into the Tiber and through Rome, giving the citizens a poignant and vivid sign of victory. Tarquinius made a pyre and burnt the spoils in sacrifices to Vulcan, sending prisoners and booty back to Rome. He then invaded Sabine territory and defeated their newly-formed army. The Sabines sued for peace; Collatia, and its surrounding land and population, were absorbed into Roman territory. Arruns Tarquinius, the king's nephew, was left there to garrison the town—Tarquinius returned to Rome to celebrate a triumph on 13 September 585 BC.[19]

The end of the Roman monarchy had significant political implications for Rome's allies and enemies, not least because existing treaties were all made under the monarchy and were now null and void. Before his murder, the disaffected Sextus Tarquinius persuaded the Sabines to help him in his attempt to restore the monarchy. After an initial defeat, Sextus enlisted the support of Fidenae and Cameria; these combined forces were defeated in 505 BC.[20] The Sabines attacked again in 504 BC, facing the two experienced Roman consuls Publius Valerius Poplicola and Titus Lucretius Tricipitinus at the River Anio. Both Livy and Dionysius agree that it was during this war that Appius Claudius Sabinus Inregillensis moved his family and clients from Sabinum over to Rome, along with 500 soldiers: the Romans rewarded him by making him a senator and gifting the Sabines citizenship and land on the far side of the Anio; Dionysius adds that the Romans promised them land beyond the Anio, in the vicinity of Fidenae, if they could capture it from the Fidenates. The war continued apace, with Tarquinius seriously underestimating the Romans in an episode where he falsely believed them all to be asleep, while his army filled the *fossum* (ditch) around Valerius' camp, attempting to gain access to the walls. In fact the Romans were lying in wait, picking off the Sabines as they came over. On a signal from the Romans, Lucretius dispatched his cavalry, driving the Fidenates into the open—where they were massacred. Casualties were 13,500 slain and 4,200 captured.

In 503 BC the consul Publius Postumius Tubertus was voted an ovation for defeating the Sabines in April, while his colleague Agrippa Menenius Lanatus celebrated a triumph (also for a victory over the Sabines). The so-called Bloodless War followed in 501 BC: a disturbance broke out amongst Sabine youths when they raped a group of courtesans during games in Rome. The Sabine ambassadors sued for peace but were rebuffed by the Romans, who demanded that the Sabines pay restitution to Rome for the costs of a war. The Sabines refused, and war was declared, but the spat seems to have fizzled out; no battle ensued.[21] This incident is significant because this was the first time the Romans had appointed a dictator to deal with a crisis.

Similarly inconclusive was the One-day War of 495 BC, in which a Sabine army invaded Roman territory—as far as the river Anio—and devastated the land. Aulus Postumius Albus Regillensis and Publius Servilius Priscus Structus rounded up the Sabines, who offered no resistance to the Roman infantry.[22] In the following year, the Volsci, Sabines, and the Aequi rose up against Rome. Manius Valerius Maximus was appointed dictator and ten legions were raised—the largest number ever recruited at any one time. Four were assigned to Valerius to enable him to deal with the Sabines, who were duly routed.

At this time, a Roman dictator was quite different from later dictators in different ages, with their associations with tyranny and absolute, undemocratic power. Roman dictators were appointed for a period of six months as an extraordinary magistrate (*magistratus extraordinarius*) to deal with a specific military or domestic crisis. They were obliged to resign the post once it was dealt with—in short, they were an expedience, and represented a focusing of the powers of the consulship. They also went by the name of 'Master of the Citizen Army (*magister populi*); they were prohibited from riding a horse during their term of office, presumably because it was felt that the head of the army should always be with his infantry— the strongpoint of the forces. One of the dictator's first tasks was therefore to appoint a *magister equitum* as subordinate cavalry commander. Dictators were created *rei gerundae causa* ('for the matter to be done'), usually leading an army in the field against a specified enemy. The practice died out around the time of the Second Punic War, although it was revived by Lucius Cornelius Sulla Felix (Sulla), who was appointed *dictator legibus faciendis et rei publicae constituendae causa*—'dictator for the enacting of laws and for the setting of the constitution'. Julius Caesar, of course, was appointed dictator a number of times.[23]

As we have noted, Rome was but one of many cities battling it out with their neighbours in the vicinity of the River Tiber. The majority of her engagements were fought with allies from other towns, against similar coalitions, largely combined with the southern Etruscans. Usually involved were the Veii; the Aequi, hill folk from the Aniene valley above Praeneste and Tibur; and the Volsci, who were originally from the Liri valley but had spread onto the Latin plain to threaten Roman territory. It is not unusual for mountain peoples to be covetous of lower-lying, flatter lands; overcrowding back home, famine, and the lack of suitable cultivatable land were the usual causes. The Volsci and the Aequi were no different, and it is their raids and incursions, in the fifth and fourth centuries BC, that caused Rome much irritation through loss of land in the Latin plain.

Despite her conquests, at the end of the fifth century BC Rome was still, like her enemies, very much an agricultural society, supported by an agrarian economy. The lower ranks of army, the heavily armed infantrymen, were made up of farmers (the *classis*), clearly indicating that there were opportunities for financial betterment—for how else would these farmers be able to afford their armour and weapons? Below the *classis* was the *infra classem*, skirmishers with less and lighter armour, requiring a smaller financial outlay. Above the *classis* were the *equites*, patricians with some wealth, who largely (but not exclusively) made up the cavalry, officers, and staff. Their wealth was usually derived from extensive land ownership. Not only were the soldiers not paid, but they also had to provide their own rations.[24]

The *classis* in particular lost out badly because of war. They were away from their lands and their livelihood for increasingly long periods, and they suffered virtual ruin when their farms were depredated by enemy action. This forced some into debt and bondage to patricians—a semi-servile arrangement (*nexum*), which involved a farmer or farm worker providing labour on the security of his person; the penalty for defaulting was being sold into slavery. Richer and bigger landowners were better-able to sustain losses, and they were also the beneficiaries of the bond-debt process which allowed them to procure yet more land and cheap labour at the expense of the *classis* and *infra classem*. In the fifth and fourth centuries Rome's incessant warring helped keep the peace at home, and delimited opportunities for social unrest. Conquered enemies and alliances provided a supply of troops either in the form of prisoners of war, forced into the Roman army, or as allies (*socii*), for whom the terms of the alliance involved military service.

We may now go on to examine the battles the Romans fought as they spread out from the immediate vicinity of Rome, overrunning most of the Italian peninsula. These would be conflicts which brought them up against the Etruscans, Volsci, Veientes, Gauls, Hernici, and Samnites, the cities of the Latin League, and the southern cities of Magna Graecia.

An amusing take on the legend of the *Rape of the Sabine Women* around 750 BC soon after the foundation of Rome.

The handle of a bronze box (*cista*) from around 350 BC: two Roman soldiers, carrying a dead comrade, found at in a grave at Praeneste. The uniforms are partially Greek.

An Etruscan chariot.

Publius Horatius Cocles defending the Pons Sublicius—a key bridge leading into Rome—against the forces of Lars Porcena, in the war against Clusium (around 509 BC).

Battles for Early Italy

Aricia (*c.* 506 BC and 495 BC)

There were, in fact, two battles of Aricia: the first was between Rome and the Etruscans, immediately following the fall of the Roman monarchy. Both were important causes of the turmoil that enveloped the area around Rome, as the various cities vied with each other for control of the lands surrounding Rome and in Etruria.

The town is named after Aricia, the wife of Hippolytus—identified as Virbius, the Roman forest god, who lived in the sacred forests nearby. According to Caius Julius Solinus, Aricia was founded by Archilocus Siculus.[1] There is evidence of a settlement there from the eighth and ninth centuries BC. The city was a member of the Latin League from the end of the sixth century until 338 BC. Aricia takes in the Lake of Nemi, home to the sanctuary of *Diana Aricina* (or *Diana Nemorensis*) and presided over by the Rex Nemorensis, immortalized in Frazer's *The Golden Bough*.[2] The cult of Diana led to Aricia becoming an influential centre of medicine.

In 508 BC Lars Porsenna, king of the powerful Etrurian city of Clusium, signed a peace treaty with Rome; he then sent one part of his army, under his son Arruns, to attack Aricia. The Aricians gained support from the Latin League, and from Cumae (under Aristodemus). The Clusians routed the Aricians outside the city walls, but the Cumaeans then attacked the Clusian rear and destroyed them. Arruns was killed; Livy tells how some survivors sought refuge in Rome, where they were given medical attention and shelter. Many stayed and settled in an area which became known as the *Tuscum Vicum*.[3] The battle was significant because it allowed the Latins to sever vital communications between Etruria and Campania. The Etruscans were now a spent force militarily, and retired beyond the Tiber; they were left only with a bridgehead at Fidenae, garrisoned by a contingent of soldiers from Veii.

The second battle took place in 495 BC, when the Romans soundly defeated the Aurunci at Aricia. The Aurunci had given Rome an ultimatum to withdraw from Volscian territory; the victorious commander was the consul Publius Servilius Priscus Structus.[4] The city then became a *municipium*, and an important stopover on the Via Appia. The Augustan viaduct there, which carries the road over a volcanic depression, still survives. Octavian's mother, Atia, was born there; Martial enjoyed Aricia's leeks and Pliny the Elder its cabbages.

Lake Regillus (496 BC)

The Battle of Lake Regillus was a decisive encounter between Rome and the cities of the Latin League, and it also marked the last of Tarquinius Superbus' attempts to restore his monarchy. The lake was close to what is now Pontano Secco, near Frascati. The Latins were led by Tarquinius' son-in-law, Octavius Mamilius of Tusculum, and by the nonagenarian Tarquinius, who had turned to the League now that the Etruscans had been defeated. The Romans were inflamed by the presence of Tarquinius and his son, Titus Tarquinius.

The Romans were led by Aulus Postumius Albus Regillensis, who had been appointed dictator to quell the Latin threat; his *magister equitum* was Titus Aebutius Elva. The Romans had 23,000 men to the 40,000 men and 3,000 cavalry of the Latins. During the battle Aebutius and Mamilius charged at one another on horseback: Mamilius was wounded in the chest, and taken from the battlefield, while Aebutius' arm was so severely injured by Mamilius' spear that he too had to retire. Mamilius eventually returned with some troops to relieve a band of Roman exiles he had deployed earlier under Titus, which were making ground against the Romans; however, he was recognised by the Roman general Titus Herminius Aquilinus, famous for fighting with Horatius at the Sublician Bridge. Mamilius was killed with a single thrust of Herminius' spear. While Herminius was despoiling Mamilius' armour he was killed by a javelin.

By dispatching his personal cavalry force to cut the deserters down, Postumius rallied the Roman forces who were fleeing the battle. The Romans turned and attacked the Latins with the help of the cavalry, who dismounted and assisted their comrades on foot. Postumius then set an important tactical precedent when he hurled a Roman standard into the midst of the enemy, where it was to be retrieved by a fervid and frenzied horde of Romans. The Latins fled, with the loss of 30,000 men.[5]

The towns of the Latin League were constantly harried by tribes coming down from the Appenines, anxious to annex more lands for themselves. The Latins could ill afford to repulse these tribes and at the same time fight with Rome, so in around 493 BC the *foedus Cassianum* was signed by the Latins and the Romans. An early example of Roman 'divide and rule', the treaty was inscribed on a bronze pillar and kept on display in the Forum for approximately 400 years.[6]

Apart from ongoing peace and mutual aid between the two signatories, the treaty provided for a common defence army, with equal numbers of soldiers from both sides, a ban on free passage or assistance to enemies, and equal shares in any booty. The treaty—Rome's first—was named after Spurius Cassius Viscellinus, consul at the time and chief negotiator on the terms, even though both Livy and Dionysius record that he was keen to have the Latin cities destroyed.[7] The treaty was hugely advantageous to the Romans, placing Rome on an equal footing with the entire League, removing as it did a long-standing enemy, and effectively strengthening the Roman army and enabling it to pursue its regional expansion. It was renewed in 358 BC but the Romans reneged soon after, sparking the Second Latin War (340–338 BC).

The battle of Lake Regillus lived long in the memories of the Romans, so much so that it was imbued with divinity. Legend has it that the Dioscuri, Castor and Pollux, came to the aid of the Romans during the battle; afterwards they watered their horses at the Fountain of

Juturna, in the Forum, and announced the victory to nervous Romans. A temple was built on the spot and dedicated in 484 BC; it still survives, in part, to this day.[8]

Macaulay gives us a taste of the bloody 'place of slaughter' in this Lucanesque extract from his *The Battle of the Lake Regillus*:

> *Little they think how sternly*
> *   That day the trumpets pealed;*
> *How in the slippery swamp of blood*
> *   Warrior and war-horse reeled;*
> *How wolves came with fierce gallops,*
> *   And crows on eager wings,*
> *To tear the flesh of captains,*
> *   And peck the eyes of kings;*
> *How thick the dead lay scattered*
> *   Under the Porcian height;*
> *How through the gates of Tusculum*
> *   Raved the wild stream of flight;*
> *And how the Lake Regillus*
> *   Bubbled with crimson foam,*
> *What time the Thirty Cities*
> *   Came forth to war with Rome.*

Macaulay called it a 'purely Homeric battle', and indeed Livy leans heavily on the *Iliad*. For example, the fight between Valerius and the young Tarquinius is based on that between Paris and Menelaus.[9]

There are similarities between Livy's description of the battle at Lake Regillus and the Battle of the Algidus Pass in 432 BC; the Romans here were led by the dictator Aulus Postumius Tubertus, who defeated the Aequi and the Volsci.[10]

Antium (482 and 468 BC)

The two battles of Antium (modern Anzio), fought by Rome against the Volsci in the fifth century BC, are characterised by battlefield guile and deception on both sides. They were important conflicts in the long-running war between Rome and the Volsci; the Volsci are well known because the exiled rebel Roman noble Caius Lucius Coriolanus defected to them. Before the battle of Lake Regillus, and the *foedus Cassianum*, the Volsci sent military support to the Latins. In 495 BC, when the consuls Appius Claudius Sabinus Inregillensis and Publius Servilius Priscus Structus invaded Volscian territory, the Volsci took three hundred children from Cora and Suessa Pometia as hostages. The Roman army pulled back. The fractious Volsci then allied with the Hernici, and sought help from the Latins. The Latins were having none of it, and seized the Volscian envoys whom they delivered to Rome; the grateful senate returned 6,000 prisoners to the Latin towns, who reciprocated by sending a crown of gold to the Temple of Jupiter Optimus Maximus.[11]

Engagements followed in 496 and 495 BC with a Roman victory at Suessa Pometia, but in 494 Rome became embroiled in the first *secessio plebis;* Manius Valerius Maximus was appointed dictator and ten legions were raised (a record for the time), three of which were assigned to the consul Aulus Verginius Tricostus Caeliomontanus to attack the Volsci.[12] Verginius captured the town of Velitrae and established a Roman colony there.

The *secessio plebis* was a form of general strike in which the plebeians downed tools, shut up shop, and deserted Rome, leaving the patricians to get on with running the city on their own—all businesses and services ground to a halt. There were five of these strikes between 494 and 287 BC. 494 BC was significant because it marked the first real breakthrough between the people and the patricians, when some of the plebs were freed from their debts and the patricians yielded some of their power when the office of Tribune of the Plebs was created. This was the first government position held by the plebeians; plebeian tribunes were sacrosanct during their time in office.

In 482 BC the consul Lucius Aemilius was dispatched to deal with the Volsci at Antium; the ensuing battle was inconclusive, with the Volsci feigning a retreat that led the Romans to believe they had won. An ill-disciplined plundering of the Volsci dead ensued, which left the Romans exposed to attack. The Romans fled, suffering heavy casualties.[13] Fourteen years later the Romans would get their revenge. Under the consul Titus Quinctius Capitolinus Barbatus, the Romans were engaged in battle with the Volsci and losing the fight. Quinctius told one wing of his army that the other wing was winning, and so redressed the balance. The Volsci attacked by night a few days later; Quinctius then dispatched some of his troops with mounted trumpeters outside the Volsci camp to create a cacophonous din, which not only confused the Volsci but also kept them awake. In the morning the somewhat fresher Romans attacked, and the Volsci retreated to higher ground. Despite heavy losses the Romans eventually won, and Antium was captured.[14]

Veii (480 BC)

In 480 the Roman army was riven by dissent and division, and so the Veians and their Etruscan allies saw their chance. Rome's two consuls Marcus Fabius and Gnaeus Manlius faced their enemy with some trepidation, probably more fearful of their own troops' reactions than anything else. During the procrastinations the Veians taunted the Romans, with the predictable result of spurring the Romans into angry action; each swore to win or die. By the end of a long and costly battle Manlius was dead, as was the former consul Quintus Fabius; nevertheless, the Romans prevailed and the Veians withdrew.[15] The battle is significant because it shows how the Roman commanders reacted when under threat of mutiny from their troops, and how the patriotism of the soldiers was converted into a suicidal will to defeat the foe.

The site of Veii, one of the richest and most powerful of the Etruscan cities, is now Isola Farnese. After centuries of conflict with Rome it finally fell to the armies of Camillus in 396

BC. It has a long tradition of belligerence, according to Plutarch: 'The first were the Veientes, a people of Tuscany who had large possessions, and lived in a spacious city; they started a war, by claiming Fidenae as theirs.'[16]

Mons Algidus (458 BC)

This was a conflict with the Aequi, who broke a truce made with Rome only the previous year. The Aequians made camp on Mons Algidus, about fourteen miles south-east of Rome. The Roman commander, Minucius, was ineffective and paid for his dithering when the enemy walled him into his own camp. There was panic in Rome, and Lucius Quinctius Cincinnatus was appointed dictator to resolve the situation. Cincinnatus was an aristocrat who became consul in 460 BC, dictator in 458 BC, and dictator again in 439 BC; he was widely regarded as a paragon of Roman *virtus* and rectitude. In 461 his son, Caeso Quinctius, was falsely accused of murder and fled to the Etruscans. His father and some friends stood bail for Ceaso, but he fled and was condemned to death *in absentia*; his father was saddled with a huge debt, which he paid by selling his lands and downsizing in retirement to a small farm. In 406 Cincinnatus put down a revolt by slaves and exiles who had taken the Capitol; he replaced a consul who had died in the turmoil but then fell out of favour with the Senate, who refused to support his levy for an army to fight the Volscians and Aequi. Cincinnatus retired, refusing to stand for consul again.

When the call came to lead Rome's army, as dictator, against the Aequi, Cincinnatus was working on his farm; he downed tools and went back to Rome, something of a returning hero. At the battle Cincinnatus led from the front, while Lucius Tarquitius, his *magister equitum*, attacked with his cavalry. Many of the Aequi were destroyed, and the surviving commanders implored Cincinnatus not to slaughter them. Cincinnatus showed clemency, telling the Aequi that they could live if they submitted to him and brought him their leader, Gracchus Cloelius, bound in chains with his officers. A yoke was set up (made of the traditional three spears), under which the humiliated Aequi passed, *sub iugum missi*. Warde Fowler neatly describes this as 'a kind of dramatised form of degradation'. Cincinnatus immediately disbanded his army, promptly resigned his office, and returned to his farm some sixteen days after assuming the dictatorship. He refused any share of the spoils—perfect behaviour for a dictator. To Livy, Cincinnatus was the ideal Roman (*homo vere Romanus*), and acted with bravery and dignity, exuding *pietas* to Rome.[17]

The name of Cincinnatus lives on, redolent as it is of civic virtue, humility, and clemency. Cincinnato in Lazio is named after him, as is the town of Cincinnatus, New York, and the Society of the Cincinnati (established in 1783 to preserve the ideals of the American Revolutionary War officers) gave its name to Cincinnati, Ohio.

The Veientes continued to irritate Rome for the next ninety or so years. There were a number of battles in the latter half of the fifth century BC. In 437 BC, one at Fidenae saw the Romans victorious under the dictator Mamercus Aemilius Mamercinus, when the Fidenates went over to the Veientes after murdering four Roman envoys (Tullus Cloelius, Gaius Fulcinius, Spurius Antius, and Lucius Roscius). They had been sent to Veii to demand the return of Fidenae, but their king, Lars Tolumnius, had them executed instead. The explanation for this outrage was that when Tolumnius' aides asked if they should execute the Roman ambassadors Tolumnius was in the middle of an untimely game of dice. He cried out "Excellent!", inadvertently ordering the execution of the Romans. When the Romans retaliated, Tolumnius was killed in close combat by the *tribunus militum* Aulus Cornelius Cossus. Cossus was one of only three Roman generals to be awarded the *spolia opima* for killing an enemy leader in single combat. After taking the cuirass from Tolumnius' body he decapitated him and stuck his head on a lance, parading it in front of the Veientes and the Fidenates—much to their horror. Cossus donated Tolumnius' armour, shield, and sword to the Temple of Jupiter Feretrius on the Capitoline, where it could still be seen during the reign of Augustus. The other two generals who were to win the *spolia opima* were Romulus (when he slew King Acro) and M. Claudius Marcellus (who slew King Britomartus, of the Insubrian Gauls).[18]

Enemies of Rome being humiliated in defeat by being led under the yoke.

Mons Algidus (431 BC)

This was another battle with the Volscians and the Aequi. The Romans were commanded by the dictator Aulus Postumius Tubertus, renowned for his strictness and appointed because the two consuls, Titus Quinctius Cincinnatus and Cnaeus Julius Mento, were unable or unwilling to agree on anything. Livy records how Postumius was wounded in the shoulder, and left the battle when his skull was fractured by a stone. Marcus Fabius, in charge of the cavalry, had his thigh pinned to his horse by a spear; Mento had his arm torn off. The Volscians were inspired by the bravery of Vettius Mettius, who fought like a tiger to defend his camp, but to no avail—the Romans were victorious, spurred on themselves by the consul hurling his spear into the midst of the enemy for them to retrieve. The Volscian and Aequian survivors were sold into slavery.

Fidenae (426 BC)

At Nomentum, in 435, Fidenae sided with the Veientes at a time when Rome was laid low by pestilence. The dictator Quintus Servilius raised an army and pursued his enemies—who were now having second thoughts—to Nomentum and then Fidenae, which Servilius captured. At Fidenae, in 426, the Fidenates and Veientes joined forces again against the Romans, who were under the command of Mamercus Aemilius Mamercinus in his second dictatorship. Mamercus had the hills to his right, the Tiber to his left, and occupied a ridge behind, unseen by the enemy. The battle marked a first for the Romans—baptism by fire in the use of incendiary tactics; this was the first time they encountered fire-brandishing women who used torches as their only weapons. The mighty enemy column, ablaze with burning torches, instilled sheer frenzy in the Romans—but after recovering from their initial surprise, and being rallied by Mamercus, the Romans seized the enemy torches and turned the tables by attacking them with their own brands. The troops on the ridge then attacked, surrounding the Veientes, cutting them down at the Tiber and forcing the Fidenae back to their city, where they surrendered.[19]

The end came for the Veientes in 396 BC. Rome had been laying siege to Veii for a decade or so; the city was finally taken by the Roman dictator Marcus Furius Camillus (*c.* 446–365 BC). His success was anticipated by amazing prodigies: for example, the Alban Lake rose although no rain had fallen to cause this, and the Veiian goddess Juno Regina defected to the Romans. The Oracle of Delphi was consulted by the Romans. Camillus eventually earned four triumphs, was dictator five times, and became known as the Second Founder of Rome.[20] Veii had been supported by Tarquinii, Capena, and Falerii.

Camillus reputedly infiltrated Veii by digging into the soft ground beneath the walls and gaining access to the city's sewage system; however, there is no real archaeological evidence to support this claim. Camillus set a terrible precedent when he refused capitulation terms, plundered on a grand scale, and destroyed the city—slaughtering all the men and enslaving the women and children. Camillus also looted the statue of Juno and established it in a temple on the Aventine. Back in in Rome, his triumph and celebrations lasted four days as he paraded himself on a chariot pulled by four white horses (a *quadriga*), the likes of which had never been seen before, nor since. According to Polybius, the Romans thought this was all somewhat haughty and hubristic: the white horses and the *quadriga* were considered to be sacred, the preserve of Jupiter.

At a stroke, Rome's territory was almost doubled. The plan was to repopulate Veii; half of the new inhabitants were to be poor Romans, but Camillus and the patricians opposed this. He made himself even more unpopular when he broke his promise to dedicate a tenth of the booty to Delphi, for Apollo. The soothsayers declared the gods' displeasure at this.

In 395 BC Camillus besieged Falerii. A local school teacher had surrendered local children as hostages to the Romans, and so the Falerians made peace with Rome. The Aequi, Volsci, and Capena all followed suit, allowing Rome to increase its territory by seventy per cent; some of this new land was distributed to the citizens. Camillus was convicted of embezzling the booty and went into exile near Ardea.[21]

The consequence of Rome's victory over Veii was that she was now the most powerful state in the central part of the Italian peninsula. Cary describes the subjugation of the Veii as 'the first definite step in Rome's career of world conquest ... a turning point in the military history of the city'.[22]

The defence budget saw significant changes around this time in the form of army pay and war tax. Pay was introduced for the soldiery, probably as a concession from the senate to the plebians. It seems very likely that the pay was paid in kind, as the minting of coinage only came one hundred years later. Apart from easing the financial burden of being a soldier, the move had the beneficial effect of increasing the numbers of men eligible for mobilization and the length of time soldiers could be kept under arms. The *tributum* was a war tax levied on all those eligible for military service—whether they were called up or not. Apart from a few instances (such as 347 BC, when there was no war) the tax was paid every year until 167, when booty paid the defence budget.[23]

War With the Gauls

The Romans did not have very long to enjoy their new hegemony over the central part of the Italian peninsula. The forces of her first external enemy, the Gauls, were massing in what was to become known as Cisalpine Gaul—the part of Italy south of the Alps. From around 500 BC, trade with places such as Massilia and Etruria drew these Celts over the mountains from parts of what is now France, southern Germany, Switzerland, Austria, and the Czech Republic, into northern Italy and the Balkans via the rivers Rhône, Seine, Rhine, and Danube.

Conflicts began some 100 years later, when tribes such as the Insubres settled in Lombardy and took Mediolanum (near Milan) in around 396 BC. These were superseded by the Boii, who crossed the River Po and settled in Bononia (Bologna). The Senones penetrated further south; they expelled the Umbrians and established the *ager Gallicus* on the east coast of Italy, between Ariminum and Ancona, and founded the town of Sena Gallica (Sinigaglia)—which became their capital. Etruscan towns further south, such as Marzabotto, were probably taken by the Boii. More significantly for the Romans, the Gauls sold their services as mercenaries to various Hellenistic powers in the eastern Mediterranean, necessitating transit through the Italian peninsula en route to rendezvous in their various theatres of war.

In 391 BC a band of Gauls led by a Senonian chieftain (probably Brennus) infiltrated Etruria as far as the city of Clusium (near modern Siena), which they besieged. Clusium appealed to Rome for help; the Romans sent envoys—three brothers of the illustrious *gens* Fabia—to negotiate. The talks broke down and so the Clusians took steps to force the Senones off their land. The Fabii discarded their neutrality as ambassadors—one of the Gallic leaders was speared by Quintus Fabius in the ensuing fight. Livy and others (notably the priesthood and the Senate) saw this as a breach of the law of nations (*ius gentium*). The Romans not only refused to hand over the culprit but added insult to injury by appointing two members of the family as consuls for the following year. The Gauls were incensed and they abandoned their siege, marching rapidly towards Rome. So great was their intent to revenge this diplomatic humiliation that their journey from Clusium was remarkable: they were so focussed on reaching the city of Rome that the Italian towns, their inhabitants, and the agricultural lands they passed through were left untouched.[1] The Romans and the Gauls met at the River Allia (the Fossa della Bettina, a tributary of the Tiber), just eleven miles north of Rome, on July 18 390 BC.

Livy was appalled by the arrogant and belligerent behaviour of the Romans in this unsavoury incident, and deplored their complacency in the face of what was plainly now a significant threat—however, no dictator was appointed. Indeed, Livy heightens and embellishes his description of the affair by rhetorically describing the Gauls as originating from the ends of the earth, as a strange enemy about which the Romans knew absolutely nothing—a far cry from the local opposition they were used to.

Strabo adds to this picture, describing the Gauls them as 'war-mad' and quick to fight, but not malevolent.[2] This image sits uncomfortably with his later description of their predilection for head-hunting and the use of other body parts of the vanquished as battle trophies. He emphasises their alleged naivety in strategy and tactics—something survivors of the sack of Rome may have taken issue with. Diodorus Siculus describes in detail the military equipment of the Gauls—or, in some cases, the total lack of it, amongst those who did battle in the nude, relying on nature's protection. He also describes their skilful use of the chariot in battle—a piece of military equipment their Celtic cousins in Britannia continued to use, to good effect, when facing Julius Caesar's invasion.[3]

Allia River (390 BC)

The battle at the Allia River on July 18th was a disaster for the Romans, a 'black day' (*dies ater*) which stained the memories of Romans for many years to come. The Roman forces under Q. Servius Fidenas, Q. Sulpicius, and P. Cornelius Maluginensis numbered 15,000, made up of Romans and Italian allies. The Gauls, led by Brennus, were at least double that strength, and possibly up to 70,000 strong. Seriously outnumbered, the Roman centre was impossibly thin; hubris too played its part, when the Romans failed to take the auspices before drawing up their lines of battle. They were cut down in their droves. The Roman flanks were crushed when Brennus attacked these first, after which the centre predictably collapsed; they also suffered from the long-reach Gallic swords. Those that could escape swam up the Tiber or drowned in the attempt, and occupied Veii or else fled back to Rome. Livy says that the Gauls were dumbstruck at the ease of their victory, and feared a trap—but there was none.

Rome (390 BC or 387–6 BC)

The Gauls pressed on to Rome in pursuit of vengeance. Those Romans who escaped had now ignominiously barricaded themselves in the citadel on the Capitol, under the command of Marcus Manlius Capitolinus. The rest of the city was wide open and undefended, as it was fortified only with a ditch and a wall made from turf. The Gauls, again astonished at the absence of security and fearing another trap, were eventually able to sack and plunder at will. The Romans in the Capitol were unaware of the survivors at Veii; Livy paints a picture of abject misery among the older non-combatant men, and lamentations from the women, who were denied a place on the Capitol. Excavations have revealed contemporary scorch marks in the

Forum and on the Palatine, which indicate extensive burning in Rome around this time. Groups of poorer citizens left the city for the surrounding countryside, rather like the city-dwellers of British cities during the Blitz: the 'trekkers', who each left their homes and took refuge in the country in the late afternoon to avoid that night's incendiaries and high-explosive bombs.[4]

The very foundations of the Roman state were in peril. The Vestal Virgins and their essential flame—symbols of the sanctity and well-being of Rome—were able to escape to Caere, with the *flamen Quirinalis* and other sacred objects. They buried what they could not carry in earthen jars, next to the Flamen's house; it has been forbidden to spit there ever since. As a measure of the awe in which the flame was held by the Romans, Plutarch tells us how crucial it was to relocate it, intact, when Rome was attacked. Livy describes it thus:

> They were seen by L. Albinius, a Roman plebeian who with the rest of the crowd who were unfit for war was leaving the City. Even in that critical hour the distinction between sacred and profane was not forgotten. He had his wife and children with him in a wagon, and it seemed to him an act of impiety for him and his family to be seen in a vehicle whilst the national priests should be trudging along on foot, bearing the sacred vessels of Rome. He ordered his wife and children to get down, put the Virgins and their sacred burden in the wagon, and drove them to Caere, their destination.[5]

Indeed, Lucius Albinus could lay claim to being the saviour of Rome, in its darkest hour, by salvaging the *sacra* and preserving the very religious foundation of the city. Rome was doomed if the Vestal fire went out.

Servius, in his commentary on the *Aeneid*, tells how in 390 BC, when the Gauls were besieging the Capitol, women banded together and donated their gold and hair to make bowstrings for the Roman archers.[6] The Gauls blockaded Rome for seven months, finally winning when the Romans surrendered in the face of impending starvation. Luckily for Rome, the Gauls were more interested in revenge and financial gain than the domination of Italy, slaying, or enslaving the population; they were accordingly paid off in gold, and promptly returned to their lands in the north. Their haste, and their disinterest in an occupation of Rome and her territories, may be explained by reports that their own lands in Cisalpine Gaul were being attacked by the Veneti; Livy prefers to explain it by illness amongst the soldiers.[7]

This episode, embarrassing and shameful to the Romans, was soon embellished and larded with fictional anecdotes to mitigate the reality of the disaster and rebuild Roman pride with *exempla pietas,* such as in the story of the Vestal Virgins and the handcart. This, and the tale of the gold-selling, hair-cutting Roman women, were no doubt invented to highlight the patriotism and *pietas* of the average Roman citizen in times of extreme danger. The Romans were not the last to convert a military disaster of the first magnitude into a morale-boosting, psychological victory: Gallipoli, Dunkirk, Singapore, and Arnhem are examples from recent British military history.[8]

To these we can add four more propagandist stories. In the first, the Gauls come across Rome's venerable senators, defiantly sitting in their ivory chairs. In what amounts to a kind of *devotio,* they stoically awaited their inevitable doom in full regalia, resplendent with their military decorations and former badges of office; the Gauls were initially impressed, but later slew them all. In the second, the Roman defenders would have been caught off guard by the Gauls had it not been for an alert and vociferous flock of geese, sacred to Juno, whose warning enabled Manlius to repel the attackers.[9] The third story describes how the Romans complained about faulty scales when the ransom gold—1,000 lbs' worth—was being weighed out, and Brennus threw his sword onto the pans and declared menacingly *'vae victis!'* ('Woe to the vanquished!'). The fourth story tells how Camillus came out of exile (one of the most daring fabrications in Roman history), was voted dictator, and enlisted the support of the Ardeans and the Romans at Veii, beating the Gauls in two battles and persuading the Romans not to relocate their city to Veii. Some sources also state that Camillus interrupted the weighing of the gold and laid his sword on the scales, asserting that Rome was ransomed by steel not gold, after which he defeated the Gauls in battle. Livy also gives Camillus a rousing battle speech, vaunting the grandeur of Rome and arguing for the preservation and restoration of the city, which led to him being celebrated as Rome's second founder.[10]

The sacking of Rome by the Gauls had significant repercussions and implications for the defence of Rome and Roman military weaponry and tactics. The most visible was the construction of the Servian Wall around the city, a much-needed fortification which was to be crucial in the Second Punic War against Hannibal.[11] The Romans also learned from the highly effective, more agile, Gallic style of combat: the vulnerable phalanx was replaced by the more versatile and manoeuvrable maniples which made up a legion, and the thrusting spear was superseded over time by the javelin (*pilum*). Close-quarter combat weaponry, including heavier long swords and full-body shields (the *scutum)*, which could be interlocked to enable tighter defense in the 'tortoise' (*testudo*), were also introduced. The infantry were supported by troops (*velites*) armed with slings and javelins. The concentration of the cream of the patricians (*principes)* in the first line of infantry was relaxed, and younger, highly-trained soldiers replaced them.[12]

Another important development released the Roman soldier from his inextricable ties to and reliance on the land, when a daily stipend was introduced. In effect this marked the start of a professional army which could fight and garrison increasingly far from home, without the need to return to farm the lands and raise money for weapons. This independence permitted Rome to take men away from their homes for long periods of time, and to therefore extend its imperialism in Italy and the wider Mediterranean arena. Booty was also becoming an incentive; as Rome extended its reach the opulent cities of the east fell under its sway, and the rich pickings often found their way back to Rome in the baggage trains of commanders. A subsequent triumph was the culmination of a successful campaign, and bestowed on the conquering hero the highest level of public approval and prestige.

The professionalisation of the army led to sophisticated levels of organisation and bureaucracy. The Romans learned much from the legacy of the Assyrians in terms of their logistics expertise: recruitment and command and supply all became more highly-organised, and permitted the Romans to expand, conquer, and annex in a systematic and largely efficient and successful way. It was always a crucial issue to recruit enough soldiers; by the time of the Punic wars a selection process (*dilectus*) was in force, which selected the best volunteers on a six year contract (later extended to up to eighteen years).

The Roman political system contributed to army recruitment—a fundamental part of the *cursus honorum* was the military tribuneship. After ten years of cadetship and training from age seventeen, twenty-four men with aspirations to the senate were elected, each year, to serve as military tribunes *(tribuni militum)*. Six were posted as commanding officers to each of the consuls' four legions, serving for a period of ten years. After this the way was open for the offices of quaestor, aedile or tribune of the plebs, praetor, and then consul. As we have noted, military success was conspicuous and prestigious, and it added much to a family's reputation and pedigree; the trappings of success were there for all to see in the form of busts, on display in the atrium of the houses of the elite, with citations recording their glorious achievements.

However, the real backbone of the Roman army was the centurion—the cream of the soldiery. Hugely experienced and battle-hardened, centurions led by example, commanding respect, and instilled discipline in their men and fear in their foes. They embodied the new professionalism of the Roman military career, where the opportunity to provide long service and exemplary training were now real possibilities. Livy provides a good example of the achievements and aspirations of the career soldier in the form of Spurius Ligustinus, in around 171 BC: he started in the Macedonian Wars and saw service in Spain, before fighting against the Greek Seleucid King Antiochus III, and going back to Spain for two campaigns in 181 and 180 BC. Spurius was much decorated and took part in a triumph; he was at the top of

The Gauls, under Brennus, weigh out the ransom value of Rome after they had sacked the city. Brennus threw his sword onto the pans and declared menancingly '*vae victis!*'—('woe to the vanquished!') Camillus, dictator, indignantly looks on.

his game at over fifty years of age, after twenty-two years in the army, and was still looking for another posting. His life was not all army-based though: in between the fighting he managed to father six sons and two daughters.[13]

The attack by the Gauls obviously left Rome vulnerable and their military diminished. It tempted and encouraged a number of previously-conquered Italian cities to rebel and attempt to regain their independence. These included old enemies such as the Etruscans, Volsci, Hernici, and Aequi. Rome methodically and effectively defeated them all, and reasserted her dominance during the next fifty years. Antium, chief city of the Volsci, was finally defeated in 338 BC; in 295 BC the Samnite Wars were brought to an end when Rome defeated an alliance of Samnites, Gauls, Etruscans, and Umbrians. Rome then became dominant in the greater part of the Italian peninsula. Stephen Oakley has estimated that, of the 130,000 square kilometres of land in the peninsula, the *ager Romanus* expanded from 822 sq km (0.6 per cent) in 510 BC to 1,902 sq km in 340 BC, and then to 23,226 sq km (17.9 per cent) in 264 BC.[14] This great swathe of contiguous territory made it increasingly difficult for enemies to threaten Rome in any meaningful way. Her population was around 347,300 in 338 BC, rising to 900,000 in 264 BC.[15]

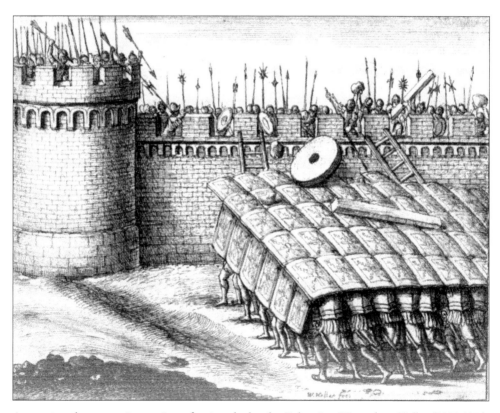

A seventeenth-century impression of a *testudo*, by the Bohemian Wenceslaus Hollar (1607-1677). Hollar lived in London for many years, and he is one of the most skilled etchers ever—remarkable, given that he was almost blind in one eye. He produced around 2,700 etchings.

The Conquest of Italy

Lanuvium (*c.* 389 BC)

Rome repulsed opportunist attacks by the Falerii and the Tarquinii to recapture land lost by their ally, the Veii. The Aequii too saw their chance, but were defeated. However, the most serious threat came from the Volsci, Hernici, and the Etruscans; Camillus was appointed dictator for a third time to deal with them, and his *magister equitum* was Gaius Servilius Ahala. Camillus' levy was unusual, as it included older men who still had strength and fight in them. The army was split into three. Taking the initiative, Camillus pursued the Volsci—who had panicked when they heard that Camillus was coming after them—to Maecium, near Lanuvium, where they hurriedly barricaded themselves behind a rampart and a wall of logs. In another display of incendiaries, Camillus burned his way through—with the aid of a strong breeze. He massacred the fleeing Volscians and distributed the booty amongst the troops, before laying waste to the Volscian lands; the Volscians surrendered.[1] According to Livy, Camillus now turned his attention to the Aequi and defeated them at Bolae, to the north-east of Mount Agidus, taking them off guard and capturing their city. The Etruscans were next—they too were unprepared when the Romans confronted them at Sutrium, forcing their surrender.

Diodorus and Plutarch have a different version of events: the Volscians march on Rome and face a Roman army bivouacked on the Campus Martius (Diodorus) or Mount Marcia (Plutarch). Rome appeals to Camillus for help; he raises an army and attacks the Volscians in the rear, driving them into massacre.[2]

As already noted, by now booty and the spoils of war were becoming as much of an obsession for the Romans as they were for the armies that came before and after. Popular support for the impending First Punic War was driven by the expectation of prodigious amounts of pillage. Oakley has calculated that Livy alone uses *praeda* (the Latin term for booty) and its cognates nearly 500 times—the same as the combined use of *nam* and *namque*—in his surviving work.[3] While commanders kept prisoners of war who were usually sold as slaves, they were at liberty to do as they wished with plunder; this usually included giving a share to the troops.[4] Some of it would be shared with his officers, friends, and relatives, while other portions would be *manubiae* (the commander's share) and spent on public works to suggest generosity and increase personal celebrity; others still might go to the public treasury (*aerarium*). Whatever its use, much of the booty had to eventually be converted into cash.[5] Predictably, by the second century BC there were disputes over the proportions given to the treasury and the troops, and disagreement over how much might be retained by the generals. As a snub to officialdom, Lucius Postumius Megellus gave all of his plunder to his troops.[6]

Sutrium (389 BC)

The Etruscans blockaded Sutrium and eventually took it, forcing the inhabitants to evacuate the city with only the goods they could carry and the clothes on their backs—a familiar picture of the defeated in war. Camillus headed for the city and met the refugees, vowing to bring misery and grief to the Etruscans in return. The confident Etruscans, who had left Sutrium unguarded, paid for their arrogance with their lives. The Romans successfully regained the city for the Sutrines, while the Etruscan survivors decided against a fight and surrendered. Camillus returned to Rome for his triumph, parading his many Etruscan prisoners, who were then auctioned off. So great was the booty that three golden bowls were made from what was left over, and were deposited in the temple of Jupiter.[7]

Satricum (386 BC)

The people of Antium joined forces with the Roman colony of Satricum. The armies here were augmented by large numbers of Latins and Hernici. The Romans had appointed Camillus dictator for a sixth time; he marched to Satricum with Publius Valerius and a force of 16,000 men. Roman morale, however, was at a very low ebb. The soldiers were concerned about the superior size of the army confronting them, and were decidedly unenthusiastic about the forthcoming battle. Camillus mounted his horse and addressed his troops, finally grabbing a standard bearer, whom he dragged towards the enemy lines. This show of courage from the aging Camillus was enough to inspire the Romans, who followed him into the fray; they regained the standard that had been hurled into the midst of the enemy, and proceeded to rout the Latins. A storm brought the carnage to a premature end, after which the Latins and the Hernici deserted the Volsci. The Volsci saw the hopelessness of their situation, threw up their arms, and surrendered.[8] Sutrium was again the centre of hostilities when the Etruscans took the town. Camillus attacked, his troops scaled the walls, and they massacred the invaders inside—as well as those who had fled into the countryside.

Signia (362 BC)

The battles of Signia in 362 were fought against the Hernici, who had defected in 366 BC after many years of friendship with Rome. Lucius Genucius Aventinensis was the first plebeian consul to take a command in war, so much depended on his performance and all eyes were focussed on him. Unfortunately Genucius walked straight into an ambush, he was slain, and his legions were routed. In Rome, news of the disaster was met with smug patrician arrogance—they ascribed the reverse to the fact that they had been denied their rightful office, and argued that the gods had not sanctioned the appointment of a plebeian.

Appius Claudius Crassus was then appointed dictator, but before he could arrive Gaius Sulpicius Peticus assumed command of the army—only to be immediately surrounded by the Hernici. Nevertheless, he was able to put them to flight. The arrival of Crassus effectively doubled the strength of the Roman army, although this was partly offset by a contingent of the Hernician force which comprised a crack unit of unit of 3,200 men. The Hernici were further motivated by the promise of double pay. The Roman cavalry charged but were unable to break through the enemy lines by normal means, so they dismounted and charged on foot, as infantry—eventually the Hernici were routed. The following day the planned attack on the Hernician camp was delayed as no favourable omens were forthcoming: the Hernici abandoned camp and withdrew under cover of the night. Despite their victory, the Romans lost a quarter of their force.[9]

Anio River (361 BC)

The following year saw the return of the Gauls. This incursion must have been met with considerable trepidation by the Romans (led by the dictator Titus Quinctius Poenus), as they encamped at the opposite end of the bridge over the river from the Gauls; they were ever-mindful of the disastrous events of thirty years before. However, the battle is more famous for the 'David and Goliath' exploits of one of the Gallic warriors and Titus Manlius. After numerous inconclusive battles over the bridge on the Anio, a giant of a Gaul emerged from the ranks and boomed out a challenge to single combat. Manlius took up the invitation—after some understandable hesitation—and, receiving permission from the dictator, met the confident, resplendently armoured, mocking giant. Against all the odds, Manlius inflicted fatal wounds to the giant's stomach and groin—consistent, no doubt, with Manlius' short reach. Manlius then removed the Gaul's torque from his neck and put it on, thus winning the agnomen 'Torquatus'—a name that was passed down to successive generations in honour of his bravery. The Gauls were stunned by this unexpected and astonishing reverse and fled to Tibur.[10]

Pedum (358 BC)

In 360 BC the Romans repelled an army of Gauls at the battle of Colline Gate—a long and bloody engagement, made all the more intense because the fighting was visible and audible to the citizens of Rome. The Roman soldiers were spurred on by the thought of their families watching. Two years later the Gauls were back; the dictator appointed to quell the threat, Gaius Sulpicius, managed to anger his impetuous troops by insisting on delaying the conflict and forbidding any action. A delegation of frustrated and impatient soldiers convinced Sulpicius to act, and in so doing triggered what was surely one of the first Roman military conflicts involving a force of muleteers. Sulpicius ingeniously ordered the saddle-bags to be removed from his donkeys, armed the 1,000 or so muleteers, and ordered them into the surrounding woods to await orders. The next day, the Romans lined up and were charged by the Gauls; the muleteers were commanded to attack, causing the Gauls to flee in the face of this 'cavalry' force. They ran straight into the *magister equitum*, Gaius Valerius, with predictable consequences.[11]

Mount Gaurus, Saticula, and Suessula (343 BC)

The Battle of Mount Gaurus was the first engagement in what is called the First Samnite War. The Samnites originated from the Sabellians, who lived a rustic life in the Apennines. In common with other mountain people they were attracted to nearby lowlands due to overpopulation and their search for more yielding agricultural land. The existence of the Etruscans and Latins on the plain below forced them into the more southerly lands of Campania, where they settled prodigious amounts of land (comparable at least to Rome's extensive territories at that date). In 423 BC the Sabellians took Capua, and Cumae three years later. Now, as Campanians, they were virtually independent and, they became urbanised, absorbing Greek and Etruscan influences and enjoying a peaceful lifestyle—in stark contrast to their country cousins back up in the mountains. Politically, the Campanians were made up of a federation of towns in which Capua was the dominant partner. By the mid-fourth century the peace was rudely shattered by the arrival of their belligerent kinsmen, the Samnites, who were looking for workable land themselves. In 343 BC the Campanians appealed to Rome for help.

The Romans and the Samnites had signed a treaty in 354 BC, perhaps to provide mutual assistance against the Gauls. For whatever reason, the Romans reneged on this in 343, enabling them to assist the Campanians. Whether this was because the Gallic threat had receded, or because of an offer of alliance with Capua, it is impossible to say; in any event Rome presumably saw it as an opportunity to take control of southern Italy. Capua was a rich city, and novice plebeian tribunes had a point to prove in their new-found military opportunities. Rome was, therefore, unlikely to pass this opportunity up. Diplomacy failed, and an army was dispatched to Mount Gaurus, west of Neapolis, under Marcus Valerius Corvus Calenus. Here, a long stalemate was eventually broken to the Romans' advantage and the Samnites were routed. In the meantime the other consul, A. Cornelius Cossus, was busy destroying another Samnite army at Saticula, having narrowly avoided an ambush, with Livy recording Samnite losses of 30,000 men. P. Decius Mus saved the day when Cossus became trapped—Decius took a force of 1,600 men and secured a mountain top, below which the Samnites had to pass. He held this position and broke through the Samnite lines to relieve his trapped colleagues. For this distinction he was awarded a unique double Grass Crown (*Corona Graminea*) by both his own army and the army of Cossus.[12]

The Grass Crown, or Blockade Crown (*Corona Obsidionalis*), is the closest Roman equivalent to our Victoria Cross—both are awarded for conspicuous gallantry. It was the pinnacle of all military rewards in the Roman Republic, and was only awarded to a commander whose valour saved a legion or army from annihilation. The crown was made from grass, flowers, and wheat picked from the field of battle.[13]

In 340 BC the Latins were demanding equal rights with Roman citizens. The consul, Titus Manlius Torquatus, dismissed this out of hand, and threatened to kill any Latin who entered the senate. Around the same time, Titus Manlius and Publius Decius Mus were striving to restore old-fashioned military discipline in the Roman army. Their objective was to reduce the chances of 'friendly fire'—the likelihood of this was high because the Latins spoke the same language, organised their armies in the same way, and wielded similar weapons. The opportunity for confusion and for blue on blue casualties was huge. The orders forbade any soldier to engage the enemy, or leave his post without permission, under penalty of death. Tragically, Manlius's son did just that, seeking glory with some comrades, and slew Geminus Maecius—a Latin champion—in single combat. He took the spoils to his father who reacted not by congratulating him, but by assembling the legion. Hiding his fatherly pride, Manlius berated his son in front of them all and handed him over to be executed. According to Valerius Maximus, he was tied to a stake and 'slaughtered like a sacrificial victim', much to the horror of the onlookers. From then on 'Manlian Orders' became synonymous with the strictest of military disciplines.[14]

The Samnites regrouped near Suessula; the Suessulani were naturally unnerved, and appealed to Valerius for help. Valerius responded with a modest force which camped close to the Samnites, who had lined up for battle. The Romans ignored this, giving the Samnites cause to underestimate their opposition; they broke ranks to forage nearby, and were cut down by the Roman cavalry.[15] Livy exaggerates that 40,000 Samnite shields and 170 standards were collected from the battlefield—true or not, all of the plunder was shared amongst the soldiers.

In 342 BC the Romans were preoccupied with a mutiny in the army—the troops were unhappy at the extended service they were having to endure so far from home. Luckily the Samnites were also preoccupied, by a dispute with Tarentum; consequently, the two factions renewed their treaty in 341 BC. The Capuans had no choice but to make their own alliance with other Latin cities, while the Samnites' request for Rome to help them against Tarentum was ignored.

The Latins too became disaffected. To them, the terms of the treaty they had signed in 358 were repeatedly translated into actions that heavily favoured the Romans: land distribution was weighted towards Rome; Rome was receiving help in wars and battles very much in her own interest rather than that of the Latins; and Rome had appropriated both Tusculum and the *ager Pomptinus* (the Pomptine Marshes and the Monti Lepini) from the Volscians for herself. In protest, the Latins threatened to withdraw support during the Gallic threat of 349. The strain on relations was exacerbated when Rome signed a treaty with Carthage in 348 BC, which allowed the North Africans to capture citizens in Latin cities for slavery. The result was an ultimatum from the Latins, demanding the restoration of parity of rights. The Romans rejected this, so the Latins formed an alliance with the Campanians and the Volsci. The Romans, having settled the mutiny in their own army, marched on the forces of the Latin alliance—supported by their old enemy, the Samnites.

P. Decius Mus devoting himself (*devotio*) in a suicide charge at the battle of Mount Vesuvius (340 BC).

Mount Vesuvius and Trifanum (340 BC)

The first of these battles took place under Mount Vesuvius, led by the consuls Publius Decius Mus and T. Manlius Torquatus. After a period of stalemate the Roman left flank appeared to be folding. Decius Mus saw this, and was spurred on by an omen which proclaimed that the war would only end when a general on one side, and an entire army on the other, were dedicated to the gods of the underworld. Mus concluded that the situation required a *devotio* (ritual self-sacrifice in battle) to turn a likely defeat into victory; he mounted his horse and charged the enemy in a suicide attack. Decius Mus died under a hail of spears, but not before his bravery had inspired his army to follow him into the fray. Both commanders had kept their crack troops in reserve, but when Torquatus sent his men forward the Latins assumed they were the cream of his force, and responded in kind. When the Romans had exhausted these Latin veterans, Manlius now sent in his crack force against the weary Latins—and cleaned up. Three quarters of the enemy were slain. A further Roman victory followed that same year, at Trifanum. Rome demanded that the Latins give up their lands, but they refused and the hostilities continued.

Livy gives us the background to the *devotio*; it was essentially a last-ditch attempt to snatch victory out of defeat, imbued with religious and magical connotations. Here is Livy's detailed description of Mus's sacrifice:

'Valerius, we need the help of the gods! Let the Pontifex Maximus dictate to me the words in which I am to devote myself for the legions.' The Pontifex bade him veil his head in his toga praetexta, and rest his hand, covered with the toga, against his chin, then standing upon a spear to say these words: 'Janus, Jupiter, Father Mars, Quirinus, Bellona, Lares, ye Novensiles and Indigetes, deities to whom belongs the power over us and over our foes, and ye, too, Divine Manes, I pray to you, I do you reverence, I crave your grace and favour that you will bless the Roman People, the Quirites, with power and victory, and visit the enemies of the Roman People, the Quirites, with fear and dread and death. In like manner as I have uttered this prayer so do I now on behalf of the commonwealth of the Quirites, on behalf of the army, the legions, the auxiliaries of the Roman People, the Quirites, devote the legions and auxiliaries of the enemy, together with myself to the Divine Manes and to Earth...' In full armour [he] leaped upon his horse and dashed into the middle of the enemy. To those who watched him in both armies, he appeared something awful and superhuman, as though sent from heaven to expiate and appease all the anger of the gods and to avert destruction from his people and bring it on their enemies.

Devotio ran in the family—Decius Mus's son was to devote himself before the battle of Sentinum in 295 BC. His son, in turn, died after a *devotio* in the Battle of Ausculum against Pyrrhus, according to Cicero. There are precedents in Greek legend, examples being: the Athenian King Codrus; the Theban prince Menoeceus, who sacrificed himself during the siege against Thebes by the Seven; and the Carthaginian general Hamilcar, who threw himself into the fire at the Battle of Himera (according to Herodotus).[16]

Pedum (338 BC)

The next confrontation was on the Fenectane Plains, in 339 BC, where Quintus Publilius Philo soundly defeated the Latins and won a triumph for his success.[17] The Latins were incensed by the confiscation of their lands, and the next year Tiberius Aemilius Mamercinus engaged the Latins at Pedum, near Tibur. However, halfway through the campaign news of Philo's triumph reached the envious Mamercinus; not to be outdone, Mamercinus returned to Rome—even though his campaign remained unfinished—and demanded a triumph of his own. The senate were outraged, and insisted that no triumph would be awarded unless Mamercinus took Pedum. Lucius Furius Camillus finally defeated the Pedani, and an army from Tibur, in 337.

Antium (338 BC)

In 338 BC the Latin threat was finally extinguished at the Battle of Antium, on the river Astura. Gaius Maenius led the Roman naval forces here, and defeated the Latin armies of Antium, Lanuvium, Aricia, and Velitrae, who were en route to Pedum. A colony was established at Antium, a bustling sea port and haven for pirates; the city was barred from further maritime activity and their warships were seized, although the inhabitants were granted Roman citizenship. Some of the vessels were sailed to Rome, while others were scuttled.

Maenius took six rams (*rostra*) from the prows of the enemy warships and placed them in what became known as the Rostra (the podium) in the Forum, from which orators addressed the people. Maenius and his colleague Lucius Furius Camillus were awarded triumphs, and both had equestrian statues erected in their honour, in the Comitia at the Forum. Maenius' statue was placed upon a column, the *Columna Maenia*, and he took the cognomen *Antiaticus* in memory of his victory.

The Latin League was dissolved in the important peace settlement that followed; Rome annexed some states, while others were allowed to remain autonomous. The Romans were perspicacious enough to see that ruthlessly suppressing the Latins would be counter-productive. Instead they divided and ruled, isolating each state and giving them the opportunity to cultivate a measure of reciprocated loyalty to Rome. The surviving Latin states were bound to Rome by individual bilateral treaties. For example, Tusculum, Aricia, and Lanuvium were granted full citizenship, and kept their municipal governments. The Campanians were reformed as a *civitas sine suffragio*—that is, they enjoyed all the rights and duties of a Roman citizen (including an obligation to military service), but they could not vote in Roman popular assemblies. Formiae, Capua, and Cumae were amongst those who followed suit. A second *colonia maritima* was established at Ostia.

Rome had finally achieved dominance in the central Italian peninsula; their new allies were obliged to provide military support, but they paid no taxes and gave no tribute to Rome. This peace settlement was to become the model for Rome's political treatment of subsequent vanquished states, a template for imperialism and Romanization.[18] Nevertheless, the Samnites—who still controlled 6,000 square miles of Italy—remained a problem.

Imbrinium (325 BC)

The Second Samnite War lasted some twenty-two years (from 326–304 BC) and involved at least eighteen battles of some consequence. The battle of Imbrinium was the first, and marked the beginning of an extended period during which Rome was at war on an annual basis. Things flared up in 327 BC, when the Samnites installed a garrison in Greek Neapolis; the Capuans protested to Rome, and the Romans began to lay siege to Neapolis. Lucius Papirius Cursor took up the dictatorship to deal with the issue, but he was detained in Rome, attending to his auspices. In his absence the *magister equitum*, one Quintus Fabius Maximus Rullianus, disobeyed orders and attacked the Samnites at Imbrinium; the rout accounted for 20,000 Samnite dead.[19] Rullianus was condemned to death by Cursor only to be saved by the intercession of the senate. Cursor was a hard man: his cognomen means 'The Runner', dedicated to him because he could walk over fifty Roman miles a day in full kit. Unfortunately, he demanded the same extreme endurance from his soldiers.

The same year saw the Romans operating on the Adriatic coast for the first time when they crossed the Appenines, allied with the Marsi and the Paeligni in the mountains, and subdued the coastal Vestini. Presumably, the objective was to attack Apulia and take the Samnites from the rear. However, the next confrontation with the Samnites was not nearly as decisive for the Romans, and any satisfaction they felt at the outcome would have been erased four years later at Caudine Forks.

Mount Tifernum and Bovianum (305 BC)

Rome spent ten years strengthening their hold in Campania and Apulia. The Samnites induced the Etruscans further north to fight Rome, but their threat was quashed with little trouble in battles at Sutrium (311 and 310 BC), Perusia (310 and 308 BC—a crushing defeat for the Etruscans), and Lacus Vadimonis (310 BC). Rome's victory at Vadimo marked the beginning of the end for the Etruscan league, as growing numbers of its cities looked to Rome to counter internal strife. Rome was increasingly able to negotiate separate and independent treaties with the individual cities, thus extending their policy of divide and rule and rendering the whole region largely dependent on Rome. The Umbrians revolted in 308 BC and were defeated at Mevania.[20] After Tifernum and Bovianum peace was restored between Rome and the Samnites, at least for the time being.

Bovianum (298 BC), Tifernum (297 BC), and River Volturnus (296 BC)

The Third Samnite War started when the Samnites unsuccessfully tried to forge an alliance with Lucania. When they were rebuffed, the Samnites threatened to take Lucania by force; the Lucanians appealed to Rome, who saw this as an opportunity to surround Samnite territory. The first battle appears to have been at Bovianum, followed by Tifernum the following year. Here, Quintus Fabius Maximus and Publius Decius Mus infiltrated Samnium country from different directions. The Samnites were cut to pieces and fled when they mistakenly believed that a contingent of Fabius' veterans was the army led by Decius Mus, attacking from the rear. Mus enjoyed more success when he defeated the Apulians, preventing them from joining the Samnites at Beneventum. Decius Mus and Fabius Maximus then joined forces and laid waste the Samnite lands over the next few months. A further victory followed in 296, at the river Volturnus, when the consul Lucius Volumnius Violens defeated the Samnites under Staius Minatius. Volumnius' assault was reinforced by the Roman prisoners taken by the Samnites; they broke free, captured Staius, and presented him on horseback to Volumnius. Apart from the victory—which was attained with minimal losses—the Romans regained 7,400 prisoners, took 2,500 of their own, killed 6,000 Samnites, and acquired much booty.[21]

Sentinum (295 BC)

The battle started when the enemy split their forces; the Saminites and Gauls attacked the Roman army, while the Umbrians and Etruscans assaulted the Roman camp. The strategy was betrayed to Fabius, who dispatched two armies to devastate Etruscan territory around Clusium—which had the effect of diverting the Etruscans to the defence of their lands. Eventually the armies clashed. On the right, Fabius drew on his experience and wore down the Samnites and Gauls by prolonging the battle—both sides were susceptible to fatigue –carrying out a successful head-on assault. Things were very different on the left, however, where the impetuous Publius Decius Mus (the son of the consul of 340 BC) played all his cards at the outset; he paid the price when his troops were overcome by a Gallic charge of chariots. Decius despaired and 'devoted' himself as his father had done at the battle of Mount Vesuvius, charging headlong into the ranks of Gauls to his death. His valour and sacrifice had the desired effect when the Romans regrouped and mounted a counter-attack, supported by reserves from Fabius' army, the Triarii, Campanian cavalry, and part of the III Legion (led by the tribune Lucius Cornelius Scipio). The Gauls formed a *testudo*, but to no avail—this was surrounded by the 500 Campanian cavalry and the third legion. Fabius then took the Samnite camp. The Samnites lost 25,000 men, including Gellius Egnatius—their commander—while Decius Mus lost 7,000 and Fabius 1,700.[22] The Mus predilection for *devotio* became so notorious that when Pyrrhus was up against the third-generation Publius Decius Mus, he commanded that in no account must he be allowed to die in the battle.

Duris, the contemporary Greek historian and ruler of Samos, puts the Samnian losses at a staggering and unbelievable 100,000 men (as quoted by Diodorus). Orosius is even more outrageous, quoting 140,330 infantry and 46,000 cavalry.[23] Whatever the toll, the Samnites suffered further heavy losses later that year when they faced Appius Claudius and Lucius Volumnius at the Battle of Caiatia; 16,000 were killed and 2,700 taken prisoner. The Romans lost 2,700 men.[24]

The *testudo* (tortoise) was a tactic in which soldiers aligned their shields to form a packed formation, encased by shields front and top. The first row held their shields from their shins to their eyes, so as to cover the front, forming a shield wall all around. The men at the back placed their shields over their heads to protect the formation from above, balancing the shields on their helmets and overlapping them. The Greeks called it *chelone*; the Byzantines the *foulkon*. In theory, the *testudo* formed an impenetrable shield which would soak up missile attacks. It could be formed either by stationary troops or by troops on the march. The disadvantage lay in the fact that, due to its density, hand-to-hand combat was difficult.

Both Plutarch and Dio Cassius describe the *testudo* for us in their accounts of Mark Antony's invasion of Parthia in 36 BC:

Plutarch: Then the shield-bearers wheeled round and enveloped the light-armed troops within their ranks, they dropped to one knee, and presented their shields out as a barrier. The men behind held their shields over the heads of the first rank, while the third rank did likewise for the second rank. What results, which is amazing, looks just like a roof and is the best defence against arrows, which just glance off it.

Dio: This *testudo* and the way in which it is formed are as follows. The baggage animals, the light-armed troops, and the cavalry are placed in the center of the army. The heavy-armed troops who use the oblong, curved, and cylindrical shields are drawn up around the outside, making a rectangular figure, and, facing outward and holding their arms at the ready, they enclose the rest. The others who have flat shields, form a compact body in the center and raise their shields over the heads of all the others, so that nothing but shields can be seen in every part of the phalanx alike and all the men by the density of the formation are under shelter from missiles. Indeed, it is so marvelously strong that men can walk upon it and whenever they come to a narrow ravine, even horses and vehicles can be driven over it.[25]

Luceria (294 BC)

However, Rome did not have it all her own way. When Marcus Atilius went to the rescue of Luceria when it was under attack by the Samnites, he suffered a terrible reverse. The Samnites fought doggedly and came out on top, but both sides were war-weary and reluctant to bring the battle to a conclusion. The Samnites were forced to pass the Roman camp on the only road out, but fortunately for the Samnites the Romans were on the verge of mutiny, and could only manage an unsuccessful cavalry charge in which many of their own troops were trampled to death. The Romans turned and fled. Orders were given that anyone approaching the ramparts—be they Roman or Samnite—should be treated as an enemy, and so Roman cavalry began confronting Roman infantry. The Romans turned again, eventually mustering enough enthusiasm to launch an infantry attack on the front and a cavalry charge to the rear. Surrounded, the Samnites lost 5,000 men and had 7,800 taken prisoner; these prisoners were forced, naked, under the yoke. The Romans also fared badly, losing 7,800 men over the two days.[26]

L. Papirius Cursor went some way here to avenging the humiliating disaster of the Caudine Forks, as he rescued the Roman hostages held in the town, recovered the standards lost at Caudine Forks, and made those 7,000 Samnites pass under the yoke.

Aquilonia (293 BC)

The Samnite threat was finally extinguished at the Battle of Aquilonia, where the Roman commander, L. Papirius Cursor, showed considerable ingenuity. The Samnite force numbered a massive 36,000 men facing Papirius, augmented by a mass conscription throughout Samnium—to which all Samnites of military age were obliged to comply. They took strict oaths to their country, and new state-of-the-art armour was issued. Any who refused or left were sacrificed to Jupiter on the spot, their bodies left in a heap as a stark warning to any others who might be contemplating refusal. In the end, 40,000 men joined up at Aquilonia. Sixteen thousand of the more-experienced men constituted the crack unit called the Linen Legion, named after their brightly-coloured linen tunics.

Cursor's colleague Carvilius Maximus attacked Cominium to preoccupy the Samnites garrisoned there. Papirius gained the upper hand at Aquilonia, inflicting carnage on the

Samnites; to add to the slaughter, he had sent Spurius Nautius with mules and muleteers and three cohorts onto a hill nearby. These soon charged back, dragging twigs and bushes behind them to raise a huge cloud of dust—which the remaining Samnites mistook for a second Roman army, thinking that Cominium had fallen. The Roman cavalry then proceeded to annihilate the Samnites: 20,340 were killed with a further 3,870 taken prisoner, and ninety-seven standards were captured. The crack Samnite Linen Legion was one of the casualties.[27] Cursor gained a triumph, and seven days of thanksgiving was declared in his honour.

The battle is also remembered for falsification of the auspices. The keeper of the auspicious chickens reported to Papirius that the omens were favourable because the chickens had greedily eaten their feed; in fact, the chickens had eaten nothing. When Papirius learned of the lie he posted the chicken keeper to the front line, where he was soon killed by an enemy spear.

The War Against Pyrrhus

The Pyrrhic War was triggered by a minor naval battle in the Bay of Tarentum and the treaty obligations between the city of Tarentum and Epirus in Greece. When Rome entered Tarentine waters Tarentum saw this as a breach of treaty, and requested pay-back from the Greek king Pyrrhus for the aid they had given him in his conflict with Korkyra. Pyrrhus saw this as an empire-building opportunity.

Tarentum was founded in 706 BC by Dorian-Greek immigrants, and was the only colony to be established by the Spartans. Its founders were Partheniae, who were traditionally believed to be the sons of virgins. They were actually the sons of unmarried Spartan women and Perioeci, free men—who were not officially citizens of Sparta—whose role it was to increase the Spartan birthrate, and thereby the number of recruits to the Spartan military, during the Messenian wars. These marriages in Sparta were later annulled, and the sons were forced to leave Greece. Phalanthus, the Parthenian leader, consulted the oracle at Delphi as to how best to handle this, and was told that Tarentum was to be the new home of the exiles.[1] Tarentum grew in stature, and by the time Roman power was spreading south it had become a major commercial and military force amongst the cities of Magna Graecia in southern Italy.

From the eighth and seventh centuries BC onwards, famine, overcrowding, and the quest for new commercial opportunities and ports led the Greeks to colonise diverse places such as the eastern coast of the Black Sea, Libya, and Massalia (modern Marseille). Sicily and the southern tip of the Italian peninsula were also settled; the Romans called this region Magna Graecia due to the number of Greeks settled there. With the Greeks came Greek culture: dialects of the Greek language, arts, religious rites, and the *polis*—all merging with native Italic culture. The Chalcidean-Cumaean version of the Greek alphabet—which was adopted by the Etruscans—and the resulting Old Italic alphabet subsequently evolved into the Latin alphabet. Prominent cities included Neapolis, Syracuse, Acragas and Sybaris, Tarentum, Rhegium, Nola, Ancona, and Bari.

Tarentum's commercial supremacy came about largely through its extensive sheep farming industry—its fleeces, dyed purple with the copious mussels obtainable from the harbour, were much sought-after throughout Italy. Ceramics were also important to the economy. Trade soon spread into the lands on the Aegean, beyond the Po, and across the Alps. This commercial prowess was matched by political stability, the ability to raise an army of some 15,000 men, and the strongest navy in the Mediterranean. The Tarentine armed forces were strengthened by numerous Greek mercenaries, allowing them to fend off incursions by the Oscans and even attempt expansion. During the First Samnite War the Tarentines formed an alliance with King Archidamus of Sparta, and then in 334 BC with his brother-in-law, King Alexander of Epirus. Alexander successfully quelled incursions by the Brutii, Samnites, and Lucanians, and forged a non-aggression pact with the Romans on behalf of Tarentum. Tarentum, however, was increasingly suspicious of Alexander's ambitions, and left him to be slaughtered by the Lucanians. Rome's expansionism was also viewed with some anxiety, and their attempts at diplomacy were rejected by Tarentum. The Battle of Tarentum followed soon after.

Pyrrhus (*c.* 319–272 BC) was crowned King of Epirus (r. 306–302, 297–272 BC) and Macedon (r. 288–284, 273–272 BC). He was the son of Aeacides and Phthia, a Thessalian woman who was a second cousin of Alexander the Great through Alexander's mother, Olympias. In 298 BC Pyrrhus was taken hostage in Alexandria, as the result of a peace treaty between Demetrius, his brother-in-law, and Ptolemy I Soter. There, he married Ptolemy's step-daughter, Antigone, and in 297 BC regained his kingdom in Epirus with Ptolemy's aid. Pyrrhus had his co-ruler—Neoptolemus II of Epirus—murdered. One of the more flamboyant of Greek brigands, whose services were readily available throughout the Mediterranean, Pyrrhus answered Tarentum's plea for support against Rome with alacrity.

The Pyrrhic Wars were notable for two reasons other than the significant Roman victory and the subjugation of Magna Graecia; they gave us the term 'Pyhrric victory', and the first deployments of elephants (elephantries) against the Roman army. The Indians were the first to use the elephant as an instrument of war and they make an appearance in the Sanskrit epics, later stories of the Mahabharata and the Ramayana in the 4th century BC. To some kings, an army without elephants was as ludicrous as a forest without a lion, a kingdom without a king, or as valour unaided by weapons.[2] From India they penetrated Persia, and featured in their wars with Alexander the Great. Their debut was at the Battle of Guagamela in 331 BC, when the Persians deployed fifteen elephants. Alexander was so astonished by the elephants that he made a sacrifice to the God of Fear the night before the battle; as it turned out, the elephants failed to make an appearance due to fatigue. Alexander won the day, and was so impressed by the war machine that he enlisted the captured fifteen elephants into his own army—adding to their numbers as he overran the rest of Persia. Up against Porus (which is now the Punjabi region of Pakistan), Alexander faced up to 100 war elephants at the Battle of the Hydaspes Rvier. This was small fry compared to what the kings of the Nanda Empire (Maghada) and Gangaridai (present-day Bangladesh and the Indian state of West Bengal) could throw against him— between 3,000 and 6,000 war elephants—which effectively halted his invasion of India. After returning home he set up a unit of elephants to guard his palace at Babylon, and established the office of *elephantarch* to take command of his elephants. War elephants made their European debut in 318 BC, when one of Alexander's generals, Polyperchon, besieged Megalopolis with the help of sixty elephants. Pyrrhus must be given credit for the introduction of the combat elephant to Italy, at the battle of Heraclea. Here the elephants were of the Indian variety, and they were given the sobriquet 'Lucanian oxen' by the awe-struck Roman soldiers.[3] We are, of course, destined to meet these formidable beasts again in the wars against Hannibal.

Carthaginian War Elephants Engage Roman Infantry at the Battle of Zama (1890) by Henri-Paul Motte (1846-1922).

The Pyrrhus troupe lands in Italian soil, complete with elephants, in 280 BC.

Tarentum (282 BC)

This naval battle erupted when the Roman admiral Lucius Valerius entered the Bay of Tarentum, with a small flotilla, and dropped anchor; he assumed the Tarentines would be friendly, and that all previous treaty obligations were null and void. Valerius sailed into Tarentine waters in response to a plea from the Greek city of Thurii—on the Gulf of Otranto—for military assistance against the Lucanians. This action violated a treaty between Rome and Tarentum which forbade Rome from entering Tarentine waters. As we have seen the Tarentines had already been agitating against the Romans, and saw Valerius' presence as a threat; they accordingly attacked the Roman fleet, sinking Valerius' flagship and other vessels. The Romans tried to contain the outrage through diplomacy, but their offers of compensation were spurned by Tarentum; Rome then declared war on Tarentum.[4]

The Romans were struck by consternation and terror when they saw what they were up against at Heraclea, Lucania, on the Gulf of Otranto. Valerius Laevinus crossed the River Siris with a lesser force of 20,000 men, but his army crumbled in the face of a 3,000-strong cavalry charge followed by infantry. The Romans were finally defeated when Pyrrhus' elephants panicked the Roman horses and the Thessalian cavalry routed the Roman troops. Despite his victory Pyrrhus lost 13,000 men to the Romans' 15,000—although the figures may be nearer 7,000 and 4,000. The Lucanians and the Samnites joined Pyrrhus on the strength of this victory.[5]

The losses suffered here by Pyrrhus give us the term 'Pyrrhic victory'—where casualties are so great in victory that the damage is greater than any gain. Plutarch puts the situation neatly:

> The armies separated; and, it is said, Pyrrhus replied to one that gave him joy of his victory that one more such victory would utterly undo him. For he had lost a great part of the forces he brought with him, and almost all his particular friends and principal commanders; there were no others there to make recruits, and he found the confederates in Italy backward. On the other hand, as from a fountain continually flowing out of the city, the Roman camp was quickly and plentifully filled up with fresh men, not at all abating in courage for the loss they sustained, but even from their very anger gaining new force and resolution to go on with the war.[6]

Recognising his dilemma, Pyrrhus is reputed to have commented: '*Ne ego si iterum eodem modo uicero, sine ullo milite Epirum reuertar*'—'Another victory like that and I'll be going back to Epirus without a single soldier'.

'Friendly fire' would have been a common occurrence in the head-on, close-combat fighting of the tightly-knit Greek and Roman fighting units. The absence of distinctive uniforms, the similar languages between enemies and allies, and the general turmoil would have heightened the chances of fighting against friends and allies. Thucydides had vividly described the mayhem of the Athenian defeat at the night-time battle of Epipolae, in 413 BC—a blueprint for battlefield confusion. He asks how anyone can really know what is going on in the dark: 'many parts of the enemy ended by falling upon each other, friend against friend, citizen against citizen'.[7] This nightmare scenario must have been repeated endlessly down the years. Despite attempts to control and to deter, the elephant only added to the opportunities for friendly fire. Despite its benefits as a psychological and physical instrument of war, the elephant was prone to panic, difficult to control, and indiscriminately deadly when on the rampage. It was common for a startled, frightened elephant to trample its own soldiers in its blind rush to flee the battlefield.

Asculum Satrianum (279 BC)

Pyrrhus invaded Apulia and attacked the Romans, who were under Gaius Fabricius and Publius Decius Mus—the son of the 312 BC consul Publius Decius Mus. The initial battle was long and bloody, but inconclusive by nightfall. According to Plutarch, Pyrrhus and his 70,000 men were able to deploy nineteen elephants the following day; these literally crushed the Roman opposition. Pyrrhus lost 4,000 men, but the Romans lost 6,000. According to Dionysius, the Romans unsuccessfully tried to stop the elephants by deploying hastily-devised anti-elephant devices. Troops let loose salvoes of javelins—carrying jibs with burning grappling hooks—at the elephants and wagons. The elephants prevailed, and furiously attacked the Romans; according to Plutarch, the Romans compared their charge to an earthquake or a tsunami, concluding that a discreet retreat was the better part of valour. However, Livy says that the battle was inconclusive, while Dio records that Pyrrhus was defeated, and Orosius states that it was a disaster for Pyrrhus.[8]

　　Whatever the true outcome, Pyrrhus realised that his costly victories had reduced his army quite considerably and that his resources were diminishing rapidly. After the battles of Heraclea and Asculum he turned to the Romans for a diplomatic solution. Not surprisingly, his condition that the Romans give up any ambitions on the cities of southern Italy was rejected by the Senate, which was led by Appius Claudius. A later, diluted demand that the Greek cities be merely granted independence from Rome was similarly rejected. It was at this point that the Carthaginians moved in. They were concerned that Pyrrhus was now eying their island of Sicily, and so offered naval and financial support to Rome in the hope that this would enable them to prolong the war, diverting attention from Sicily.

Eryx (277 BC)

The Carthaginians were not wrong. After Asculum Pyrrhus envisaged richer pickings from Sicily, where Syracuse had invited him to dispel the Carthaginians. His crossing in the Straits of Messina was attacked by the Carthaginian navy, resulting in the loss of approximately seventy of his 110 ships. He was nevertheless crowned King of Sicily, and in 277 BC captured the Carthaginian stronghold of Eryx (modern-day Erice). This success persuaded other Greek cities under Carthaginian rule on the island to join him. Negotiations with the Carthaginians began the following year—they were ready to supply Pyrrhus with money and ships but, in accordance with what was agreed with Syracuse, he demanded that Carthage leave Sicily completely. The Greek cities were against peace with Carthage because they still held the strategic stronghold of Lilybaeum (Marsala). Pyrrhus ceded to them and broke off the Carthaginian peace negotiations. However, his tyrannical attitude and the rough-handed way he treated the Greeks—not least when recruiting oarsmen for his under-manned ships—began to lose him support.

Eryx is built on the summit of Mount Erice, some 750 m above sea level. Today it boasts two castles—the Saracen Pepoli Castle, and the Norman Venus Castle. The latter is built on the ancient Temple of Venus and was—according to legend—founded by Aeneas. In his *On the Nature of Animals*, Aelian records that animals selected for sacrifice would voluntarily walk up to the temple altar to be slain.

Pyrrhus then laid siege to fortress Lilybaeum, but after two months he realised he needed to blockade the fortress from the sea as well from land; he requested troops and money from the Greek cities to enable him to build a fleet. The Greeks refused, so Pyrrhus exacted compulsory contributions and set up a military dictatorship with garrisons in the Greek cities. The Greeks were so enraged by this that they were willing to parley with the Carthaginians, who promptly unsuccessfully attacked Pyrrhus. Pyrrhus had had enough and returned to Italy on the pretext of aiding Tarentum, who were again in trouble from a coalition of Samnites, Bruttians, and Lucanians. As his boat left the island, he remarked presciently: 'What a wrestling ground we are leaving, my friends, for the Carthaginians and the Romans.'[9]

The Carthaginians attacked again in the Straits of Messina, inflicting heavy losses on Pyrrhus' fleet. The Mamertines (sons of Mars), who inhabited the lands around the straits, anticipated Pyrrhus by crossing ahead of him with an army of 10,000 men and proceeded to harry him. Pyrrhus took a blow to the head in one of the skirmishes, but responded to a challenge from one of the Mamertines—a giant of a soldier—for one-to-one combat. Pyrrhus squared up to him and delivered a blow to his head which cleaved the Mamertine clean in half, from head to foot. According to Plutarch, the giant literally fell apart. Pyrrhus then continued to Tarentum.

Beneventum (275 BC)

In 275 the two Roman armies were in Samnite Beneventum, under Manius Curius Dentatus, while the other was in Lucania. Pyrrhus sent a unit to preoccupy the latter while he attacked Dentatus with his main force. Pyrrhus' circuitous route to attack the Roman camp under cover of night was exposed when dawn broke, enabling Dentatus to defeat one of Pyrrhus's wings. However, Pyrrhus' elephants were active on the other wing; Dentatus was able to turn them with a salvo of javelins, and they trampled their own men as they fled in panic.[10] Pyrrhus then returned to Epirus and home, leaving Rome, victorious, to deal with the encroaching threat of the Carthaginians.

The First Punic War

Rome had conquered the central and southern parts of the Italian peninsula. Her success lay in the ability to pick off individual enemies on a piecemeal basis; rarely did she have to face combined armies or coalition forces. Camerinum and Sentinum were examples of unusual strategic alliances against Rome. Rome's infantry was also a major contributor to her success; the legions, while not up to the calibre of the Greek armies under Pyrrhus, were highly trained and disciplined, and kept up to strength by ceaseless recruitment in the city of Rome and from her allies—Pyrrhus's generals complained that by fighting the Romans they were merely cutting off the Hydra's heads. Polybius writes that in 225 BC Rome had 700,000 infantry and 70,000 cavalry at her disposal.[1] Discipline was rigorous and strict; the death penalty awaited anyone who broke ranks in battle or fell asleep while on guard, and mutiny by entire legions was often punished by decimation. Significantly, the Romans were also wise enough to learn from their mistakes and to incorporate the practices of their enemies if they thought they were worth it; apart from the obvious benefits to tactics and strategy, this brought with it the most advanced armour, weapons, and military equipment.

Other beneficial developments included the military road, the *colonia,* and the marching camp. The earliest roads were the Via Latina and the Via Appia—arteries which maximised the Romans' reach, mobility, and ability to respond effectively to various military situations, and which were the precursors of a network of all-weather roads throughout the empire. At the zenith of the empire, twenty-nine military highways radiated from the city of Rome—while the 113 provinces of the late empire were connected by 372 roads, measuring over 400,000 km. In Gaul there was 21,000 km of road, and in Britannia there was at least 4,000 km.

The *colonia* were built to consolidate territorial gains and usually accommodated 4,500–6,000 inhabitants. They were often built in places of strategic importance, such as at the heads of mountain passes (Ariminum), river confluences or crossing places (Interamna), road junctions (Venusia), or coastal landing places (Antium). According to Livy, Rome's earliest colonies date from around 752 BC at Antemnae (two miles north of Rome at the confluence of the Tiber and the Anio) and Crustumerium (near the Allia and the Tiber).[2]

The marching camps (*castra*) were essential to security while an army was on the move; their construction at the end of a day's marching followed a text-book plan, with every man knowing his particular responsibility and the position of his billet.[3] The camp built after the battle of Asculum saved the Romans from annihilation by Pyrrhus's cavalry. Josephus describes the daily routine:

> …as soon as they have marched into enemy territory, the Romans do not fight until they have fortified their camp; nor is the fence they construct poorly built or uneven…. Their individual places [in the camp] are not assigned at random; but if the ground happens to be uneven, it is first leveled: the camp is four-square, and many carpenters are ready with their tools to build the buildings for them.[4]

Carthage was Rome's first overseas enemy. The city was founded by Phoenicians from Tyre in 814 BC, on the Gulf of Tunis (outside what is now the city of Tunis) at the junction of a number of Mediterranean trading routes. From about 600 BC Carthage began a 300-year process of eliminating Greek influence from the coasts of Spain and the islands of the western Mediterranean, leaving the Greeks with a tenuous presence in eastern Sicily. They established colonial cities along the Mediterranean coasts to provide safe harbours for their merchant fleets, to extract a region's natural resources, and to trade without outside interference. Carthage was unusual amongst ancient societies of the time because of its focus and dependence on overseas trade. The Carthaginian empire that came up against Rome, in the third century BC, comprised southern Spain, North Africa, Malta, Sardinia, Corsica, and western Sicily; colonies included cities on Cyprus, Sardinia, Corsica, the Balearics, Crete, and Sicily, as well as at modern-day Genoa and Marseille.

Prodigious quantities of silver, lead, copper, and tin ore— which was essential for the manufacture of bronze objects—were mined in Carthaginian Spain, notably at Tartessos (modern Andalusia, at the mouth of the Guadalquivir River). Preserving and maintaining this monopoly was obviously a priority for Carthage as their power and prosperity depended on it; their powerful navy defended it, while Carthaginian merchants did everything they could to keep the locations of the tin mines an industrial secret. Carthage was the Mediterranean's largest producer of silver, which was mined in Spain and on the North-African coast; one mine in Iberia provided Hannibal with 300 Roman pounds of silver every day. Other lucrative trades included Cornish tin from the Cassiterides—or Tin Islands—and gold and ivory from West Africa. Exports included wine, textiles, and pottery; from the fourth century these were bolstered by agricultural produce from the fertile North-African hinterland.

The Carthaginian fleet then was essential to the Punic economy. This navy was serviced by seasoned shipwrights and crewed by experienced sailors; unlike the army, the sailors of the Carthaginian navy were mainly recruited from local Carthaginians. The navy provided a stable profession which offered financial security to its sailors, and contributed to the city's economic and political stability, largely eliminating the disaffected underclasses who tended to support reactionary leaders. The navy had succeeded Syracuse and Tarentum as master of the Mediterranean. Polybius tells that the Carthaginians were more preoccupied with maritime affairs than any other nation, and that their fleet numbered up to 350 vessels. The navy was a professional, permanently-manned senior service, while the army was enlisted for a particular campaign and then demobilized—exactly the opposite to the Roman military set-up. According to Eratosthenes of Cyrene (*c.* 276–*c.* 195 BC), in defence of their mastery of the waves the Carthaginians would seize every ship sailing towards the Straights of Gades or Sardinia—and throw everyone on board into the sea.

The army was made up of motley conscripts from Numidia—mainly highly-effective light cavalry—and mercenaries from around the Mediterranean, as well as Gallic, Balearic, and Iberian troops. Numidia was a Berber kingdom, largely occupying modern-day Algeria and part of western Tunisia. The Numidians comprised two great groups of tribes: the Massylii in the east of Numidia and the Masaesyli in the west. During the early Second Punic War, the Massylii (under King Gala) were allied with Carthage, while the Masaesyli (under King Syphax) were allied with Rome. However, in 206 BC the new king of the Massylii—Masinissa—moved over to Rome, while Syphax switched his allegiance to the Carthaginians.

The dependence on mercenaries and conscripts came about during the reign of King Hanno the Navigator in 480 BC, after the Carthaginian reverses in the Sicilian Wars of the fifth and fourth centuries—in which there were significant Punic casualties. Recruiters attracted mercenaries and fugitive slaves from the whole Mediterranean region with financial contracts, and through treaties with other states. The three extensive Sicilian Wars—or Greek-Punic Wars—were fought between the Carthaginians and the Greeks (led by the Syracusans), for control of Sicily and the western Mediterranean from 600 BC to 265 BC. Generals were elected to assume military commands, and they in turn were regulated by a panel of 104 judges to restrict the prospect of military coups.

Carthaginian soldiers were trained by career officers of considerable experience—their continuity of service over long periods was a distinct advantage over the Roman annual consular system.[5] The Carthaginians deployed the now-extinct small North-African elephant; to minimise episodes of 'friendly fire' their riders were equipped with a spike and hammer, used to kill the elephants if they ever charged towards their own troops. In 550 BC, Mago I took steps to establish Carthage as a major military power in the region and allied with the Etruscans against the Greek city-states in southern Italy; the alliance lasted until Rome expelled its kings and established the Republic. Carthage's military was based on the Greek phalanx. We can estimate how many troops Carthage was able to conscript in the fourth century from the archaeological remains: 24,000 infantry, 4,000 cavalry, and 300 elephants. This does not include mercenaries and auxiliaries. Appian records that 40,000 infantry, 1,000 cavalry, and 2,000 chariots were deployed in the invasion of Agathocles of Syracuse.[6] An exception to the usual Carthaginian army was The Sacred Band of Carthage—a 2,500-strong infantry unit of Carthaginian citizens, operational from the fourth century BC and made up of men from wealthy Carthaginian families. They were trained to be warriors from an early age, and were able to afford high-quality armour and weapons. The Sacred Band was massacred at the Battle of the Krimissus in 341 BC.[7]

Historically, Carthage was always ready to defend its commercial assets but generally toed a diplomatic line in preference to conflict. As the Romans expanded along the Latin coast the Carthaginians kept relations amicable by signing treaties with them, the first of which was in 509 BC—the same year as the Republic was established. The objective was to preserve each other's interests and co-exist commercially and militarily. Things started to change when

Carthage formed an alliance with Rome against Pyrrhus in 279 BC. Rome was suspicious of Carthage's intentions, believing that their aim was to control the Italian coast. To that end the Romans established a chain of coastal colonies, from Etruria to Campania, between 350 BC and 270 BC; in each of the treaties, Rome stipulated that Carthage must not settle on Italian soil. In 311 BC a flotilla was commissioned to patrol the Italian coast, and the insignificant Roman navy was beefed up with the establishment of the *classici* to supervise naval fortifications. From the Carthaginian perspective, Rome's capture of lands on the Italian side of the Straits of Messina looked threatening and exposed the Carthaginian territories on Sicily.

Messana (264 BC)

The First Punic War started with the battle of Messana. Messana (modern Messina) had been something of a rogue state since 288 BC, when it was ruthlessly and mercilessly taken by a group of discharged and unscrupulous Campanian mercenaries. They called themselves Mamertines (children of Mars) after the Oscan god of war (Mamers); they had originally been hired by Agathocles of Syracuse. The surviving Messanians were evicted, and their property and women were shared out between the mercenaries. In 264 BC the ambitious, expansionist King Hiero II of Syracuse laid siege to Messana with a promise to execute the inhabitants when it fell. The Mamertimes were notorious pirates with 'mafiosi' tendencies, so unsurprisingly they had few genuine friends on Sicily. Nevertheless, a Carthaginian flotilla, led by Hanno, helped out by persuading Hiero to end the siege; the Mamertines were then stuck with Hanno and the Carthaginians. To get rid of them they enlisted the help of the Romans, who were increasingly anxious over the proximity of Carthaginians to Italy. Hiero II then allied with Carthage. However circuitous and accidental the route that brought them to this point may have been, the Romans and the Carthaginians were now potentially at loggerheads. The Senate and the popular assembly were divided over what action to take— war-weariness and the unsettling prospect of Carthage sitting on Rome's doorstep, opposite the very foot of Italy, were equally powerful considerations. In the end, the Romans were finally swayed into action by the consuls of the day, who desired military kudos and were seduced by the prospect of much booty. A timid commander sailed away in the face of Rome's relief expedition, but his government back home were somewhat angered at having lost Messana in such an undignified fashion. The Carthaginians accordingly sent their own force, supported by King Hiero; the Romans responded by sending a consular army, and in so doing embarked on their first overseas military operation. Ennius, with characteristic simplicity, described this momentous event: *Appius indixit Karthaginiensibus bellum* (Appius declared war on the Carthaginians).[8] Polybius later called the wars against Carthage 'the longest and most hotly contested war in history'.[9]

Messana was now under siege from the Carthaginians, and from Hiero, but the Roman consul Appius Claudius Caudex easily put both armies to flight. He was no doubt helped by the mutual distrust which thrived between the two allies, which came to a head when the Carthaginians crucified Hanno for cowardice and poor judgement. The Romans had achieved their military objective in invading Sicily; they were buoyed by their easy victory here, and, under the consul Manius Valerius, foolishly lay siege to Hiero in fortress Syracuse. Resorting to diplomacy, Valerius succeeded in winning Hiero over to the Romans' side—in exchange for territory in the east of the island, from Cape Passaro to the foothills of Mount Etna. Syracuse was now a Roman ally, paying an indemnity of 100 talents of silver, but most crucially they would also help supply the Roman army in Sicily—thus solving, at a stroke, Rome's logistic problem of provisioning an overseas army. The Carthaginians were now isolated; they reacted by sending a force of 50,000 troops to Agrigentum, a city of major strategic importance on the south coast of the island and a trading partner.[10] In the meantime, Claudius consolidated his success by attacking and defeating the Carthaginians.[11] His cognomen 'Caudex' means 'blockhead', or even 'thick as a plank', in Latin.

Agrigentum (262 BC)

Hanno procrastinated for two months, but was eventually spurred into action to relieve his fellow general Hannibal Gisco, whose army was starving to death in the besieged city of Agrigentum. However, the Romans were able to repulse Hanno, his mercenaries, and his elephants, with great loss to the Carthaginians; the survivors stole away and lived to fight another day. According to Polybius the Romans lost 3,000 infantry and 200 cavalry, against Carthaginian losses of 30,000 foot soldiers and 540 cavalry, with 4,000 men taken prisoner. The Romans sacked the city and enslaved the inhabitants (25,000, according to Zonaras)— perhaps not the best advertisement for an invading army which hoped to win over other strategic ports and cities on the island.[12]

It is safe to say that now the Roman war machine and military policy were to some extent being dictated by personal military ambition—ambition which recognised no boundaries, and which was increasingly fuelled by the prospect of military celebrity and lucrative plunder. The conquest of the whole island of Sicily now seemed a very real prospect.

The Carthaginians were descended from the Phoenicians, who themselves had a long maritime and mercantile tradition, much of which was centered on the port of Tyre. We have seen how the Carthaginians maintained a sizable fleet to run its extensive overseas trade and to service its colonies up and down the Mediterranean. The Romans, on the other hand, had little foreign trade to speak of and therefore no prior requirement for a standing fleet. However, they quickly realised the need for a navy in their new-found thirst for overseas expansion. In 262 BC the Carthaginian fleet comprised 120 or so quinqueremes—crewed by 250 rowers, working sixty large oars—and 120 fighting sailors; crucially, the Romans resolved to build a fleet at least as large as the Carthaginians', becoming a naval power for the first time in their history. Ancient battleships carried no artillery, but this absence of firepower was compensated by using the actual vessel as a weapon of destruction; naval battles were won by ramming and by boarding, in what has been called a 'land battle on planks'.[13] The alacrity with which the Romans pursued their new naval policy can be partly explained by the sheer necessity of being able to fight at sea, but also because the Romans had been winning land battles for centuries—the fact that they could now be fought within the confines of a ship's deck posed no problems for them.

Mylae (260 BC)

The engagement at Mylae (Milazzo) later that summer was Rome's second naval success. Led by Gaius Duilius, the general in Sicily who surrendered his army command to join the navy, the Romans took their fleet of 120 ships to meet the slightly-larger Carthaginian force of 130, who were under Hannibal Gisco. The Carthaginians had expected a victory over the inexperienced Romans, but they failed to bargain for the *corvus* (raven)—a grappling gangplank, carried vertically and hinged to the prow of each Roman boat. Polybius describes it in some detail: a bridge 4 feet wide and 36 feet long, with a small parapet on both sides. The engine was in the prow, where a pole and pulleys allowed the bridge to be raised and lowered. There was a heavy spike—like a bird's beak—underneath the device. This was designed to pierce the enemy ship's deck when the bridge was lowered, giving a grip between the vessels and a route for the soldiers to cross to the enemy ship and do close battle. The Carthaginians turned and fled, with the loss of fifty quinqueremes.

Duilius was rewarded with a *columna rostrata* (victory column) in the Forum—the first Roman decoration for victory in a naval engagement, and Rome's first naval triumph.[14] The inscription is now preserved in the Capitoline Museum:

> …and the Segestaeans … he (Duilius) delivered from blockade; and all the Carthaginian hosts and their most mighty chief after nine days fled in broad daylight from their camp; and he took their town Macela by storm. And in the same command he as consul performed an exploit in ships at sea, the first Roman to do so; the first he was to equip and train crews and fleets of fighting ships; and with these ships he defeated in battle on the high seas the Punic fleets and likewise all the most mighty troops of the Carthaginians in the presence of Hannibal their commander-in-chief. And by main force he captured ships with their crews, to wit: one septireme, 30 quinqueremes and triremes: 13 he sank. Gold taken: 3,600 [*and more*] pieces. Silver taken, together with that derived from booty: 100,000 … pieces. Total sum taken, reduced to Roman money … 2,100,000.… He also was the first to bestow on the people a gift of booty from a sea-battle, and the first to lead native free-born Carthaginians in triumph.

Later that year Hamilcar replaced Hannibal, who was arrested and executed in Carthage. Hamilcar attacked an army of Roman allies at Thermae Himerienses, slaying 4,000 of them in a decisive battle.[15] After Mylae, rather than following up his victory Duilius sailed round Sicily to relieve Segesta, which had been under siege from the Carthaginians. The Romans then relieved Macella and proceeded to Thermae, where they were defeated by Hamilcar; in 259 Hamilcar followed this up by taking Enna, in the centre of the island, which the Romans regained in 258 BC.

Camarina (258 BC)

Two years later the Romans were locked into their objective of taking the whole of Sicily. The battle of Camarina (modern Kamarina) on the south coast is notable for two events at opposite ends of the military skills spectrum. Firstly, the foolish decision by Aulus Atilius Calatinus—the consul and first Roman dictator to lead an army outside Italy in 249 BC—to march his troops into a steep valley, where they were ambushed and all but massacred. Secondly, the wisdom and bravery of the military tribune Marcus Calpurnius Flamma, who identified the strategic advantage of a nearby hilltop and led 300 men to the summit. In doing so he diverted the Carthaginians from Atilius, thus allowing the main force to escape from the ravine. All 300 of Calpurnius' troops died on the hill, while he was left for dead; but he survived, and was taken prisoner by the Carthaginians. Livy gives these words to the courageous Calpurnius as he encourages his men before the suicide mission: He cried 'Let us die, my men, and in dying, save our trapped legions from their peril'. Pliny the Elder tells us that he was awarded the Grass Crown; he leaves us in no doubt about the importance of the decoration, and the honour due to its bearer:

> But as for the crown of grass, it was never conferred except at a crisis of extreme desperation, never voted except by the acclamation of the whole army, and never to anyone but to him who had been its preserver. Other crowns were awarded by the generals to the soldiers, this alone by the soldiers, and to the general. This crown is known also as the 'obsidional' crown, from the circumstance of a beleaguered army being delivered, and so preserved from fearful disaster. If we are to regard as a glorious and a hallowed reward the civic crown, presented for preserving the life of a single citizen, and him, perhaps, of the very humblest rank, what, pray, ought to be thought of a whole army being saved, and indebted for its preservation to the valour of a single individual?

Strabo tells how Camarina had been destroyed by the Carthaginians in 405 BC: not long beforehand, the city was plagued by a mysterious disease. The marshes of Camarina had protected it from attack via the north, but it was suspected that the marsh was the source of the disease. Draining the marsh to eradicate the disease was a popular suggestion; the oracle was consulted, but it advised against draining it and said that the plague would pass. However, the Camarinans were impatient and they disobeyed the oracle. Now there was nothing to stop the Carthaginians—they marched across the drained marsh and erased the city, killing everyone.[16]

Tyndaris (257 BC)

According to Polybius, the following year the consul Gaius Atilius Rutilius was honing in to a cove off Tyndaris when the Carthaginian fleet sailed past him, oblivious to his presence. He immediately gave chase with ten of his fastest vessels. The Carthaginians turned on Atilius, surrounded his flotilla, and sank nine of his ships. When the main Roman force arrived, soon after, they sank eight of the Carthaginian ships and captured ten more.[17]

Cape Ecnomus (256 BC)

Inspired by their naval successes, the Romans made plans to attack the Carthaginians in their homeland; their 230-warship fleet sailed to Cape Ecnomus (Poggio di Sant' Angelo) on the Sicilian south coast, from where they planned to launch their invasion of North Africa. The Carthaginians anticipated the Romans' plans and sailed to Heraclea Minoa, about 40 miles to the west, with a similarly-sized armada. Led by the consuls Marcus Atilius Regulus— another great Roman patriot, and brother or cousin of Gaius—and Lucius Manlius Vulso Longus, the Romans eventually defeated the Carthaginians, once again employing the *corvus* to good effect. Polybius describes the strategies and the battle in some detail, particularly the Carthaginian tactic of feigning retreat in the centre, drawing the Romans in, and surrounding them with their flanks. The plan failed here, but it served the Punic forces well in the land battles of The Second Punic War. Suffice to say that at Ecnomus the Romans lost twenty-four ships to the Carthaginians' thirty plus; the Romans also captured sixty-four ships, complete with crews. After resupplying, the Romans continued on to the North African coast.[18] Ecnomus was one of the biggest sea battles in ancient history.

Adys (256 BC)

Rome's first action on the African mainland was forty miles east of Carthage, at the town of Clupea, which they captured, devastating the surrounding lands. After moving on to Adys, they lay siege to the city of Carthage. Under Hasdrubal (the son of Hanno), Bostar, and Hamilcar, the Carthaginians marched out of their capital city to confront the Romans; they occupied ground that was patently unsuitable for the deployment of cavalry or elephants. An enthusiastic attack by the Carthaginians was repulsed when the charging mercenaries extended themselves too far. The Romans won the day, and offered terms which were rejected on account of their severity; one of the punitive conditions was that the Carthaginians vacate Sicily.[19]

Cape Hermaeum (255 BC)

The year ended badly for both the Romans and the Carthaginians. The latter were anxious to follow up their success at Bagradas, and engaged the Roman fleet at Cape Hermaeum (Cape Bon). However, the outcome was disastrous as they were routed by the Roman fleet, which was on its way to relieve Regulus—114 of the Carthaginian vessels were captured by the Romans. The Roman fleet had been rebuilt to the tune of 350 vessels, and sailed under the commands of Marcus Aemilius and Servius Fulvius. The Romans, for their part, could do little more than ignominiously pick up their survivors from the Bagradas disaster. However, on the way home they sailed into a terrific storm in which they reputedly lost up to 90,000 men, 150 of their own vessels, and the 114 captured Carthaginian ships. The Roman fleet was reduced to eighty ships.[20] The Carthaginians sacked Agrigentum and departed.

Panormus (250 BC)

In 254 BC the Romans attacked Panormus (Palermo) by land and sea, and took the city. Four years of virtual stalemate followed. The Punic elephants took centre stage when Hasdrubal marched from Lilybaeum to confront the Romans, who were under the command of Lucius Caecilius Metellus. Mistakenly attributing the Romans' inaction to pachydermophobia (fear of elephants), Hasdrubal drew his troops ever closer to the Roman lines and into Metellus' hands. The Roman light cavalry, which had dug an elephant-proof trench near to the city walls, fired on the beasts and then retired to their trench, while the archers rained arrows down on them from the walls. The elephants soon stampeded and turned, trampling on their own troops; those that survived fled in the face of a Roman charge. Around 130 elephants were captured, most of which were shipped back to Rome. Morale was boosted, and all fear of elephants evaporated.[21] The cities of Ietas, Solous, Petra, and Tyndaris all went over to Rome. Hasdrubal was recalled to Carthage and executed. His successor, Adhubal, withdrew the garrison from Selinus and sacked the town. This reverse effectively ended significant Carthaginian military activity in Sicily.

When he was Pontifex Maximus in 213 BC, Lucius Caecilius Metellus saved a number of priceless and irreplaceable Roman icons. A fire consumed the Temple of Vesta, threatening the *Palladium* and other sacred buildings; Metellus leapt into the flames without hesitation, re-emerging with the treasures. He went blind, paying for his bravery and *pietas* with his eyes, but the Senate granted him the privilege of a chariot when coming and going to the Curia.

Drepana (249 BC)

In 249 the Romans, led by the consuls Publius Claudius Pulcher and Lucius Junius Pullus, laid siege to Lilybaeum—but to no avail. Leading a small flotilla, Hannibal (son of Hamilcar) broke the siege by day and replenished the garrison by night. Indeed, the only real consequence of the now-humiliated Roman efforts was to encourage the Carthaginians to rebuild their fleet. Claudius attacked Drepana, the site of the Punic shipyards. Adherbal, the Carthaginian commander, headed out of the harbour, and when Claudius saw this he ordered his fleet to leave the harbour for the open sea. The result was a Roman naval calamity of massive proportions, with multiple collisions and total confusion. The Romans were exposed along the shoreline; Adherbal captured ninety-three of Claudius' vessels and their crews. The remaining thirty Roman ships, under Junius Pullus, were attacked by the Carthaginian admiral Carthalo and driven onto rocks off Cape Passaro, where they were wrecked in a strengthening gale. However, not to be outdone, Pullus assailed lofty Eryx by land, taking the fortress and with it its strategic importance. Lucius Iunius Pullus committed suicide rather than returning to Rome in disgrace. The war-weary Romans had, for the time being, gone as far as they could—militarily and financially.[22]

In his *De Natura Deorum*, Cicero tells us that the defeat was due to Claudius' disrespect for the pre-battle auspices. The sacred chickens refused to eat the grain—a terrible omen which indicated that the gods were clearly not in favour of a battle. In a foolish bid to calm his frightened crew, Claudius unceremoniously threw the chickens overboard, pronouncing: '*bibant, quoniam esse nolunt*' ('Let them drink, since they won't eat'). Claudius survived the battle but not the aftermath; he returned to Rome in disgrace, and was charged with treason— not for his ineptitude, but for his sacrilege in the chicken incident. He was exiled.

Aegates Islands (241 BC)

In 247 BC Hamilcar Barca assumed command of the Carthaginian forces in Sicily. He marked his appointment with a series of guerilla raids which forced the Romans to establish a number of defensive coastal colonies—the most important of which was Brundisium. Hamilcar then took the stronghold of Mount Hercte, near Panormus, and retook Mount Eryx. In the meantime the Romans were refitting their fleet, realising that naval supremacy was essential in this war. They turned out 200 swifter galleys to a superior Carthaginian design; these were immediately deployed in 241 BC under Gaius Lutatius Catulus, during the ongoing sieges of Drepana and Lilybaeum. However, the treasury was empty so money for the fleet was raised by a kind of public subscription, where wealthy citizens—individually or in consortia— financed the construction of one ship each.

Catulus and his praetor, Quintus Valerius Falto, wisely insisted on thoroughly training their crews before setting sail; the *corvus* had now been abandoned. With staggering myopia, the Carthaginians had laid up their fleet and paid off their crews. Of course, it was now too late for them to save either Drepana or Lilybaeum. Therefore Hanno cobbled together a small force, loaded with supplies, to relieve his compatriots at Eryx and pick up some mercenaries. Lutatius Catulus engaged their ramshackle, over-loaded flotilla at Aegusa (Favigagna) in the Battle of the Aegates Islands, off Drepana. Victory came easily; fifty Punic ships were sunk and seventy were captured, complete with crews—according to Polybius, the Romans took 10,000 prisoners. Diodorus says that the Romans lost thirty ships, with fifty badly damaged. Nevertheless, they now had a clear sea to Africa and a second attempt on Carthage. To mark his victory, Catulus built a temple to Juturna in the Campus Martius, now in the area known as Largo di Torre Argentina.

Without the precious supplies and ordnance they needed to re-equip their army, the Carthaginians had no choice but to accept defeat and surrender on the Romans' terms.[23] The terms were particularly stringent, and included the demand that the Carthaginians renounce all claims to Sicily and pay an indemnity of 1,600 cwt of silver (80 tons) over the following decade. The Romans, on the other hand, sailed away from the First Punic War with an overseas province, a source of substantial annual revenue, and a fleet which was the strongest naval power in the Mediterranean. The war had lasted a long twenty-three years, its duration explained in part by Carthage's strategy to wear down her enemy with exhaustion and war-weariness. Huge armies, and fleets of up to 70,000 men, were pitted against each other in a war over which the victorious Romans lost more ships (over 600) than the defeated Carthaginians. A constant and prodigious supply of troops once again served the Roman war machine well, as did their facility for learning from the enemy, and their enthusiastic taking of the initiative. The reliance on potentially unreliable mercenaries did not help the Carthaginians.

The next contentious issue for the Romans lay in the islands of Sardinia and Corsica. When Hamilcar attempted to pay off the mercenaries he had employed, they mutinied over the amounts owed to them and besieged the Carthaginian authorities. The Romans helped their former enemy raise more loyal mercenaries, and even rejected a request from disaffected mutineers in Sardinia to allow them to take over the island. However, in 238 BC Hamilcar went a step too far when he restored Carthaginian sovereignty, giving Rome pause for thought. The renegade mutineers on Sicily repeated their request, which this time was granted by the Romans; they dispatched a force to occupy the Carthaginian posts on the island's south-west coast. Carthage protested, and Rome responded belligerently by declaring war on Carthage and refusing further diplomacy. The Carthaginians had no option but to cede to Rome's further demands, unreasonable and unfair as they were. Carthage was forced to withdraw all claims not only on Sardinia, but on Corsica too, and—to add insult to injury— they were required to pay a further indemnity of 1,700 talents. Plutarch described Rome's actions here as 'contrary to all justice'. If Carthage ever needed cause for revenge then they now had it in spades.

Latin warriors from the third century BC—ivory plaques found in a grave at Praeneste.

The Gauls and Illyria

Fortunately for the Romans, their victory over the Gauls at Arretium in 284 BC was conclusive enough to obviate the need for opening an unwelcome second front while they were preoccupied with Pyrrhus and the Carthaginians. The more bellicose tendencies amongst the Gauls were probably satisfied by enlistment in various Punic mercenary units. In 236 BC the Boii made a half-hearted attempt at insurrection, but the mere appearance of a Roman army at Ariminum put an end to all that. Unusually, the temple doors at the Temple of Janus were able to remain firmly shut for a while. It was not until 225 BC that the spectre of the Gallic threat returned.

Telamon (225 BC)

The ensuing Battle of Telamon (Talamone) was decisive. Lucius Aemilius Papus pursued the Gauls north while Gaius Atilius Regulus, returning from Sardinia with his army after successfully quelling a revolt, landed at Pisae (Pisa), en route to Rome but diverted to reinforce Papus. The Gauls were effectively sandwiched. Atilius' troops took a hill in the vicinity of Telamon; the Gauls were now forced to stand back to back to face both Roman armies. The Roman javelin-throwers wreaked considerable slaughter, particularly amongst the 30,000 Gaesatae—Gallic mercenaries from Transpadine Gaul whose name means 'spearmen', and who reputedly fought naked, 'trusting nature's protection'. Their small shields were a distinct disadvantage against salvoes of Roman missiles.[1] Polybius prefers to believe that the reason they wore no clothes was because they kept getting snagged in brambles. The Romans eventually won through when their cavalry charged down from the hill, successfully breaking the bloody deadlock between the two infantries. The Gauls lost 40,000 men, with a further 10,000 taken prisoner. One Gallic king, Concolitanus, was captured; another, Aneroëstes, fell on his sword. Regulus was killed and decapitated, with his head presented to the Gallic leaders.[2]

Clastidium (222 BC)

The Romans were now intent on ridding Italy of the Gauls and subduing northern Italy—a huge task, considering that the territory involved was almost the size of the peninsula it had taken them many years to conquer. Once again, the Romans were able to take advantage of an enemy that was unwilling or unable to form a united front against them; the Gauls were hopelessly divided. In 224 BC Cispadane Gaul fell, and in 223 BC the consul Gaius Flaminius crossed the River Padus (Po) and defeated the Insubres. The consuls for 222 BC were the pugilistic Marcus Claudius Marcellus and Gnaeus Cornelius Scipio Calvus, who disregarded Flaminius' attempts at peace and lay siege to Acerrae; the Gallic response was to besiege Clastidium (Casteggio). Claudius headed there and was met by the Gauls, a force which included 10,000 Gaesatae. Although considerably outnumbered, the Roman cavalry surrounded the Gauls and cut them down. Plutarch describes the hand-to hand single combat in which Marcellus slew Viridomarus, an Insubrian chieftain, and so won the rare honour of dedicating the *spolia opima* to Jupiter Feretrius.[3]

Scipio's younger brother was Publius Cornelius Scipio, father of Scipio Africanus. Gnaeus Cornelius Scipio got his nickname 'Calvus' ('the bald') to distinguish him from his uncle, another Gnaeus Cornelius Scipio—who had the embarrassing sobriquet Asina ('donkey'). Gnaeus Cornelius Scipio had to endure further lifelong embarassment because *asina* was the feminine form of the adjective. His son was Publius Cornelius Scipio, who became consul in 191 BC and was nicknamed 'Nasica' because of his pointed nose.

Mediolanum (222 BC)

The Gauls—or at least the Insubres—gave up the fight later that year, at Mediolanum (Milan). Gnaeus Cornelius had taken Acerrae and now chased the Gauls to Mediolanum, where they surprised the Romans by attacking their rearguard. The Roman van responded, so the Gauls fled into the mountains and sued for peace.[5] Colonies were established at Cremona and Placentia, and Rome's great road in the north—the Via Flaminia—was built as far as Ariminum and the Via Aurelia, along the coast of Tuscany to Pisae. Naval stations were established at Luna (La Spezia) and at Genua (Genoa).

Rome's imperialism and expansionism naturally led to greater concerns regarding trade and its protection. The trade routes of the Adriatic were constantly harried by the institutional piracy of the Illyrians, who dominated the coastline from Dalmatia southwards. In 230 BC, in what was Rome's first significant political contact with Greece, the Romans had protested to Queen Teuta (r. 231–227 BC) about the piracy which she openly condoned. Apparently she told the ambassadors that it was never the custom of royalty to prevent its subjects from gaining advantage from the sea. She then imprudently sanctioned the murder of one Roman envoy, Coruncanius, and imprisoned the other.[4] The Romans mobilised and set sail with an army of 20,000 troops, 200 cavalry, and the whole Roman fleet of 200 ships, under the command of consuls Lucius Postumius Albinus and Gnaeus Fulvius Centumalus. They set up Demetrius of Pharos as a client king to challenge Teuta's power. Demetrius had enjoyed a similar position under Teuta, and was renowned as a pirate. The Romans took Corcyra, Apollonia, Epidamnus, and Pharos, and finally laid siege to Scodra, Teuta's capital city. She surrendered in 227 BC, and was subjected to restrictions on military and naval activity (not to sail south of Lissa), while her lands were limited to the region around Scodra. However, the Romans did not quash the Illyrians but set up a protectorate instead. This meant that the Illyrians, as *amici* (friends), remained free, unoccupied, and untaxed, but had a moral obligation to show practical gratitude to Rome. The benefits of this diplomatic solution were far-reaching for all parties in the region, not least to traders in Greece and Magna Graecia. Corinth admitted Rome to the Isthmian Games—a sure indication of the goodwill generated in the region.[5]

Pharos (219 BC)

The situation in the Adriatic was later complicated by the troublesome Demetrius, who soon resumed his piratical ways and broke the terms of the treaty with Rome by sailing beyond Lissus—on the assumption that he was at liberty to do so as an *amicus* of Rome. Rome quickly disabused him of this when they sent Lucius Aemilius Paulus to deal with the situation. The fortress at Dimale (Krotina) was soon taken, allowing Aemilius to turn his attention to Demetrius, who was at the garrison town of Pharos (Starigrad), on the island of Pharos off the Illyrian coastline. Aemelius surreptitiously disembarked the majority of his troops and then sailed into Pharos with twenty ships, to be met by Demetrius with virtually the whole of his garrison. The main Roman force then appeared and took a hill above the harbour. Demetrius broke off his battle in the harbour and assailed the hill, only to find himself under attack on two sides. He fled the island in a boat he had standing by for such an eventuality, and arrived at the court of Philip of Macedon.[6] Rome's requests for extradition were refused.

Aemilius was the father of Lucius Aemilius Paullus Macedonicus; his daughter, Aemilia Paulla (*c.* 230–163 BC), married Scipio Africanus.

The Second Punic War

Meanwhile, the Carthaginians were not idle. Far from licking their wounds after the catastrophic 241 BC Battle of the Aegates Islands, they set about expanding their empire in the Iberian Peninsula, extending their interests beyond the southern coast and the mines of Andalusia in 237 BC. Hamilcar Barca ('The Thunderbolt') was the driving force behind this policy, and set out for Spain via what are now the Straits of Gibraltar; he was to be succeeded in the enterprise by his son-in-law Hasdrubal, and by Hannibal, his son. Apart from compensating for the lands lost to the Romans—particularly lucrative Sicily—the expansion into the Spanish hinterland would bring in much-needed overseas revenues, through exploitation of the peninsula's rich mineral wealth (not least in the gold and silver mines of Sierra Morena). Moreover, Spain gave Carthage a vital source of military manpower. The soldiers here had a sound reputation for physical toughness, and they brought with them the famous thrusting swords; the usually temperamental and disputatious Spanish warmed to Carthaginian discipline and training. A combination of conscripted southern Spanish troops, renowned volunteer Celtiberians from the Castilian plateau, and veteran Africans was to give Carthage its best armies yet. Hamilcar died in battle in 228 BC, having subdued a good part of the peninsula; he was apparently thrown from his horse and drowned in a river while attacking the Oretani near Toledo. Among his manifold achievements he founded the port of Barcino (modern Barcelona). Hasdrubal ('The Handsome'), Hamilcar's son-in-law, took over the command.

Rome's gaze was elsewhere, focussed on resurgent Gauls and buccaneering Illyrians. The Greek colony of Massilia complained to Rome, their ally, in 231 BC about the vulnerability of its dependencies on Spain's eastern coast. However, Rome was happy with Hamilcar's explanation that the Carthaginian government was doing no more than seeking new revenue streams to help pay the crippling indemnity to Rome. In 226 BC Hasdrubal reassured Rome when he promised not to cross the Ebro bearing arms. More proactively, three years later Rome took Saguntum under its wing, and into its *fides*, when the city complained of feeling threatened by heightened Punic visibility and activity. Saguntum, however, was to be the touch paper that ignited further Roman-Carthaginian conflict.

Hannibal succeeded as leader of Carthage on his father's assassination in 221 BC; importantly, the twenty-five-year-old warrior had already won the full confidence and respect of his armies. He had nurtured a deep hatred for Rome since the age of nine, when he allegedly signed an oath of lifelong hostility towards the Romans. This and an overwhelming demand for revenge, after the settlement of the First Punic War, are possibly the chief underlying causes of the second war, and explain the actions of the Carthaginians. However, it is equally likely that at this time the Carthaginians were simply doing what they said they were doing: looking for replacement lands and ways of paying the indemnity.

In 221 BC Rome was called to arbitrate between Saguntum and the Torboletes, a tribe loyal to Carthage. Saguntum was the only city south of the Ebro not in Carthaginian hands. Rome found in favour of Saguntum, evoking, for the Carthaginians, vivid memories of Rome's meddling in Messana. Saguntum again felt threatened and appealed to Rome, who sent envoys to Hannibal in New Carthage (Cartagena) in 220 BC to warn him to stay away from Saguntum. The message was reiterated in Carthage, where the Carthaginians stubbornly supported their leader's stance. In 219 BC Hannibal saw that Rome was embroiled with Illyria, in the Adriatic, and decided to act. He began an eight-month siege of Saguntum; they naturally appealed to Rome for help, but—despite the *fides* involved—help never came. At the end of the siege Hannibal sold all the inhabitants into slavery and shared out the slave market proceeds amongst his soldiers. Hannibal took some of the booty from the sack of the city back to Carthage, and distributed it to the people to win support for his war aims; the rest ended up in his war chest.

When Illyria had been subdued the Senate woke up to the fact that something was not quite right in Spain. Livy sums up the shock and trepidation felt in Rome at this realisation:

> The commissioners who had been sent to Carthage, on their return to Rome, reported that everything breathed a hostile spirit. Almost on the very day they returned the news arrived of the fall of Saguntum, and such was the distress of the senate at the cruel fate of their allies, such was their feeling of shame at not having sent help to them, such their exasperation against the Carthaginians and their alarm for the safety of the State—for it seemed as though the enemy were already at their gates—that they were in no mood for deliberating, shaken as they were by so many conflicting emotions. There were sufficient grounds for alarm. Never had they met a more active or a more warlike enemy, and never had the Roman Republic been so lacking in energy or so unprepared for war ... the Carthaginians ... were now crossing the Ebro fresh from the sack of a most wealthy city, and were bringing with them all those Spanish tribes, eager for the fray. They would rouse the various Gaulish tribes, who were always ready to take up arms; there would be the whole world to fight against; the battleground would be Italy; the struggle would take place before the walls of Rome.[1]

The Senate identified the capture of Saguntum as a *casus belli*, and demanded the extradition of Hannibal through the envoys Publius Valerius Flaccus and Quintus Baebius Tamphilus. Carthage refused the ultimatum. A decree was passed in Rome to raise six legions: 24,000 infantry, with 1,800 cavalry, and the recruitment of 40,000 allied infantry and 1,800 cavalry. The Romans voted for war. A further delegation was then sent to Carthage, invested with the power to declare war. Quintus Fabius offered peace or war, and the Carthaginians—according to Livy—affected indifference; Fabius responded:

'Here we bring you war and peace, take which you please.' He was met by a defiant shout bidding him give whichever he preferred, and when, letting the folds of his toga fall, he said that he gave them war, they replied that they accepted war and would carry it on in the same spirit in which they accepted it.

So began the Second Punic War.[2]

Hannibal had decided to invade Italy from the north and so deny Rome its best resource—a seemingly fathomless pool of recruits for its armies. Between the Ebro and the Pyrenees the Carthaginians swiftly subdued the Illergetes, the Bargusii, the Aeronosii, and the Andosini, and took a number of cities—all with considerable losses, though, to Hannibal. As he moved north and east, he left his brother Hanno in command of what is now roughly Catalonia, with 10,000 infantry and 1,000 cavalry. From 220 BC Hannibal had been preparing for this phenomenal challenge by sending envoys to the Gallic tribes in the Po valley, from whom he secured promises of money, food, and guides. It was hardly a difficult sell for Hannibal; Rome's high-handed treatment of the conquered Gauls and the cavalier disposal of their lands made it easy for the Insubres and the Boii, in particular, to support the Carthaginians. Polybius describes the diplomacy as follows:

[Hannibal] conducted his enterprise with consummate judgement; for he had accurately ascertained the excellent nature of the country in which he was to arrive, and the hostile disposition of its inhabitants towards the Romans; and he had for guides and conductors through the difficult passes which lay in the way of natives of the country, men who were to partake of the same hopes with himself.

Rhodanus River (218 BC)

After a relatively uneventful march from the Pyrenees, Hannibal reached the Rhodanus (Rhone). He had friendly natives on the right bank, who helped the Carthaginans build boats and canoes for the crossing, but the hostile, pro-Roman Volcae were hovering on the left. A small detachment under Hanno (son of Bomilcar) was sent 25 miles upstream to modern-day Pont St Esprit, where they crossed the river on rafts, doubled back along the opposite bank, and gave a pre-arranged smoke signal to Hannibal. The main force crossed the river and successfully engaged the Volcae, who fled.[3] Five days of meticulous preparation was brought to successful fruition in a few hours. Hannibal was now on the right side of the Rhodanus; the road to the formidable Alps was clear.

Apart from the unrelenting steepness on ascent and descent, the unforgiving toughness of the terrain, the snow, the cold, and the avalanches, the epic crossing was made all the more difficult by the unwelcome attentions of the Allobroges. Nevertheless, Hannibal succeeded in defeating them and finally descended near what is now Bourget. Many of the baggage animals perished—with their loads—on the mountains, so it was imperative that he found new supplies. Moving on to Chambery, he was able to replenish there by plundering the city; he then destroyed it as a warning to any future Italian resistance. The hostile Taurini provided another object lesson in

Carthaginian diplomacy; Hannibal offered them peace, but when it was refused he surrounded and razed their settlement to the ground, executing all the inhabitants. Hannibal had crossed the Alps, but he lost more half his army in the attempt. Polybius says that the total march was 9,000 stadia, or 993 miles, from New Carthage to Italy in five months. This is equivalent to 200 miles a month, averaging 6–7 miles a day, Alpine mountains notwithstanding.

Rome selected a dictator (the first since 249 BC) to take control of the worsening situation. Unusually, the dictator was elected by the Senate instead of by one of the consuls; the reason being that one of the consuls had been killed while the other was away with his army. Hannibal's progress was painstakingly shadowed by the dictator appointed to deal with the crisis, Quintus Fabius Verrucosus Maximus—who by his stolid patience earned the sobriquet, *Cunctator* (the Delayer).[4] His cognomen, Verrucosus, came about from the wart on his upper lip. Fabius' success at plundering enemy supply lines to replenish his own reserves earned him the honour of being called 'the father of guerilla warfare'. One of his first actions was to appease the gods. Plutarch records that Fabius put the disaster at Lake Trasimene down, in part, to Flaminius' impiety; apart from his cavalier attitude to the omens before leaving Rome, a series of portentous lightning bolts had been ignored. Fabius— characteristically taking no chances—orchestrated a prodigious sacrifice: the equivalent to Italy's whole agricultural production for the next harvest season, including cattle, goats, pigs, and sheep. In addition he decreed that musical festivities should be celebrated, and told everyone to spend precisely 333 sestertia and 333 denari.

Fabius recommended that the Senate should consult the *Sibylline Books* (the *libri Sibyllini*). The original was a collection of oracular responses, in three books, brought to Rome by Tarquinius Priscus—after some haggling about their value with the Sibyl at Cumae. Virgil dignifies them by including them in the list of religious initiatives Aeneas will take when he establishes Rome: 'A great sanctuary awaits you too in our kingdom; for this is where I will put your oracles and the mysterious prophecies told to my people; here I will ordain chosen men, propitious Sibyl'. The *Books* were kept underground, in a stone chest, under the temple of Jupiter Optimus Maximus on the Capitoline, which was guarded by ten men. The *Books* could only be accessed by fifteen specially-appointed augurs (*quindecimviri sacris faciundis*). Consultation took place by Senatorial decree, at a propitiatory ceremony in times of civil strife, external threat, and military disaster, or on the appearance of strange prodigies or phenomena.

The city walls were fortified; the Master of Horse Marcus Minucius Rufus was delegated to raise two Roman and two allied legions, with cavalry units, to defend the city at Tibur. The un-walled towns in Latium were abandoned, and their inhabitants relocated into fortified settlements. Bridges at strategic points were destroyed. Publius Servilius Geminus took command of the fleet at Ostia, as proconsul.

Wherever Hannibal went, Fabius followed. As a child Fabius had been nicknamed *ovicula* ('Little Sheep'), because of his docility and his habit of following others about; this stood him in good stead for his strategy against Hannibal, resisting the temptation to engage even in the fertile Falernian Plain around Capua, which Hannibal had entered through a pass near Mount Callicula and proceeded to lay waste to. Fabius' tactics were simple; despite intense provocation, Fabius declined pitched battles, shadowed the Carthaginians at a safe distance, kept to the high ground, and maintained a position between Rome and Hannibal. The Roman army camped on grounds unlikely to suffer Punic attack, and Roman forage parties were always protected by flying columns of light infantry and cavalry. Carthaginian foragers were cut down at every opportunity. However, the down-side to this was the wholesale and economically-crippling destruction of considerable tracts of agricultural land by the Carthaginians, and the increasing frustration felt by Fabius' colleagues and the anxious Roman people.

Fabius knew that the Carthaginians had only three options by which to exit the Falernian plain; he blocked off two of them, Casilinum and Cales, and posted a unit of 4,000 troops at Callicula. Fabius began a waiting game, content to wait until Hannibal took desperate measures after his provisions had slowly ran out. Nevertheless, Rome demanded decisive action now; the Carthaginians were trapped and more and more land was being devastated.

However, Hannibal realised his predicament with his usual resourcefulness and perspicacity, exiting the plain by enlisting the service of 2,000 cows, to whose horns he had tied bunches of twigs. The cattle were herded by 2,000 camp followers, while the whole force was protected by 2,000 spearmen. Appian records how Hannibal had 5,000 prisoners executed to prevent them escaping. The kindling was set alight, and the terrified cows stampeded over the hills towards the Roman camp—the Romans were terrified. Fabius refused a night battle. Meanwhile, Hannibal marched back through the pass with his army, having pulled off one of the most audacious decoys in military history. To make matters worse for the Romans, Hannibal sent a detachment of Spanish troops, experienced in mountain warfare, back to help the Carthaginians who had herded the cattle; the Romans lost 1,000 men in the ensuing battle. Fabian tactics persisted, but now the dictator implemented a scorched earth policy in Apulia—destroying the land ahead of Hannibal in a bid to deprive him of food and other supplies.

The *Cunctator* was criticised for his lack of aggression and proactivity; for his refusal to engage, he was vilified as Hannibal's lap-dog (his *paedagogus*), so-called after the slaves who accompanied Roman children to school, carrying their books. One of his biggest critics was the frustrated and hostile Marcus Minucius Rufus, Fabius' second-in-command, who petulantly complained: '*audendo atque agendo res Romana crevit, non his segnibus consiliis quae timidi cauta vocant*' ('Rome grew great through audacity and action, not through the lazy plans the timid describe as caution'). The poet Ennius, writing in 170–180 BC, showed rather more perceptive hindsight when he described Fabius as '*unus homo nobis cunctando restituit rem*' ('the one man who gave us back our Rome by holding back'). The simple truth of the matter is that while Fabius was shadowing him Hannibal was constantly irritated, and unable to take one single Roman town. Furthermore, Fabius' close attentions raised morale and inspired confidence in the extremely anxious Italian and Roman populations. *Cunctando* became a byword for military sagacity, and a badge of the Roman way of doing things, taken up later by Livy, Sallust, Cicero, Virgil, and others.[5] Fabius' name—as in 'Fabian strategy'— was adopted as the military term to describe delaying tactics, a war of attrition with a view to avoiding pitched battles and instead wearing the enemy down, continually keeping him at arm's length, and keeping him guessing. When he died, in 203 BC, every Roman citizen allegedly contributed to the cost of his funeral; they were burying the father of their country.

The years 218-216 BC were undoubtedly the worst period in Rome's military history, with four of her worst military disasters following one after another. The calamitous battles at the

Ticinus River, the Trebia River, Lake Trasimine and, worst of all, Cannae, all combined to deliver a blow the likes of which the Romans had not seen since the annihilation at the River Allia and the subsequent sack of Rome. The Romans would not suffer such an ignominious reverse again until the Battle of the Teutoburg Forest in AD 9. These black days (*dies arteres*) were to have an almost indelible impact on Roman pride, morale, and confidence, apart from the significant effects on troop numbers, equipment, and reputation. Rome had to bounce back with a vengeance and restore faith in herself, not just as a global civilisation and vital society, but as an effective fighting force. Rome's enemies were watching very closely.

After Cannae it is reasonable to assume that the Roman military command vowed to never again fall foul of encirclement or double envelopment. Accordingly, the clumsy infantry phalanx was dropped, and there was a change from the manipular system to that of the cohort, made famous under Gaius Marius, as the basic infantry unit of the Roman army. Just as significantly, the days of the potentially divisive two consular armies were numbered; a unified command was obviously needed to ensure unity, morale, and strength in numbers as required. Scipio Africanus was promoted to commander-in-chief of the Roman armies in Africa, as a permanent appointment for the duration of the war. After Cannae, the Roman army began its development into a professional fighting force.

In the wake of the battle, Maharbal was frustrated by what he saw as vacillation on the part of Hannibal, and suggested to the commander that he march on Rome without further ado. According to Maharbal, within five days Hannibal could have been taking dinner on the Capitol. Livy records that a more circumspect Hannibal responded by saying, 'I like your passion but need time to think about your plan'. Maharbal, somewhat deflated, replied, 'No one man has all of God's gifts. You, Hannibal, know how to win a victory, but you have no idea how to use it' ('*vincere scis, Hannibal, victoria uti nescis*').

No-one doubts Hannibal's brilliance on the field at Cannae, but the debate rages on over his actions in the aftermath. Should he have marched on to Rome, or was he right to resist the temptation? On balance, it seems that his judicious decision not to take the city was the right one, despite the insistent urgings of Maharbal and no doubt others. In reality, Hannibal's army was exhausted, and it would have taken much longer to travel the 400 km to the city than Maharbal's fleeting five days. Rome's defences would have been strengthening all the time, and a siege could have been drawn out over months, or even years. Meanwhile casualties would accumulate, and matériel and supplies would diminish; if the Carthaginians did finally manage to breach the walls, they would have been hard-pressed to succeed in 'house-to-house' fighting. Hannibal would also have been hard-pressed to organise effective lines of supply anyway; perhaps, in reality, it was his strategy to subdue Rome on the battlefield, and thereby destroy her network of alliances (through opportunistic defections), extinguishing her aspirations to hegemony on the Mediterranean.

Having buried his many dead, having taken care of many of his wounded, and having arranged for an honourable burial for Paullus, Hannibal attempted a dignified settlement with the Romans over the question of repatriation of prisoners of war. Ten representatives were chosen from the approximately 8,000 captives, and they were led by the the cavalry commander Carthalo to negotiate with the Romans on prisoners and on wider terms of peace.

Roman women imploring the gods to save Rome from Hannibal. Their aim was to persuade the Senate to accept Hannibal's ransom demand, in exchange for 8,000 Roman prisoners of war (Livy 22, 57).

Given the three recent battles in which Rome had been virtually annihilated and humiliated, Hannibal could have been forgiven for thinking he was on safe ground.

However, Rome seized the day and began the slow and painful rebuilding of its forces. The experienced Marcus Claudius Marcellus took over Varro's ramshackle army. Marcus Junius Pictor was appointed dictator, and his *magister equitum* was the skillful Tiberius Sempronius Gracchus. Boys as young as seventeen years old were called up, while 8,000 slaves were bought, emancipated, and enlisted. Six thousand prisoners were released from jail, and given their freedom in exchange for military service. Gallic weapons were 'plundered' from temples, where they had been displayed as war trophies from previous victories. However, a telling fact was that only 1,000 cavalry could be mustered, indicative of the extensive losses suffered by the equestrian order.

In a show of defiance reminiscent of their rejection of Pyrrhus's proposals sixty years earlier, the Romans unequivocally refused to negotiate with the Carthaginian delegation. Carthalo was flatly rejected. There was to be no ransom, and Rome lived to fight another day—perhaps buoyed up by its own determination to rise again, phoenix-like, from the hell of their virtual annihilation.

In the final analysis, Cannae was as indecisive as it was apocalyptic in terms of the Second Punic War. Hannibal's crushing victory gave him dominance in the south, but he still remained cut off from the north (and a potential source of Gallic manpower) by the Roman allies in central Italy. Crucially, his power in the south failed to deliver the allied recruits he badly needed to redress the significant imbalance in military strength. For the Romans, Fabian *cunctatio* tactics and guerrilla warfare became the order of the day, and this only served to frustrate and restrict the Carthaginian war effort going forward.

Nola (216 BC and 215 BC)

To make matters worse for the Romans, hitherto staunch allies in southern Italy now showed their fickleness by defecting to the Punic cause. Arpi, Salapia, Herdonia, Uzentum, Capua, and Tarentum all deserted Rome for Carthage. Capua was a particularly difficult loss for the Romans to stomach. Seduced by Hannibal's promise to make it the capital city instead of Rome, it became Hannibal's winter headquarters and, as an important industrial centre, an excellent supply base for the Carthaginians. Hannibal again had a clear road to Rome, but resisted the temptation once more—well aware, no doubt, that his army was insufficiently large to storm the capital, and that the allies of Rome were standing by to rebuild its shattered armies. Rebuild is exactly what the Romans did; they introduced a levy which soon raised four legions, including some conscripts who were mere boys. Slaves were even eligible—8,000 joined up in exchange for a promise of liberty after the war. The fortunate 10,000 who escaped the carnage of Cannae were also available.

Hannibal resumed his devastating activity, taking towns here and there until he arrived at Nola, 9 miles north of Vesuvius. This was held by Marcus Claudius Marcellus—winner of the *spolia opima*—and his army. Ugly rumours were circulating that the inhabitants of Nola were planning to defect, close the gates on the Romans, requisition their supplies, and man the walls after they had left to do battle. Marcellus took the necessary action to forestall this treachery, restricting the movements of the inhabitants to within the walls. Hannibal lined up for battle, but after three days of Roman delaying tactics he could wait no longer and advanced. At that, the Roman infantry and cavalry surged out of the middle gate to deliver a reeling blow to the Punic army; the allied forces streamed out of the other gates, sending the Carthaginians back to their camp with the loss of 2,800 men (although Plutarch says 5,000). Roman casualties were a modest 500, small recompense for Cannae.[6] The following year Hannibal was back again, reinforced by Hanno. The Romans were victorious again, and it seems this was largely because they were armed with long-range long spears while the Carthaginians were equipped only for close combat. They lost 5,000 men to the Romans' 1,000, while 300 Spanish and Numidians deserted to the Romans.[7]

Cornus (215 BC)

This battle was a result of Carthaginian support for a local uprising in Sardinia. The Carthaginian commander was Hasdrubal the Bald, while his counterpart was Titus Manlius Torquatus. The rebel cities surrendered to the Romans, enabling Manlius to send much-needed soldiers back to Italy. Cornus was significant because it left the crucial Sardinian grain supply intact, while the Carthaginian navy was also denied bases on Sardinia, close to Italy. With the damage to Roman agriculture, the protection of overseas grain supply was crucial. Carthage did not threaten Roman rule in Sardinia again.

Carales and Beneventum (214 BC)

The Romans won a decisive victory at Carales, in Sardinia, under Titus Manlius Torquatus. The slaughter was extensive: 12,000 Sardinians and Carthaginians were killed, and Hasdrubal the Bald, Hanno, and Mago were all taken prisoner—along with 3,700 others. Hamsocora, the local chief who instigated the conflict, committed suicide when he learned that his son had been killed in the battle. At Iberia (also called Dertosa) in Spain, Gnaeus and Publius thwarted a plan by Hamilcar Barca to invade Italy. They then went on to relieve the starving townsfolk of Iliturgi, which had been besieged by Hasdrubal, Mago, and Hamilcar. In the ensuing battle, the Romans were victorious despite being outnumbered 16,000 to 60,000.

The following year Tiberius Sempronius Gracchus faced Hanno at Beneventum (Benevento). Gracchus' army consisted largely of the slaves who had joined up after Cannae. In an attempt to still their restlessness, and satisfy their yearning for their promised freedom, Gracchus declared that immediate liberty would be granted to every man who brought him a Carthaginian head. Mass decapitation followed; so intent were the slaves to deliver a head that they neglected to deal with the still-rampant living enemy, and were encumbered by the heads they were carrying under their arms. Gracchus had to back-pedal: he ordered the slaves to leave the corpses intact, and promised freedom to all—but only if the battle was won. The Carthaginians were slaughtered, with the massacre pursuing them all the way back to their camp. They lost 16,000 men to the Romans' 2,000. Gracchus kept his promise and freed the victorious slaves.[8] Some 4,000 others, with whom he was less than pleased, were less fortunate—he ordered that they should eat their evening meal standing up, instead of sitting down, for the rest of their service in the legions. This same year, Marcellus stormed Leontini and put 2,000 Roman deserters—who were hiding in the city—to the sword.

The Siege of Syracuse (213–211 BC)

King Hiero II of Syracuse (r. 270–215 BC) had been a good ally to the Romans from 263 BC, but his death in 215 BC led to the accession of his naive grandson Hieronymous. Hieronymous was seduced by Carthage's offer of half of Sicily in return for his support. Before things could go much further, he was assassinated, and his policy regarding Rome was reversed. However, the Carthaginians still retained some influence, and reported with some zeal that the Romans—under Claudius Marcellus—had taken Leontini, over-enthusiastically sacking and pillaging the settlement. The Syracusans responded by massacring a number of Romans and renewing their alliance with Carthage. Marcellus tried to limit the damage he had caused by laying siege to Syracuse, by land and by sea. But Hiero had looked after his city during his long reign; he had installed catapults which outranged the Roman artillery, and a formidable array of anti-siege machinery. This war work was the brainchild of the brilliant Archimedes (*c.* 287 BC–212 BC), a Syracusan citizen now focussing largely on military machinery—on a sabbatical from less bellicose studies.[9] Marcellus was at a loss, and continued the siege.

The Romans made another diplomatic blunder when they carried out a massacre in Enna, with even more gusto and butchery than at Leontini; the effect was to persuade more Sicilians to support Carthage. Marcellus did not wait any longer outside Syracuse, and took the city's outer defences by night. Carthaginian reinforcements were cut down by malaria in the swamps to the south of the city, and a Punic fleet of 130 warships flinched from engaging the Roman fleet of 100 vessels. However, after some months cracks began to show when the Syracusans let their guard down during the festival of Artemis. A small squad of Roman soldiers infiltrated the city by night, and were quickly reinforced; however, the citadel remained intact. Eight months later an Iberian officer named Moeriscus let the Romans in, near the Fountains of Arethusa. Marcellus allowed his troops to sack this gem of a city, birthplace of Theocritus and—according to Cicero—the greatest and most beautiful Greek city of them all. One of the victims was Archimedes, who was run through by a legionary despite orders to spare him. Valerius Maximus takes up the story:

> At the capture of Syracuse Marcellus had been aware that his victory had been held up much and long by Archimedes' machines. However, pleased with the man's exceptional skill, he gave out that his life was to be spared, putting almost as much glory in saving Archimedes as in crushing Syracuse. But as Archimedes was drawing diagrams, with mind and eyes fixed on the ground, a soldier who had broken into the house in quest of loot, with sword drawn

A rare collection of copperplate engravings showing various Roman army matériel. They relate to the siege of Syracuse (214-212 BC) by Marcellus, and are probably by Antoise Humblot, who signed one of them. He died in 1758. These are *The Use of a Sambuca by Marcellus in the Siege of Syracyse Between 214-212 BC*.

(A) *Different Types of Covered Galleries* and (B) *Types of vinea to Cover the Assailants.*

over his head, asked him who he was. Too much absorbed in tracking down his objective, Archimedes could not give his name but said, protecting the dust with his hands, 'I beg you, don't disturb this', and was slaughtered as neglectful of the victor's command; with his blood he confused the lines of his art. So it fell out that he was first granted his life and then stripped of it by reason of the same pursuit.

Tradition has it that his last words actually were: 'Do not disturb my circles' ('μή μου τοὺς κύκλους τάραττε', or in Latin, *'Noli turbare circulos meos'*). A less well-known version, related by Plutarch, suggests that he may have been killed while trying to surrender to a Roman soldier. Archimedes was carrying mathematical instruments at the time, and may have been killed because the soldier thought that they were booty worth having.

The Romans had never been in doubt that Syracuse was going to be extremely difficult to break. They brought their own siege instruments to bear, including the *sambuca*—a floating siege tower with grappling hooks, invented by the Greek physician Heraclides of Tarentum— and ship-mounted scaling ladders which were lowered, by pulleys, onto the city walls. Despite these innovations, however, they were no match for Archimedes' inspired defensive devices. These included a huge crane-operated hook—the Claw of Archimedes—which lifted the enemy ships out of the sea, before capsizing them or dropping them to their destruction. He also created a giant mirror, used to deflect the powerful rays of the sun onto the ships' sails and set fire to them. These inventions, combined with the firepower of ballistas and onagers, frustrated the Romans for months.

Himera (211 BC)

By 211 BC the Romans had most of Sicily under its control, the main exception being Agrigentum, which was held by Hanno, Epicydes, and the Numidian general Muttines—an acolyte of Hannibal's. Muttines led the Carthaginians out of the city to the river Himera (Salso), where the Numidians harried the Romans relentlessly. After three days Muttines was called away to deal with a mutiny of his troops, and left instructions not to attack. The instructions were ignored, and the Carthaginans offered battle. At this point, a contingent of disaffected Numidians approached Marcellus and offered to withdraw from the battle; the Carthaginians suffered a serious reverse without these crack troops, losing thousands of men.[10]

Ilorci (211 BC)

The Carthaginians had not quite finished yet, though. Gnaeus was forced to flee because the Celtiberian mercenaries had deserted, leaving him badly under-strength; this was exacerbated when the armies of the two Hasdrubals joined forces with Mago. The Numidian cavalry caught up with the Romans at Ilorca (Lorca), and hacked them to death—Gnaeus Scipio was among them.[11] The two Scipios had made a significant contribution to the Roman victory in the Second Punic War. For a long period, they had prevented reinforcements reaching Hannibal from Spain; and they had, by their presence, detained the crack Numidian horsemen, keeping them away from their overstretched comrades in Italy.

Capua (211 BC)

The focus in Italy was all on Capua, the most prestigious of the cities which had defected to Hannibal after Cannae. Hannibal abandoned his siege of Tarentum to concentrate his forces on Capua, and to engineer a mass exit by the town's inhabitants. In opposition, Appius Claudius attacked Capua, building a highly-effective ring of trenches around the city while Quintus Fulvius faced Hannibal. The former easily achieved his objective, forcing the Capuans back into the town and starving them into surrender. The latter, after a setback caused by a penetrating force of Spaniards and three elephants, also succeeded, with the result being Hannibal's withdrawal. The Romans took Capua soon afterwards.[12] Tarentum would fall to the Romans in 209 BC.

Colline Gate, Rome (211 BC)

Now Hannibal headed for Rome, establishing his camp on the River Anio 3 miles from the city. His plan was not to take the city, but to divert the Romans from Capua and engage them in open battle. Fabius Maximus Cunctator was able to convince the anxious Romans that Hannibal's advance and unsettling proximity to the city was simply a ploy. In the event, Fulvius returned with 15,000 men and camped between the Colline and Esquiline Gates. With breathtaking audacity, Hannibal approached the walls of Rome with 2,000 cavalry on a reconnaissance mission, ostensibly to assess the strength of the defences ranged against him.[13]

Cartagena (209 BC)

Scipio was blockaded by land, and Gaius Laelius by sea. Polybius' description of Scipio's capture of the city shows it to have been particularly brutal; the butchery was not confined to the men and women of Cartagena:

> [Scipio] directed [his soldiers], according to the Roman custom, against the people in the city, telling them to kill everyone they met and to spare no one, and not to start looting until they received the order. The purpose of this custom is to strike terror. Accordingly, one can see in cities captured by the Romans not only humans who have been slaughtered, but even dogs sliced in two and the limbs of other animals cut off. On this occasion the amount of such slaughter was very great.[14]

Carmone (207 BC)

Further conflicts followed in 210 BC at Herdonia—where the Carthaginians were victorious and the Roman consul, Gnaeus Fulvius Centumalus Maximus, was amongst the dead—and at Numistro, which was inconclusive; the Carthaginians stole away in the night. Herdonia was the last Carthaginian victory of the war. The Romans again inflicted a severe punishment on some of their survivors: over 4,000 men were sent to Sicily, to join the survivors of Cannae in their penal regiment. Many of these were Latins, and their exile had ramifications—the Latin colonies were war-weary after ten years of continuous battles fought on their lands. Manpower was short, and much of their agricultural land had been devastated; as a consequence, twelve out of thirty colonies declined to send further recruits or money to Rome. This moratorium lasted for five years, badly compromising the Roman war effort.

In Spain the twenty-five-year-old Publius Cornelius Scipio (later Africanus) took command after the deaths of his father and uncle. His first success was the capture of Cartagena in 209 BC, which he assaulted by land and sea after a speedy dash. In doing so he took control of the Carthaginian arsenal, and deprived them of the revenues from the nearby mines.

The precocious Scipio had been fast-tracked along his *cursus honorum*, side-stepping the usual service as praetor and consul to be invested with proconsular *imperium*. As one of the greatest military commanders of all time, Scipio's greatest quality was surely his ability to inspire those around him and to adapt Hannibal's own battle tactics, recycling them against him. Scipio was, of course, no young hot-head. Tellingly, he now spent time training his troops in Hannibal's tactics and perfecting the use of the superior Spanish sword—which had become regular issue. A diplomat too, he resumed his father's practice of winning the support of local tribes, thus weakening the Carthaginians. The training was to pay off in 208 BC, in his victory at Baecula (Bailen), where the troops were able to employ a new flexibility of movement—unheard of in the strict three-line formation characteristic of the legions, which was annihilated at Cannae. The local Spaniards in Scipio's army celebrated him as king—an honour which he declined. At the same time, he was probably hailed as *imperator* by his own men—an honour which later was to become commonplace for victorious commanders.

Back in Italy there were further battles against Hannibal at Canusium (209 BC), a bloody conflict in which the Carthaginian elephants again turned on their own forces. Roman losses were considerable. The Romans were ambushed at Petellia, and fought at Venusia and Locri Epizephyrii (Locri)—all in 208 BC. The same year Valerius attacked Clupea, on the North-African coast, capturing eighteen Carthaginian ships which were then taken to Lilybaeum as trophies. In Spain, Hasdrubal Barca was facing increasing defections from the Spanish ranks, and collided with Scipio at Baecula, suffering a reverse. After this he headed for the Pyrennes, to join his brother; he was Hannibal's only hope of significant reinforcements, and represented the only chance of a victory in Italy.[15]

After Hasdrubal Barca had left, Hasdrubal (son of Gisgo) prepared for a showdown at Carmone, which involved all the remaining Carthaginian troops, Spaniards led by Mago, and Numidians under Masinissa. When Scipio arrived, he delegated Laleius to face Mago while he took on Masinissa; he was able to repulse the Numidians by ordering his cavalry to level their spears and advance slowly in the face of the Numidian charges. Scipio then camped, concerned no doubt by the strength of the enemy—70,000 infantry alone, compared to his inferior numbers. Nevertheless, he managed to surprise the enemy, defeating the Numidians again with the same tactics. However, the infantry were greatly outnumbered. To raise their flagging morale, he courageously grabbed a shield and ran into the no man's land between the two armies, exhorting his troops to rescue him. The resulting frenzied charge proved too much for the Carthaginians—they lost 15,000 men while the Romans lost 800.[16]

Metaurus River (207 BC)

A further conflict followed at Grumentum, in which Hannibal's army (apparently in considerable disarray) suffered a reverse at the hands of the consul Gaius Claudius Nero.[17] Hasdrubal had reached Italy unopposed by now, and was heading to Sena Gallica (Senigallia) for what promised to be a momentous and decisive meeting with Hannibal in Umbria. However, in a piece of luck for the Romans, the messengers carrying details of the rendezvous were intercepted en route. With a force of 6,000 infantry and 1,000 cavalry, Nero covered 250 miles in six days to join his colleague, Livius, in Sena. The Carthaginians, meanwhile, were incommunicado and in tactical disarray. A battle followed at the river between Nero and Hasdrubal, but was inconclusive despite the heavy loss of life on both sides. Nero then deployed a number of cohorts to the Carthaginian flank and rear, slaughtering large numbers of Spaniards and Gauls. In the Punic equivalent of a *devotio*, seeing that all was lost, Hasdrubal charged into the midst of the Romans and was slain. Nero returned north with the head of Hasdrubal. This he unceremoniously threw into Hannibal's camp, thereby giving him the breaking news of his brother's death. Metaurus was the defining moment of the war, paving the way for the Romans' eventual success; Hannibal retired to the mountains of Bruttium for the next four years.[18] Marcus Livius Salinator, the other consul, and Nero were each awarded a triumph. Here is Lord Byron's conclusion:

> The consul Claudius Nero, who made the unequalled march which deceived Hannibal and deceived Hasdrubal, thereby accomplishing an achievement almost unrivaled in military annals. The first intelligence of his return, to Hannibal, was the sight of Hasdrubal's head thrown into his camp. When Hannibal saw this, he exclaimed, with a sigh, that 'Rome would now be the mistress of the world.' To this victory of Claudius Nero's it might be owing that his imperial namesake reigned at all. But the infamy of the one has eclipsed the glory of the other. When the name of Claudius Nero is heard, who thinks of the consul? But such are human things.

Ilipa (206 BC)

Meanwhile, in Spain, Scipio was squaring up to Hasdrubal (son of Gisgo) and Mago (son of Hamilcar); their huge armies numbered 48,000 Romans and up to 50,000 Carthaginian

Publius Scipio Africanus—Roman military genius.

Hannibal—Carthaginian military genius. The bust was found at Capua.

infantry, with 4,000 horses. The Carthaginian government was no doubt impatient for success, urging Hasdfrubal to act. After an initial skirmish the battle began in earnest, and Scipio's inspired and skillful tactics—a reverse Cannae—won the day. Refining his action at Baecula, he ordered an early breakfast for his men and successfully deployed a complicated double-outflanking movement, which smashed the enemy flanks, seemingly weakened by the early attack and by not having time for breakfast. Only a heavy storm prevented the Romans from invading the Carthaginian camp and wreaking further havoc.[19] Nevertheless, the Carthaginians were now left without a credible army. Scipio's illness, and premature rumours of his death, led to brief unrest amongst the Spanish and Roman troops. He recovered and proceeded to take Gades (Cadiz), effectively ending any remaining Carthaginian presence in Spain.

Astapa (206 BC)

The battle of Astapa was an unusual conflict. The inhabitants of the city nursed a particularly hateful grievance against the Romans, and opted to fight to the death. They built a bonfire of all their possessions in the middle of the city, at the forum, atop of which they forced all their women and children to sit. If things went badly, the intention was to set the bonfire ablaze, women and children included. Things did go very badly. The gates were flung open, and the men of Astapa charged out in a mad frenzy, taking the Romans by surprise and hurling themselves onto the Romans weapons. The Romans rallied, and the fire was lit; a bizarre conclusion saw those who had ignited the pyre flinging themselves onto it.[20]

Utica (203 BC)

In 205 BC Scipio returned to Rome and was elected consul. His priority was to get the Senate to agree to an invasion of North Africa, in order to avenge the Carthaginian devastation of Italy. At first they sensibly refused; Hannibal was still on their doorstep, and the defence budget was fast running out. An appeal by Scipio to the people in the Comitia, however, forced the Senate to allow him to take the two penal legions exiled in Sicily after Cannae— plus any volunteers. After a period in Sicily of intense training in the finer tactics of Baecula and Ilipa for his new armies, Scipio set sail and landed near Utica in 204 BC.

That year Masinissa defected to the Romans, reading the writing on the wall—this was a decisive move in the war. Scipio was able to use his forces to good effect at the Battle of Salaeca, when he had the Numidians approach the Carthaginian lines under Hanno (son of Hamilcar), drawing them into a bloody ambush. Hanno and 1,000 more died, with a further 2,000 slain by the pursuing Romans.[21] Meanwhile, the leader of the Numidian Masaesylii, Syphax, deserted the Romans and sided with Hasdrubal, an alliance cemented by the betrothal of Hasdrubal's daughter, Sophinisba, to Syphax—although until 206 BC she had been engaged to Masinissa. At Utica, Scipio had to extricate himself from the Castra Cornelia, a promontory on which he had chosen to spend the winter. He found himself cut off by Hasdrubal and Syphax, while a Carthaginian fleet blocked any retreat by sea. Nevertheless, Scipio managed to escape by raiding both Punic camps with incendiaries, taking the enemy completely by surprise. Soon after, Scipio soundly defeated the Carthaginians at the battle of Campi Magni. Syphax was captured at the Battle of Ampsaga, where he made a last ditch, desperate attempt to inspire his men by charging into the enemy ranks. He was unseated from his horse and taken prisoner. Syphax was expelled from his capital at Cirta (Constantine), which capitulated at the sight of their leader in chains; he was replaced by Masinissa as King of Greater and Lesser Numidia.

Syphax died at Tibur in 202 BC. Bizarrely, Sophinisba then married Masinissa; however, Scipio had other ideas and demanded that she be sent to Rome as a trophy for his triumph. Masinissa—who obviously feared Rome more than he loved Sophinisba—helped her to evade this ignominy by urging her to die like a true Carthaginian princess, supplying her with the poison which killed her. Sophinisba died with dignity. In terms of the number of tragedies and operas Sophinisba later inspired, she is on a par with Cleopatra.[22]

A sea battle of sorts followed later that year, off Utica. In order to repel the Carthaginian fleet Scipio lashed his boats together in groups of four, thus forming a running surface in which a kind of land battle could be fought. The Carthaginians managed to restore some of their pride when they grappled the Roman ships, and towed sixty of them away.[23]

Zama (202 BC)

Everything looked to be over in early 202 BC, when the Carthaginians agreed a ceasefire, sought peace terms, and ordered Hannibal to return from Italy. He landed at Hadrumentum (Sousse), and marched to Zama with an impressive force of 15,000 seasoned troops. However, the Carthaginians broke the armistice while negotiations were still underway. Scipio responded by detailing Masinissa to raise as large a force as possible and rendezvous at Naragara (Sidi Youssef), 50 miles west of Zama. A parley between the two leaders came to nothing, leaving war as the only option. The scene was set for a showdown between Hannibal and Scipio. Hannibal's army comprised 36,000 infantry, 4,000 cavalry, and eighty elephants. Scipio had 29,000 infantry and 6,100 cavalry.

Significantly, Scipio had chosen to encamp on a hill that had a plentiful supply of water; Hannibal was on a hill opposite, which was considerably less well-irrigated. Scipio was determined to minimise the impact of the elephants and arranged lanes—elephant breaks—within his ranks, through which the beasts might pass, leaving his troops unscathed. Hannibal took the initiative by orchestrating a charge led by his eighty elephants; however, Scipio panicked them by orchestrating his trumpeters and buglers to create a cacophonous din. Some of the elephants charged back on their own lines, while others rampaged through the Roman cavalry. The long and bloody battle was finally brought to a finale when the consul Laelius and Masinissa returned from pursuing the Carthaginian cavalry, and attacked the Carthaginian rear.

The Roman casualties were 2,000 men in total; the Carthaginians ten times that number, with a further 20,000 taken prisoner. Carthage had lost its army and had no option but to surrender. The terms of the earlier peace settlement were re-imposed, but with the indemnity doubled to a crippling 10,000 talents and the required naval reduction increased from twenty ships to ten. The total withdrawal from Spain was retained, with the added stipulation that any war waged by Carthage had to be with the permission of Rome. Masinissa was gifted all the land in Africa that he or his ancestors had held. Scipio rubbed salt in the wound by parading his forces around the city.[24]

One of the positive factors which Rome was able to take from her victory in the Second Punic War was the performance and healthy status of the Roman fleet. After a decidedly late and hesitant start in naval matters, Rome was able to launch and maintain a fleet of some 160 battleships in 218 BC—decidedly more than the complacent Carthaginians, who could only muster 130 at best. This performance provides yet more evidence of Rome's facility and willingness to learn from their mistakes, to learn from their enemies, and to turn disadvantages and miscalculations to their advantage. The deterrent factor of the Roman fleet was instrumental in preventing the transportation of Punic reinforcements from Africa and Spain to Italy, and helped contain Philip V of Macedon by deterring the monarch from joining forces with Hannibal—an alliance which might well have tipped the scales against Rome.[25]

There is no doubt that the war also exposed a darker side of Rome's military; their not infrequent indiscriminate plunder, butchery, and, no doubt, rape, in some of the towns and cities they had taken. More positively though, in Hannibal and Scipio Africanus it threw up two of history's best commanders. Hannibal excelled in his leadership of a—often motley—conscripted army, made up of non-Carthaginians and foreign mercenaries. He never once had to deal with a mutiny, despite the make-up of his army. Scipio was a master of imitation, learning from Hannibal all the while, and fine-tuning his foe's skills and successes to his own advantage. Training was always high on Scipio's agenda, and it was rigorous and robust training which helped him win the day. The Carthaginians, on the other hand, made costly mistakes in neglecting their fleet—just as Rome was emerging as a major naval power—and in reinforcing armies in Spain, when their armies in Italy may have used them to a greater advantage. The Roman Senate, the Roman people, and the Latin allies showed a steely determination and concord, which were major factors in helping them to consistently bounce back, despite suffering unbelievably high casualties across a number of theatres. The selfless sacrifice of the Roman people, in times of grinding anxiety and taxing austerity, was another key element in the victory in the Second Punic War.

Above: *The Spoils of War*, photographed by Gabriel Moulin (1872-1945).

Right: A Carthaginian warrior.

Next pages: Four dramatic scenes from the Second Punic War, depicted on Liebig trade cards. Published by the Compagnie Liebig (later Oxo), manufacturers of meat extract.

DE TWEEDE PUNISCHE OORLOG - 1. Hannibal trekt over de Alpen.
LIEBIG PRODUCTEN: verbeteren de keuken.

Nadruk verboden.   Uitleg op keerzijde.

DE TWEEDE PUNISCHE OORLOG - 3. Slag bij de Metaurus-rivier (207 v. Chr.).
LIEBIG PRODUCTEN: kracht en smaak van 't vleesch

Nadruk varboden.   Uitleg op keerzijde

DE TWEEDE PUNISCHE OORLOG - 2. Scipio redt het leven van zijn vader.
LIEBIG PRODUCTEN: verminderen de uitgaven

Nadruk verboden. Uitleg op keer

DE TWEEDE PUNISCHE OORLOG - 5. Slag bij Zama.
LIEBIG PRODUCTEN: " Het beste van het vleesch "

Nadruk verboden. Uitleg op keerz

Gaul, Macedonia, Greece, and Spain

The Punic Wars gave Rome hegemony in the western Mediterranean. However, the years between the Second and Third Punic wars brought little peace to the Romans, and the doors of the Temple of Janus remained resolutely open. Rome now began to exert power in the eastern Mediterranean; for the Romans, the Mediterranean truly was *Mare Nostrum*.

Cremona (200 BC)

In the year after Zama the Gauls became restless, and there were skirmishes with the Boii at Mutilum. This exploded into a serious conflict in 200 BC, when 40,000 Gallic troops made up of the Boii, Cenomani (from around Verona), and the Insubres joined forces under the Carthaginian Hamilcar. Having sacked Placentia, they had the Roman colony of Cremona next in their sights. However, the Roman consul Lucius Furius Purpureo managed to repel the Gauls, killing 35,000—including Hamilcar. Later battles followed in 197 and 196 BC at the Mincio River, near Mantua, and at Comum (Como) under M. Claudius Marcellus (son of the hero of Clastidium). In the former, 35,000 Insubres were killed and 5,200 captured; in the latter, 40,000 more Insubres perished, according to Valerius Antias—a historian whom Livy reports as famous for his hyperbole.[1] This marked the end of the threat from the Insubres and the Cenomani; they were allowed to retain their lands, but were required to provide occasional military aid.

In 194 BC the Boii rose up again, but they were heavily defeated by Valerius Flaccus at Mediolanum. The following year Lucius Cornelius defeated the Boii at Mutina (Modena), taking 14,000 lives and 1,092 prisoners. This was at some cost, though: the Romans lost over 5,000 men, including two military tribunes, twenty-three centurions, and four allied generals.[2] The Boii conceded half of their lands to Rome, after which they migrated to the Danube—where their name survives in 'Bohemia'. Cremona and Placentia were repopulated, while new *colonia* were established at Bononia (189 BC), Mutina, and Parma (183 BC). A major new road—the Via Aemilia Lepidi—was built, extending the Via Flaminia from Ariminum to Placentia.

Athacus (200 BC)

The First Macedonian War was indecisive. It merely showcased the expansionist ambitions of Philip V of Macedon, who signed an alliance with Hannibal after Cannae—perhaps with an eye to invading southern Italy, in the footsteps of Pyrrhus. The Roman admiral Valerius Laevinius signed treaties with the Aetolian League and with Attalus I of Pergamum in 211 BC. Philip concluded a peace treaty with Rome in 205 BC. In 203 BC he signed a secret treaty with the Seleucid King Antiochus III, with a view to taking Egypt from Ptolemy V. Antiochus had recently captured various Ptolemaic possessions in Asia, as well as southern Syria and Palestine. Ephesus was taken and made a second capital city; Antiochus then married into the Ptolemaic family. Meanwhile, Philip won no friends with his piratical attacks on Greek shipping, or with his routine enslavement of the inhabitants of the towns and cities he took. Rhodes was one of the states attacked by Philip, and in 201 BC they joined with Pergamum in a naval battle in against him. The Treaty of Phoenice ended the war.

The Second Macedonian War opened with the Battle of Athacus, which came about after Rome agreed to help the Rhodians and Attalus against an increasingly aggressive Philip. The previous year, the Romans had flatly rejected a request for armed assistance by the Aetolian League due to war-weariness and commitments in the western Mediterranean. This situation had not changed in 200 BC, so it seems likely that they agreed to help now because they knew of the clandestine alliance between Philip and Antiochus III—and because they were alarmed by an attack on Athens by the Acarnanians, allies of Philip. The Romans may have been overawed by Antiochus after his recently concluded invasion of India—or, more specifically, of the Kabul Valley—and his victory over Bactria and Parthia. On his own he may not have posed a threat, but in an alliance with Philip he was considerably more worrying.

Philip attacked Athens again and moved into what is now the Dardanelles, laying siege to Abydus; his reputation for barbaric cruelty preceded him here. He announced to the inhabitants that the walls were about to be stormed, and that anyone contemplating suicide (to avoid the rapine of his troops) should do so within three days. Fearing the worst, the Abydans killed all their women and children and threw all their possessions into the sea. All the remaining men fought until the end.

Philip rejected an ultimatum from Rome which insisted he indemnify Rhodes and Pergamum and desist from action against any Greek state. Sulpicius Galba then landed in Illyria—with a modest force of 30,000 men, conveyed by an equally modest fleet—and moved east, into Macedonia. Philip had an army of some 20,000 infantry and 2,000 cavalry, including Illyrians and Cretans. The two armies met head on, but the battle was inconclusive; the next day, the Macedonians declined to engage in battle. Following this they were defeated at the Battle of Ottolobum.[3]

River Aous (198 BC)

The Romans were back in Greece two years later, and invaded Macedonia under the consul Titus Quinctius Flamininus. After weeks of delay, Philip sued for peace, but the Roman terms were so exacting that continuing the war was the only option. Flamininus eyed the Macedonian catapults lining the ravine of the River Aous with some trepidation and concern. However, the day was saved by a turncoat shepherd, who agreed to take the Romans safely down the river to emerge at the rear of the enemy. They attacked on arrival, and Philip fled on hearing the clamour of more Romans converging from behind.[4] In the meantime, Flaminius secured the support of the Aetolians and the Achaean League. The Romans again resorted to diplomacy, but Philip rejected terms which entailed surrendering his three 'Fetters of Greece': Demetrias, Chalcis, and Acrocorinth.

Flamininus, a philhellene, was much more proactive than Galba had been, and insisted that Philip renounce his claim to the Greek cities and stay within Macedon. Peace in Greece and liberty for the Greeks were his watchwords.

Cynoscephalae (197 BC)

The decisive battle of the war came the following year, at Cynoscephalae. Flaminus's army was nothing if not international. It comprised troops from the Aetolian League, light infantry from Athamania, mercenary archers from Crete, and elephants and cavalry supplied by Masinissa of Numidia. On the other hand, Phillip had about 16,000 heavy infantry drawn up in a phalanx formation, with 2,000 peltasts, 5,500 light infantry from Illyria, Thrace, and Crete, and 2,000 cavalry. After a number of minor skirmishes, the 25,000 Macedonians (strengthened by 6,000 Aetolians) charged the Romans and inflicted heavy casualties. However, Flamininus rallied and returned the favour by successfully deploying his elephants and his infantry; a military tribune made the decisive move, when he fortuitously detached two maniples and brought them to bear at the Macedonians' rear. The Romans lost 700 men that day, but the Macedonians lost 13,000. Philip asked for a ceasefire, and peace was signed in 196 BC. Philip was confined to Macedonia under the terms of the treaty, as well as being obliged to withdraw from all Greek cities and to give up his conquests in Thrace and Asia Minor. The Macedonian fleet was confiscated, and an indemnity of 1,000 talents was to be paid, while Philip's son was sent to Rome as a hostage.[5] Greece now belonged to Rome. Nevertheless, the Romans kept garrisons in the strategic cities which had belonged to Macedon—Corinth, Chalcis, and Demetrias—and the legions were not completely evacuated until 194 BC. Rome had succeeded in its pretext for war, its spurious *casus belli*, which was the defence of the freedom of the Greek cities. In 196 BC, when Flaminius announced the freedom of the Greek cities at the Isthmian Games in Corinth, he received an ovation the likes of which had never been given before—even to a Greek. The Romans finally withdrew from Greece in 194 BC, showing that Rome had no expansionist intentions there.

The significance of Flaminius' achievement shines through in Appian's description:

> When he had arranged these things with them he went to the Isthmian games, and, the stadium being full of people, he commanded silence by trumpet and directed the herald to make this proclamation, 'The Roman people and Senate, and Flamininus, their general, having vanquished the Macedonians and Philip, their king, order that Greece shall be free from foreign garrisons, not subject to tribute, and shall live under her own customs and laws.' Thereupon there was great shouting and rejoicing and a scene of rapturous tumult;

and groups here and there called the herald back in order that he might repeat his words for them. They threw crowns and fillets upon the general and voted statues for him in their cities. They sent ambassadors with golden crowns to the Capitol at Rome to express their gratitude, and inscribed themselves as allies of the Roman people. Such was the end of the second war between the Romans and Philip.[6]

Emporiae (195 BC)

Spain was now a major problem for the Romans, who were anxious to retain the mineral wealth of the country and the resulting lucrative flow of revenue. They divided the peninsula into two praetorian provinces for administrative purposes: Hispania Citerior in the east, and Hispania Ulterior in the south (roughly, modern Andalusia). However, they were winning few friends due to the heavy-handed, intrusive administration imposed after the departure of the disciplined Scipio. The consensus amongst Spaniards was that they had simply exchanged one oppressive ruler for another, with an obvious effect on loyalty. However, it was those who had not been won over or subdued so far who were the biggest thorn in Rome's side: the Celtiberians in Castile and Aragon, and the Lusitanians in the west. The Romans were also operating and fighting in uncharted territory, with long marching distances, with all the logistical and military problems that unfamiliarity and distance brings.

The first of two minor battles claimed the life of the praetor Tuditanus; the second, at Turda, was a convincing victory for the Romans. A third battle, at Iliturgi, saw Marcus Helvius and his 6,000 troops attacked by 20,000 Celtiberians. Helvius came out on top despite the odds, slaying 12,000 of the enemy, and he followed this up by taking Iliturgi and slaughtering all of its adult inhabitants.

Spain was then elevated to a consular province with the appointment of Marcus Porcius Cato to Hispania Citerior, with an increased army of 50,000 men; Cato camped at Emporiae (modern Ampurias), south-east of the Pyrenees. His force joined battle in support of the Ilergetes—Roman allies—who were being constantly harried by Spanish forces. Cato won the day and gradually subdued Spain north of the Ebro, improving communication between the two provinces.[7] But the Spaniards would not lie down; in 193 BC, P. Cornelius Scipio Nasica (the son of Gnaeus Scipio, who died at Ilorci in 211 BC) took over the praetorship of Hispania Ulterior. He attacked a detachment of the Lusitani near Ilipa (Alcala del Rio), inflicting an estimated 12,000 casualties to Scipio's seventy-three—despite being outnumbered. That same year, Marcus Fulvius lay siege to Toletum (modern Toledo) and routed an army of Vaccaei, Vettones, and Celtiberi nearby, before sacking the city.[8]

Thermopylae (191 BC)

Over on the other side of the Mediterranean, the Aetolian League was feeling aggrieved at the settlement they received following the Second Macedonian War. They had been Rome's allies, and were hoping to annex all of Thessaly under the terms of the peace agreement—but they received considerably less. They subsequently enlisted the support of Antiochus III, ostensibly to help them liberate Greece from the Romans. Antiochus, elevated to commander-in-chief of the Aetolian League, landed with 10,000 men at Demetrias, in Thessaly, and overran it. However, he found no Greek support; he and the Aetolians were on their own, and the Romans—concerned that Antiochus had designs on Italy—were advancing under Manius Acilius Glabro, with an army of 20,000 men and a squadron of elephants. Philip V entered into an alliance with the Romans. Antiochus retreated to Thermopylae, where the Aetolians manned the mountains above the pass. Marcus Cato and Lucius Valerius attacked them, and the victorious Cato then charged down the pass, causing Antiochus to flee with the loss of nearly his entire army. Antiochus then returned to Asia, leaving the Aetolians to sort out the mess.[9]

Glabro demanded unconditional surrender, which the Aetolians refused. The resulting war was cut short by L. Cornelius Scipio, the brother of Africanus and consul for 190 BC, who offered an armistice so that the legions could be deployed against Antiochus in Asia Minor. M. Fulvius Nobilior then reduced the Aetolian League to virtual impotence, with his treaty confining the members to their borders and stipulating they have the same allies and enemies as Rome. The Romans pulled out in 188 BC, and seventeen years of peace in Greece followed.

Corycus (191 BC) and Panormus (190 BC)

The Romans followed up their success here by invading Anatolia. Under Gaius Livius Salinator, their fleet won a naval battle against the exiled Rhodian Polyxenidas (Antiochus' admiral) at Cape Corycus. It was here that Hannibal re-emerged, in command of one of Antiochus' Phoenician squadrons. In 190 BC the Rhodians sent reinforcements of thirty-six ships, under Pausistratus, to the Romans at Panormus. Polyxenidas led Pausistratus into a trap, causing him to hastily man his ships and force a way out of the harbour. Only seven ships made it—these were those which were equipped with urns suspended on poles; the urns contained burning liquids, which were poured onto the enemy boats and their crews. Pausistratus' ship was sunk, taking the captain with it.[10]

Cape Myonnesus (190 BC)

The Roman fleet of eighty ships (supported by twenty-two Rhodians) under L. Aemilius Regillus was in search of supplies, and anchored in a harbour close to the promontory of Myonnesus. On hearing that Polyxenidas was nearby with his fleet, the Romans immediately set sail and engaged the enemy force, using their incendiaries to good effect. Significantly, this defeat was to cost Antiochus control of the seas, rendering him incapable of defending his empire.[11] Rome now ruled the waves after what turned out to be their final naval victory, leaving the path clear for an invasion of Asia.

Magnesia ad Sipylum (190 BC)

The Romans were keen to follow their naval victory with a decisive win on land, and for this they landed on Asian soil for the first time. The extremely long march to the Dardanelles area was supported through Greece by supplies from Philip V, and led by L. Scipio—younger brother of Scipio Africanus. Antiochus' army was strong: 60,000 infantry and 12,000 cavalry. Nevertheless, he was cautious, withdrawing beyond the River Phrygius, and camping near Magnesia. What Antiochus' army had in numbers it lacked in cohesion; individually the different units were fine, but they had had no training in working together as one fighting force. Antiochus tried for peace, but the Roman terms were unpalatable. The ensuing battle saw Antiochus annihilated, with the loss of 53,000 men; 350 Romans died. Antiochus sued for peace again, and the final treaty, the Treaty of Apamea, was ratified in 188 BC.[12] Its terms included the largest indemnity ever imposed by Rome; 15,000 talents, and stipulations that Antiochus would reduce his fleet to ten vessels and surrender his elephant herd. All territory west of Mount Taurus was to be evacuated, and he was prohibited from waging war in Europe or in the Aegean. Syria was, in effect, politically and militarily emasculated. The Romans withdrew from Asia later that year.

The constitution of Antiochus' forces at Magnesia demonstrates perfectly the multi-nationalist and multi-functional nature of some of the armies at the end of the second century. According to Livy and Appian, there were 1,500 Gallograecian infantry, 3,000 Galatian armoured cavalry (*cataphracti*) and 1,000 *agema* cavalry, his royal household guards; there was a cavalry squadron Livy calls *argyraspides*, Dahae horse-archers, 3,000 Cretan and Trallean light infantry, 2,500 Mysian bowmen, Cyrtian slingers, and Elymaean archers; tribesmen of the Tectosagi, the Trocmi, and the Tolistoboii; 2,000 Cappadocians; scythed chariots and a unit of dromedary-riding Arab archers; a regiment of Tarentines, 2,500 Gallograecian cavalry, 1,000 Cretans, 1,500 Carians and Cilicians similarly armed, Tralles, 4,000 peltasts, Pisidians, Pamphylians, and Lydians; and Cyrtian and Elymaean troops.

The Galatean Expedition (189–188 BC)

These four battles, in what became known as the Galatean Expedition, followed hard on the victory over Antiochus III. The Galateans were Gauls who entered Macedonia, moved through Thrace, and then went into Asia. Gnaeus Manlius Volso was charged with subduing them, and made for their strongholds at Mount Olympus, Cuballum, and Magaba. Manlius was successful at the first battle at Cuballum, which he followed up with an attack on the Tolostobogii on Olympus—deploying his Cretan archers with deadly effect. The Gauls could only respond by throwing stones back, and the fact that they fought naked did not help them. Returning to his base at Ancyra (Ankara), Manlius agreed to talks with the Tectosages. On the first two arranged dates they failed to appear, but on the third they charged against Manlius' delegation of 500 men with 1,000 cavalry; the fortunate nearby presence of 600 Roman cavalry saved the day. The Gauls were pursued, but no prisoners were taken. Manlius followed this up with a successful assault on the Tectosages, in their stronghold on Mount Magaba. The Gauls sued for peace after this reverse.[13]

Tagus River (185 BC)

In 186 and 185 BC the Romans were preoccupied once more in Spain. There were minor battles at Hasta, in the extreme south (where Gaius Atinius lost his life), at Calagurris (where the Celtiberians lost 12,000 men and had 2,000 captured), and at Toletum (where the two Roman armies, under Gaius Calpurnius and Lucius Quinctius, were soundly defeated despite their superior numbers).

When the Romans had rebuilt their armies and their morale, they marched to the Tagus (Tajo) to face the enemy. They crossed the river by two fords—the Spaniards missed an opportunity here to exploit the vulnerability of the Roman armies. In the end, the Romans' victory ushered in a four-year period of relative calm in Spain.[14]

Aebura (181 BC)

This calm was shattered when the Celtiberians began recruiting, amassing a 35,000-strong army. Quintus Fulvius Flaccus marched with his army to a point near Aebura, and the Celtiberians came to meet him. After a few days of inactivity, Fulvius took the initiative when he ordered Lucius Acilius to steal behind a hill at the enemy's rear—with cavalry and 6,000 auxiliaries. Gaius Scribonius was sent to the enemy rampart, drawing out the Spaniards; Fulvius then attacked, Acilius charged down the hill, and the enemy camp was easily captured. The Celtiberians were now surrounded, with nowhere to go. This success was followed by the siege of Contrebia, where the Romans destroyed the force that had come, somewhat late, to relieve the town. After this, much of Celtiberia surrendered to the Romans.

Fulvius had something of a chequered and tragic career. He won two triumphs for his victories in Liguria and Spain, but his cavalier attitude towards protocol and tradition let him down badly. In 184 BC he attempted to hold two magistracies in the same year, which was strictly prohibited. In 173 BC he built his temple to Fortuna Equestris with marble tiles that were quarried from a temple of Juno Lacinia. His two sons were serving in Illyricum, in 172 BC, when he was informed that one had died and the other had contracted a life-threatening illness. The next day his slaves found him in his bedroom, hanging by a noose. There was nothing noble about Fulvius's suicide, and it was taken as evidence of his mental instability. Livy says that 'grief and fear took over his mind' ('*obruit animum luctus metusque*'); the anger over the plundered Juno Lacinia had driven him insane.[15]

Manlian Pass (180 BC)

However, some pockets of resistance remained—which Fulvius Flaccus set about winkling out. The time came for him to return to Rome, so he turned around and headed back to base via the Manlian Pass; but the Celtiberians were waiting to ambush him. Flaccus stood firm, and his cavalry destroyed the enemy's wedge formation; the Spaniards lost 17,000 men. Tiberius

Sempronius Gracchus succeeded Flaccus in 179 BC, continuing where Flaccus had left off. At Complega, the 20,000 or so townsfolk came out to meet him, bearing olive branches and seeking peace. They then attacked the Romans, causing Gracchus to flee; however, he soon turned the treacherous Celtiberians to slaughter. Later that year, Gracchus routed the enemy at Alce and delivered a further decisive victory at Mount Chaunus.[16] The Celtiberians sued for peace, leaving only the west coast of Spain outside Rome's control. Twenty or so years of relative calm followed the settlement drawn up by Gracchus, who was the first Roman to win the confidence of the Spaniards since the departure of Scipio. Gracchus founded Gracchuris, on the Ebro, which was to become a leading centre of Roman culture.

The Istrian and Ligurian Wars (178–173 BC)

Between 178 and 171 BC the Romans fought the minor Istrian and Ligurian Wars. Aulus Manlius was dispatched to Istria (largely modern-day Croatia) to quell outbreaks of unrest. He pitched up at the Timavus River, near the coast, and set up outposts. The Istrians attacked these outposts and the Roman guards fled; the Istrians then attacked the Roman garrison, killing everyone inside. The table in the mess happened to be set for a banquet—which the Istrians ate. It turned out to be their last meal; the feast rendered them replete, drunk, and easy prey for the Romans, who returned to kill them.[17]

The Ligurian Wars were unfinished business after a battle near Pisae in 192 BC, a Roman victory in which Quintus Minucius had slaughtered 9,000 Ligurians. In 177 BC the consul Gaius Claudius was persuaded to help his brother Tiberius (proconsul at Pisae) rid himself of the Ligurians, who had come down from the mountains and camped at the River Scultenna. Fifteen thousand Ligurians died and 700 were captured in the battle, with the survivors fleeing back into the mountains. The following year the intractable Ligurians descended again, this time occupying two mountains—Letum and Ballista—near Campi Macri. The consuls—Quintus Petilius and Gaius Valerius—split the army into two, to attack from different directions. The Romans won the day, despite the death of Petilius from a javelin. The war came to an end after the Battle of Carystus (north of modern-day Genoa), in 173 BC; losses of a further 10,000 men, with 700 captured, persuaded the Ligurians to surrender unconditionally.[18] With its unforgiving terrain, Liguria had been fertile ground for Roman triumphs and booty hunters—in 173 BC the venal consul M. Popillius attacked a peaceful tribe, with no other purpose than to acquire plunder.

A revolt in Corsica was quashed in 181 BC. Sardinia was secured in 176 BC, after two years of attrition by Tiberius Sempronius Gracchus—who sold most of the inhabitants off into slavery.

Callinicus and Phalanna (171 BC)

Hostilities resumed against the Macedonians in 171 BC. Philip had spent the last seventeen years peacefully economically and politically strengthening his country, reinforcing his borders, exploiting mineral resources, introducing new taxation, and settling Thracians in Macedonia to ease a manpower problem. Philip had two sons, Perseus and Demetrias; Demetrias built up strong diplomatic relations in Rome, so all augured well for the future. However, Perseus saw this as complicating his own designs to succeed his father, and had his brother executed on spurious charges of treason. Philip was plagued by guilt, and planned to disinherit Perseus, but it was too late. Perseus acceded to the throne on Philip's death in 179 BC. Initially cautious, Perseus carried on his father's good work—but he was always viewed with suspicion by Rome. His marriage to Laodice, daughter of Seleucus IV of Syria (successor to Antiochus III), and his sister Apame's marriage to Prusias II of Bythinia were not helpful, nor was the fact that his pro-Roman neighbours were spying on him, spinning everything with an anti-Perseus twist. Most active was Eumenes III, of ever-hostile Pergamum, who turned up at Rome and delivered a character assassination of Perseus in person. This, and the translation of suspicions into belligerent action, led to a declaration of war in which the Macedonians—thanks to the prudent domestic war preparations of Philip and Perseus—fielded an army of some 40,000 men and 4,000 cavalry.

Perseus antagonised the Romans by invading Thessaly and setting up a garrison at Mount Othrys. P. Licinius Crassus marched to meet him from Epirus, and camped at Larissa with 30,000 men in total. After several days' procrastination the two armies clashed at Callinicus, in what was to be a disaster of the first magnitude for the Romans. They lost 3,000 men to the Macedonians' sixty. Perseus offered peace, but the Romans flatly rejected it.

The Romans restored some of their pride later that year at Phalanna, when they were attacked by Perseus while out foraging. The tribune, Lucius Pompeius, withdrew to a hill where he was besieged by the Macedonians. Crassus relieved his colleague, and proceeded to route Perseus' forces. The loss of 8,000 dead and 3,000 taken prisoner was enough to make Perseus retreat back into Macedonia.[19]

Uscana (170 BC), Scodra, and Pythium (168 BC)

Another disaster was waiting for the Romans at Uscanian Illyria. Appius Claudius Cento opposed a force led by Gentius, King of the Illyrians, who was now an ally of Macedonia. Claudius fell for a trap in which the inhabitants of Uscana pretended to be willing to betray their city to him. As Claudius approached what he believed to be an empty city, his army was overcome by a charge of the inhabitants. Only half of Claudius' 4,000 men escaped with their lives.[20] In 168 BC, Gentius, the King of Illyria, was attacked in Scodra, his capital, captured, and taken to Rome. Two years later, Aemilius Paullus faced Perseus across the Elpeus, a dried-up river which was impossible to cross. He sent Scipio Nasica, with 8,000 infantry and 120 cavalry, ostensibly to the coastal town of Heracleum—but really they went in the opposite direction, to Pythium, and the sanctuary of Apollo on Mount Olympus. Persius could still see Paulus, and was quite unaware of Scipio's position until a deserter revealed the plan. Perseus sent 2,000 Macedonians and 10,000 mercenaries after Scipio; however, Scipio overcame the Macedonians and they fled. Perseus withdrew to Pydna.[21]

Pydna (168 BC)

The battle-hardened Aemilius Paullus joined Scipio at Pydna to confront Perseus. Paullus allegedly caused a horse to bolt, and thus triggered the start of the one-hour afternoon battle. In a battle reminiscent of Cynoscephelae, the consul exploited gaps in the Macedonian centre and caused them to discard their long, unwieldy pikes, forcing them to depend on their short swords in the close combat that followed. The flexible Roman maniples and the use of tempered steel, as opposed to iron, won the day for the Romans. Perseus fled in the rout that followed, leaving 25,000 Macedonians dead; he later surrendered, and brought the Third Macedonian War to an end.[22] All royal officials were excommunicated, while Perseus was detained under virtual house-arrest in Alba Fucens. On a wider scale, the Romans carried out a rigorous and ruthless purge of inconvenient Greek citizens, many of them denounced by neighbours and friends of Rome.

   In 150 BC a pretender to the Macedonian throne, Andriscus, claimed to be a son of Perseus. In what became known as the Fourth Macedonian War, Andriscus defeated a small Roman force dispatched to deal with him. His success was short-lived, however, as a second army under Q. Cacilius Metellus expelled him from Macedonia in 148 BC, catching up with him in Thrace. This minor war was important because it brought it home to the Romans that a more robust and permanent political system was required in Greece. Macedonia accordingly became a Roman province, incorporating Thessaly and Epirus. The Via Egnatia was built, leading from Apollonia to Thessalonica, and remained the only decent road in Albania until the Italian invasion of 1916.

Cauca (151 BC)

The Lusitanians defeated Servius Sulpicius Galba in 151 BC. That same year L. Licinius Lucullus, a man with a reputation for brutality, arrived in Spain as consul. Unprovoked, and without senatorial authority, he attacked the Vaccaei even though they had no quarrel with Rome. Lucullus attacked Cauca on a spurious pretext for war, and slew 3,000 of the Vaccaei; the following day they requested peace, and agreed to all of the Roman terms. However, this did not stop Lucullus inveigling his way into the town and butchering the adult male survivors.[23]

Intercatia (151 BC)

The townsfolk at Intercatia, who were only too aware of his atrocity at Cauca, refused to agree a treaty with Lucullus. Lucullus was outraged, and laid siege. The Intercatians refused Lucullus' angry demands for battle; however, one giant of a man rode out, in splendid armour, with a challenge to single combat. Scipio Aemilianus accepted, and beat the Spaniard. The Romans then battered their way into the city, but were unable to defeat the Intercatians—both sides were suffering from malnutrition. Scipio formed a treaty and gave his word that it would not be violated.[24]

In 150 BC Lucullus reinforced Galba with such ferocity that the Lusitanians surrendered. In the negotiations, however, Galba showed himself to be just as duplicitous as Lucullus. The Lusitanians were persuaded to leave their homes with the promise of better lands in other regions; however, a trench was dug around them, to prevent escape, and they were massacred. All that this early example of ethnic cleansing actually achieved was a stronger resolve among the Lusitanians to resist the Romans. Their time was to come in 147 BC, when Viriathus—a natural guerrilla fighter—burst onto the scene.

Numantia (141–133 BC)

The natural fortress of Numantia was the last Spanish city to hold out against the Romans. Twelve years after the shambolic Fulvius Nobilior—'his was the first grave in the cemetery of Roman reputations at Numantia'—Q. Pompeius found himself under siege by the defenders as he now besieged the city.[25] Nevertheless, Pompeius managed to extricate himself and draw up a treaty—which he quickly reneged on, again with the blessing of the Senate. In 137 BC Hostilius Mancinus did likewise when escaping from a similar trap; the Senate was yet again complicit. In 133 BC, P. Cornelius Scipio Aemilianus, adopted grandson of Scipio Africanus, was posted to Spain with 60,000 men to bring Numantia to a conclusion. He built seven camps linked by a wall to strengthen the blockade, and took the surrender of the starving inhabitants—who were then sold as slaves. Thus ended the resistance in Spain; the peninsula was now in Roman hands.

Alpheus River (146 BC)

In view of the decidedly loose control under which the Romans left the Greek towns and cities, it was hardly surprising when a dispute arose after Rome's deportation of 1,000 Achaean citizens to Rome after the Third Macedonian War. The Achaean league naturally protested, but their citizens remained incarcerated, without trial, for fifteen years. Seven hundred died as a result of the conditions of their confinement; the survivors were released in 150 BC, but this was too late to moderate the anger felt by the Achaeans. Corinth was particularly militant, and appointed a dictator, Critolaus, who invaded central Greece in 146 BC. However, he was defeated by Caecilius Metellus at the Alpheus River. Florus is mistaken when he says that this ended the Achaean War.[26]

Scarphea and Chaeronea (146 BC)

Undeterred, Critolaus then attacked Heraclea, a town which had declined the offer to join the Achaean League. Critolaus was once again soundly beaten by Metellus, and took refuge

The statue of Viriathus at Viseu, in central Portugal—Lusitanian scourge of the Roman army around 140 BC, and one of the most successful enemies of Rome.

in Scarphea; he was never heard of again. A force of 1,000 Arcadians, on its way to reinforce Critolaus, was also massacred by Metellus.[27]

Isthmus or Corinth (146 BC)

Diaeus replaced Critolaus, and raised an army of 14,000 infantry and 600 cavalry. Four thousand were sent to garrison Megara, but these fled to Corinth on the approach of an army under Lucius Mummius, who had 23,000 on foot and 3,500 on horses. The Achaean cavalry fled the field, leaving their infantry to its fate. Mummius then proceeded to remorselessly sack and raze the virtually-deserted gem of a city.[28] There is some mitigation in the fact that many of the exquisite works of art were shipped back to Rome before the bonfires were lit. The men were killed, while the women and children were sold as slaves. The Achaean League was disbanded, and its towns were absorbed into the province of Macedonia; Corinth was erased in order to prevent it becoming a future commercial rival to Rome. Mummius received the *agnomen* Achaichus, in recognition of his victory over the Achaean League.[29] Julius Caesar refounded the city as *Colonia Laus Iulia Corinthiensis* (Colony of Corinth in Praise of Julius) in 44 BC, just before his assassination.

Titus Quinctius Flaminius feted at the Isthmian Games in 196 BC; a show of concord and appreciation by the Greek states after Rome released them from Macedonian power.

The Third Punic War

In Rome, in 149 BC, Marcus Porcius Cato spoke for many Romans when he said, '*Ceterum censeo Carthago delenda est*' ('Moreover, I am of the belief that Carthage has got to be destroyed'). In stating this he signed the death warrant on the North-African civilisation, and helped rid Rome of its most effective and threatening enemy. He was opposed in the Senate by Publius Cornelius Scipio Nasica Corculum, who wished Carthage to be spared.

Before that, however, Carthage was busy reinventing itself. The treaty they signed at the end of the Second Punic War made no reference to Carthaginian trade, nor did it impose any restrictions on it; therefore, Carthage was at liberty to carry on as the centre of Mediterranean commercial activity. The hinterland was now exploited aggressively, with more intensive agricultural methods harvesting larger revenues. Hannibal himself introduced efficiencies and greater transparency in the city's financial administration. In 191 BC Carthage was able to repay forty instalments of its indemnity in one transaction; there were frequent gifts of corn to Roman forces in the area, attempting to curry favour and highlight their non-aggressive intent. However, Hannibal was a victim of this new age—his enemies trumped up charges against him of fraternization with Rome's enemies, which were upheld by the Carthaginian senate. He fled. When the indemnity was paid-up in 151 BC, Carthage assumed that their Roman treaty had expired; this was not so, as the Romans believed it stood in perpetuity. Moreover, the Romans eyed the fertile hinterland of Carthage as a bountiful food source for Rome; the indemnity was repaid, so the Romans had nothing to lose there if hostilities were to resume.

The exile of Hannibal seemingly reassured the Romans that all was well in North Africa, but the rise of Masinissa should have disabused them. After Zama, Masinissa worked tirelessly to strengthen Numidia in every way, no doubt taking advantage of the loose and clumsy wording which described the territories handed to him in 201 BC. Supported by his 50,000-strong army, he subdued the tribes on his borders and forced neighbouring nomad tribes to settle and work the coastal lands. His ambition was to overrun large swathes of North Africa—taking in what is now Libya—around Tripoli, Tunisia, and Algeria. Carthaginian land was poached, Carthage's complaints to Rome were ignored. Rome had an obligation to defend Carthage, but Masinissa softened them up with corn gifts of his own and unsettled them with warnings of the perils of a resurgent Punic state. In 150 BC Carthage ran out of patience and declared war on Numidia. Their reduced forces were no match for Masinissa, and the resulting peace treaty saw them surrender more land in Tunisia—including the fertile Bagradas Valley. Carthaginian territory was now reduced to some 5,000 square miles.

To make matters worse, Carthage was technically in breach of the 201 BC treaty when they took up arms against Numidia. Motivated by fear, and hypnotised by Cato's mantra on the need to destroy Carthage, the Roman senate agreed to war in 149 BC. The Roman expeditionary force was met by a formal Carthaginian declaration of surrender, with terms that included hostages and the surrender of 2,000 catapults and other matériel. The hostage deal meant that 300 well-born Carthaginian children would be sent to Rome in return for the rights to their land and self-governance. The city of Utica—a Carthaginian ally— defected to Rome, and was occupied by a Roman army of 80,000 men. However, the Romans kept on raising the stakes; they requested that all arms and weapons be surrendered, and finally demanded that the Carthaginians vacate their city—which would then be erased—and relocate to a site 10 miles inland. Carthage was a maritime, mercantile nation, and the sea was their livelihood and their lifeblood; they declined the offer. The 50,000 outraged citizens began a frenzied replenishment of their arsenals, raised an army largely made up of Libyans, and fortified their defences—all in preparation for the inevitable war. Appian tells that they turned out 300 swords, 500 spears, 140 shields, and 1,000 projectiles for their catapults every day. Masinissa remained on the sidelines, a mere spectator, no doubt sulking because his prize had been stolen before his very eyes.

Nepheris (149 BC)

The war opened with the Romans laying seige, in vain, to the fortress that Carthage had now become. The consul, Manius Manilius, moved against Hasdrubal the Boeotarch (a tactician of some note) and Himilco Phameas at their camp in inhospitable Nepheris, to the south of Carthage. Manilius lost over 500 men after they were attacked by the Carthaginian cavalry, while gathering timber around the Lake of Tunis; then the Roman fleet was set on fire by Punic fire ships. Publius Cornelius Scipio Aemilianus Africanus Numantinus, a military tribune at the time, argued against the suitability of Nepheris as a battlefield—but he was accused of cowardice for his trouble. A wadi, which was difficult for armed and armoured troops to negotiate, stood in the way of the Romans, leaving them vulnerable to enemy fire and ambush during the crossing. Manilius pressed on and engaged Hasdrubal, with considerable loss of life in both armies. Hasdrubal followed up when the Romans retreated to the exposed river, but Scipio was able to save the day—albeit with some difficulty, on account of the terrain. It took the Romans a further two years before Scipio captured Nepheris, in 146 BC.[1] Manilius was replaced by Calpurnius Piso in 149 BC.

Manilius was the unfortunate senator who Cato had expelled from the senate for kissing his wife in public, in front of their daughter. Cato, however, admitted that he only ever kissed his wife during thunderstorms.[2] Manilius was also the author of a work on contracts of sale, which was cited by Varro, Cicero, and Brutus.[3]

Carthage (147 BC)

Scipio Aemilianus was now consul, despite being underage for the post, and was in charge at the siege of Carthage. His naval blockade was proving ineffective, so he built a huge stone mole at the entrance to the harbour. However, to circumvent this the Carthaginians built a new exit from the port, directly into the open sea—a project which astonishingly went unnoticed by the Romans until it was completed. The sight of the fifty-trireme-strong Punic fleet, sailing past them into open waters, staggered the Romans. The Carthaginians missed a golden opportunity here to destroy the Roman fleet, which was berthed and in a state of unreadiness. A battle took place three days later, in which the nippy Carthaginian ships were able to inflict considerable damage by breaking off Roman oars and rudders and holing the sterns of many Roman vessels. The following day turmoil ensued in the harbour mouth, with the smaller Carthaginian craft blocking the larger boats. The Romans proceeded to destroy them, but they also found it difficult to turn and exit. The Romans finally extricated themselves by towing their ships out, stern-first, on ropes extended from five allied ships outside the harbour entrance. The Carthaginian fleet was reduced to such an extent that it ceased to be an effective force.

On land, Scipio eventually breached the outer walls of Carthage. At the end of a week of bitter house-to-house and street-to-street fighting—a scenario similar to that which played out in Stalingrad two thousand years later—the Romans eventually reached the citadel, where the 50,000 survivors had taken refuge. Scipio took their surrender, sold them into slavery, and erased the city; it burned for seventeen days. The Carthaginian threat was over.[4]

During the battle 900 of the survivors, who were mainly Roman deserters, took refuge in the temple of Eshmun, in the burning citadel of Byrsa. They surrendered, but Scipio was unable to show clemency. Hasdrubal left the citadel to pray for mercy and to plead forgiveness for torturing Roman prisoners. At this point Hasdrubal's wife—obviously disgusted by her husband's behaviour—came out, insulted her husband, and jumped into a burning building with their two children. More followed her into the flames. Scipio Aemilianus wept when he saw this, and was moved to quote the two lines from Homer's *Iliad* prophesying the destruction of Troy—highly appropriate, and resonating with the final days of Carthage. Scipio realised that the fate of Carthage might one day befall Rome.[5] Polybius, an eye witness, reports it as follows:

Scipio, when he looked upon the city as it was utterly perishing and in the last throes of its complete destruction, is said to have shed tears and wept openly for his enemies. After being wrapped in thought for long, and realizing that all cities, nations, and authorities must, like men, meet their doom; that this happened to Ilium, once a prosperous city, to the empires of Assyria, Media, and Persia, the greatest of their time, and to Macedonia itself, the brilliance of which was so recent, either deliberately or the verses escaping him, he said:

'A day will come when sacred Troy shall perish,
And Priam and his people shall be slain.'

And when Polybius speaking with freedom to him, for he was his teacher, asked him what he meant by the words, they say that without any attempt at concealment he named his own country, for which he feared when he reflected on the fate of all things human. Polybius actually heard him and recalls it in his history.[6]

Scipio was obviously a cultivated individual. He was a man of culture and taste; his acquaintances formed the Scipionic circle, and included Polybius, the Stoic philosopher Panaetius, and the poets Lucilius and Terence. Cicero gives him a leading part in his *De Re Publica*—Scipio Aemilianus is the chief speaker. His Latin was apparently excellent and pure. After the Battle of Carthage he restored the works of art which Carthage had plundered to the Greek cities of Sicily.

The area surrounding Carthage was subsumed into the new province of Africa, a modest acquisition which could have been more extensive had the Romans so desired. Rome's expansionist restraint here confirms that her attack on Carthage was not motivated by a desire to expand her territory on the Mediterranean seaboard. Utica was given a large slice of the Carthaginian trade, a bounty which Rome could have easily retained if she had been keen to increase her commercial influence in the region. It seems that, in destroying Carthage, Rome was only really interested in destroying a force that instilled fear in her and remained a serious threat. The story that the Romans sowed the city with salt, to render the land barren, is a fiction: the land in fact became *ager publicus*, shared between local farmers.[7] North Africa became the vital source of grain Rome had always hoped it would be.

Transalpine Gaul and the War Against Jugurtha

Rome was unable to relax after the Third Punic War. In 133 BC Attalus III of Pergamum died, and bequeathed his city to Rome. Aristarchus led a revolt amongst the servile and lower classes, in which he soundly defeated a superior army, under Publius Licinius Crassus, at Leucae in 130 BC—despite support from Bithynia, Pontus, and Cappadocia. Crassus was killed in the battle. Later that year his successor, Marcus Perperna, took revenge for the disaster and defeated Aristarchus at Stratonicea. The city was razed, and Aristarchus surrendered.[1]

Suthul (109 BC)

Masinissa's son, Micipsa, succeeded his father after the destruction of Carthage, along with his brothers Gulussa and Mastarnable. Micipsa extended the Numidian friendship with Rome, peacefully developing burgeoning agriculture and consolidating Cirta, his capital, as a centre of the Mediterranean grain trade. On his death in 118 BC, Micipsa had indecisively allowed the kingdom to be divided between his sons, Hiempsal and Adherbal, and Mastarnable's illegitimate son Jugurtha, who was fourteen years old. Jugurtha promptly had Hiempsal murdered at Thirmida, and drove Adherbal out of the country; he then headed for Rome. Jugurtha, it seems, shared many of the virtues of Masinissa—his vitality and military skills in particular—but his belligerent stance in the subsequent negotiations left the Romans with no choice but to declare war. Under a commission headed by Lucius Opimius, Rome had decided to split the kingdom, offering Adherbal the eastern and richer half. But Jugurtha was no fool: he was quick to appreciate the Romans' weakness for bribes, calling Rome 'urbem venalem et mature perituram, si emptorem invenerit,' ('A city up for sale and destined to an early death, if a buyer should come along').[2] Opimius was suspected of and found guilty of bribery, and exiled to Dyrrhachium. This was not his first indiscretion; in 121 BC, as consul, he had ordered the execution of 3,000 supporters of Gaius Gracchus without trial—the pretext he used was the state of emergency—the senatus consultum ultimum—declared after Gracchus's murder.

Jugurtha resumed hostilities against Adherbal, detaining him in Cirta along with a number of Italian residents who anticipated relief by the Romans. However, this was not forthcoming and Rome's inadequate diplomacy failed to prevent either the subsequent massacre of the Italians or the murder of Adherbal. Cirta had become an economic centre for Roman trade in North Africa, and was populated with Roman and Italian merchants and businessmen—as well as with native berbers. Failure also met the first two Roman generals sent there, who were incompetent and achieved nothing: L. Calpurnius Bestia in 111 BC, and Spurius Postumius Albinus in 110 BC. Calpurnius nearly saved the day when he offered an armistice; but in the end it only exacerbated matters, when it brought to light a scandal stoked up by an opportunist tribune-elect, C. Memmius, who alleged that a number of senators (including Calpurnius) were in Jugurtha's pay. The Roman people were outraged at this rampant corruption. An attempt to resolve the issue, by allowing Jugurtha to give evidence in Rome, became a legal farce when an associate of Memmius' deployed his veto, and Jugurtha himself openly planned the assassination of his cousin Massiva—a rival for the Numidian throne who was in Rome at the time. Jugurtha was given safe passage, but the Romans now demanded nothing less than his unconditional surrender.

The following year, Aulus, brother of Spurius, decided to besiege Jugurtha in his treasury stronghold at Suthul. The timing could not have been worse—it was the middle of a ferocious winter which had reduced the surrounding lands to a giant lake, and (in common with many treasuries) Suthul could boast the impregnability of Fort Knox. Feigning the promise of a treaty, the wily Jugurtha led the Romans out into woodland and then attacked their camp, aided and abetted by bribed traitors. Jugurtha gained access and the Romans fled, only to be surrounded by the Numidians. Jugurtha smugly allowed them to go free—but only after they had passed under the yoke, in utter humiliation.[3] A number of senators were convicted of corruption in Rome, while Spurius, Calpurnius, and Opimius were exiled under the *Lex Mamilia*—passed to prosecute those suspected of Jugurthine corruption.

Muthul River (109 BC)

Q. Caecilius Metellus Numidicus, a man of rare integrity and the sworn, life-long enemy of Marius, took over the command. He proceeded to attack Jugurtha's towns, including Cirta, while simultaneously restoring much-needed morale and efficiency within his armies. However, Jugurtha led the Romans into an ambush at the River Muthul. A long and inconclusive battle followed, but the day was lost by the Numidian elephants which lumbered into woodland and were easily picked off by the Romans—forty elephants died that day, while a further four were captured. The Numidians fled, denied of one of their most effective weapons of war.[4] Publius Rutilius Rufus was responsible for incapacitating the elephants at the Muthul; he was also responsible for introducing an improved system of drill to the Roman army. Rufus wrote an autobiography and a history of Rome, which covered the Jugurthine War, in Greek. He was an expert in law, and wrote treatises on the laws of bankruptcy as well as other forensic subjects.

Cirta (104 BC)

The decisive battle took place at Cirta, some five years later. Gaius Marius was in command, at the head of an army comprised in part of volunteer *proletarii* whom he had rigorously trained. Jugurtha's brother-in-law, King Bocchus, ruled in neighbouring Mauretania (Morocco), and was persuaded to help by the offer of land. Marius first took the southern fortress of Capsa and levelled it; other cities joined the toll. Unlike Aulus Postumius Albinus before him, Marius did manage to take a Jugurthan treasury fort close to the River Moluccha—this compromised Bocchus' ability to pay his mercenaries. Marius had decided to spend winter some 600 miles to the west; during his march he was attacked twice by Jugurtha and Bocchus. Marius won a resounding victory in the first, while the second took place at Cirta—another Roman victory, in which Marius was assisted by the quaestor, Lucius Cornelius Sulla Felix, and his cavalry. Bocchus read the future and slyly defected to the Romans, in delicate negotiations deputed to and adroitly conducted by Sulla; Marius was no diplomat. Sulla persuaded Bocchus that the way into Rome's confidence lay in the betrayal of Jugurtha, and eventually Bocchus put any misgivings or conscience behind him; Jugurtha was kidnapped, sent to Rome, dumped in a pit under the Tullianum prison and left to die. Bocchus received a sizeable part of Numidia in payment for his treachery, and so ended the Jugurthine War.[5] The seeds of the enmity between the precocious but talented Sulla and Marius probably were sown here, when Sulla ostentatiously had a signet ring made which showed Jugurtha kneeling in submission to him. He also suggested that the Numidian defeat was down to him, even though the victory officially belonged to Marius.

The appointment of Marius was significant for two reasons. Firstly, he was elected by the popular Tribal assembly in defiance of the senate, thus setting a sinister precedent which would eventually lead to the undermining of the senate's authority. Secondly, Marius set another consequential precedent himself, by extending the qualification of enlistment to include volunteers from the *proletarii*—some of the poorest men in Roman society, the *capite censi*, and those citizens with little or no property. As we have noted, these people obviously had no lands of their own to go back to when they were discharged; they were effectively in the army for life, and could look forward to settlement on the lands provided by their commanders when they retired.

Booty was captured movable goods which often needed to be converted into cash—it included precious metals, property, and prisoners of war who were sold at the slave market. The disposal of booty (*manubiae*) was under the control of the commander, and could be distributed between himself and his troops with a contribution to the war chest in Rome. Occasionally the commander cut his troops out of the distribution, although this was obviously the least-popular option. By the second century BC plunder provided significant financial gain for many commanders, but only rarely were campaigns launched just for the sake of wealth management. In 264 BC Appius Claudius used the prospect of booty in his arguments for war in Sicily. Lucius Licinius Lucullus, consul for 151 BC, provides one of the few examples of a predatory commander, in a campaign in Nearer Spain.

Booty had other indirect benefits; its judicious distribution converted soldiers into loyal troops, and strengthened political ties and obligations amongst fellow officers. It offered an outward show of military prowess, and enabled commanders to curry popular favour by the financing and construction of public and religious buildings. Caecilius Metellus offers a notable example: after the end of the Fourth Macedonian War, in 146 BC, he built two temples in the Campus Martius which honoured Juno. The display of booty during triumphs was a highly-visible indicator of military success, with the audiences entertaining themselves by making comparisons to previous hauls. The prospect of plunder occasionally had an effect on morale; before the battle of Telamon, the anxious Romans were uplifted by the sight of gold collars and armbands worn by their Gallic enemies. Booty also had an effect on recruitment— raising troops for the wars in Spain and the European theatres of the western Mediterranean was notoriously difficult, while the levy for the Third Punic War triggered an outbreak of voluntary enlistment. Rome's allies also benefitted, with a percentage of booty often going to them; the strengthening of the bonds between Rome and her allies was a benefit of this.

Polybius provides us with a template for the pillaging of cities by Roman forces in his description of the sack of New Carthage, by Scipio Africanus, in 209 BC.[6] A number of troops are detailed to do the plundering while at least half of the force remains in formation, guarding against enemy attack.

By training up a volunteer army of *proletarii* to the highest standards, Marius took the first significant step towards converting a conscript militia into something approaching a standing professional army. The size of the Roman army increased dramatically, as did the numbers of reserves that commanders could call upon. The rise of the private armies, deployed by unscrupulous commanders in the first century BC, had begun—while the Senate's control over the Roman army receded.

But the devil was in the details, and it was the military refinements Marius introduced which paved the way for the armies of the late Republic and the Empire. All soldiers now carried a pilum and a sword; the maniple was scrapped and replaced by the cohort, of which there were ten in every legion, now around 6,000 men strong, led by sixty battle-hardened centurions. The emphasis was now on close combat cut and thrust—skills perfected by the gladiatorial schools. Marius understood the value of regimental pride and rivalry, and introduced the silver eagle. Mobility and speed were also crucial, so henceforth each legionary carried his own spade for digging his share of the marching camp; as a result, dependence on the cumbersome baggage train was reduced. Marius's troops became known as 'Marius' mules' (*'muli Mariani'*).

The Invasion from the North

The Northmen (or, more exactly, the Cimbri and Teutones) had vacated their lands in Frisia and Jutland in the second century BC, when the sea had begun to encroach—possibly due to climate change. After many years of wandering along the Danube and the Rhine, they found themselves on the borders of Italy, near Noricum (modern Austria and part of Slovenia), where they defeated the Taurisci (or Norici) in 113 BC. The Taurisci were allies of Rome, and made their appeal for assistance. Despite a conciliatory gesture of the offer to retreat, the Cimbri and Teutones were attacked by a Roman army, under Gnaeus Papirius Carbo, at Noreia (modern Ljubljana). The Northmen won convincingly, but stopped short at advancing into Italy.[1] The Romans were saved from total annihilation by the onset of an opportune storm. Carbo committed suicide by drinking vitriol (*atramentum sutorium*, or sulphuric acid).[2]

Four years later the Cimbri and Teutones, supported by the Helvetian Tigurini under Divico, invaded eastern France at the borders of Gallia Narbonensis. M. Junius Silanus attacked when the Senate refused an offer of mercenaries in exchange for Italian land. The Northmen defeated the Romans again, and once more they prudently desisted from invading Italy. However, the Tigurini raided Roman territory on the Rhone and caused a revolt in Languedoc, amongst the Volcae Tectosages. In 107 BC Lucius Cassius Longinus was killed in an ambush by the Tigurini, at the battle of Burdigala (Bordeaux). His second in command, Gaius Popillius Laenas, was released, but only after he and his men were forced to surrender half of their baggage and pass under the yoke in humiliation. The Tigurini fell back, allowing the consul Q. Servilius Caepio to sack the Tectosage headquarters at Tolosa. The booty was estimated at 100,000 lbs of gold. According to Strabo, the *aurum Tolosanum* (allegedly the 'cursed gold' looted by the Gauls during the sack of Delphi in 279 BC) never made it back to Rome, and Caepio was the prime suspect. This is Strabo's account:

> …and it was on account of having laid hands on them that Caepio ended his life in misfortunes—for he was cast out by his native land as a temple-robber, and he left behind as his heirs female children only, who, as it turned out, became prostitutes … and therefore perished in disgrace.

Caepio did actually have a son, who turned out to be the maternal grandfather of Marcus Junius Brutus—the assassin of Julius Caesar. Caepio ended his life, exiled, in Smyrna.[3]

Aquae Sextiae (102 BC)

Meanwhile, Marius was elected consul by the people five times between 104 and 100 BC. He raised another army of *proletarii*; their rigorous training programme included digging a canal, to bypass the silted up Rhone estuary. The Cimbri, Teutones, Ambrones, and the Tigurini launched a bold three-pronged attack on the Romans. However, Marius took advantage of the fact that the enemy forces were now split into three manageable armies, and having allowed the huge army to pass (it apparently took six days), he lured the Teutones into an area near Aquae Sextiae, from which there could be no retreat. The Teutones were massacred or taken prisoner in droves; their king, Teutobodus, was among the captured. The casualty figures are once again subject to arrant exaggeration and inflation; Livy says 200,000 died, with 90,000 made prisoners of war.[4] The bookish Quintus Lutatius Catulus was less successful against the Cimbri—he failed to secure the Brenner Pass, and retreated to the south bank of the Po. Luckily for the Romans, the Cimbri were happy to pause and indulge themselves in the fertile Alpine foothills, giving Marius time to join up with Catulus and form an army some 55,000 men strong. Writing in the early fifth century AD, Jerome describes the tragic fate of the captured women and children as a paradigm of German valour:

> By the conditions of the surrender three hundred of their married women were to be handed over to the Romans. When the Teuton matrons heard of this stipulation, they first begged the consul that they might be set apart to minister in the temples of Ceres and Venus, and then when they failed to obtain their request and were removed by the lictors, they slew their little children and next morning were all found dead in each other's arms, having strangled themselves in the night.[5]

Vercellae (101 BC)

Marius and Catulus, waiting for the hot and energy-sapping summer, engaged the Cimbri at Vercellae, where they were victorious—killing many (60,000) and enslaving even more (120,000). Those who escaped fled back to their camp, only to be killed by their womenfolk, who then killed themselves. Sulla, meanwhile, defeated the Tigurini in the eastern Alpine ranges.[6] With this defeat, the threat posed by the Northmen was extinguished; however, it also served to fan the flames of rivalry between Marius and Sulla. Marius, in true cavalier style, granted Roman citizenship to his Italian allies after the battle, without the permission of the senate. To Marius, the voice of an ally on the battlefield was indistinguishable from the voice of the law.

Like Publius Rutilius Rufus before him, Catulus was a distinguished literary figure and a philhellene. He was orator, a poet, and an author of works including a history of his consulship, the *De Consulatu et De Rebus Gestis Suis*. He introduced the Hellenistic epigram to Rome, and the personal verse made famous by Catullus some fifty years later. Catulus is also remembered for the architecture he financed and commissioned; the *Monumenta Catuli*, the Temple of *Fortuna Huiusce Diei* (the 'Fortune of This Day') to commemorate the Battle of Vercellae, and the *Porticus Catuli*, paid for by proceeds from the sale of Cimbrian booty.

Epilogue

The next seventy-three years, leading up to Octavian's establishment of the Roman Empire in 27 BC, saw no reduction in military activity and war-mongering. However, now the wars (Mithridates and Caesar's Gauls apart) were not against a foreign enemy or an invader, but rather often Romans against Romans (The Civil Wars), Romans against Roman allies (The Social Wars), and Romans against slaves, rising up in revolt (Spartacus and The Servile Wars). In The Civil Wars Romans battled each other, first with Sulla, and then in two triumvirates, which marked a protracted period of internecine conflict, savage proscriptions, and near anarchy in Rome itself. The legacy of Marius allowed individual commanders to raise private armies, and to deploy them against the armies of rival commanders. Sometimes this was in alliance with other commanders in the two triumvirates, the first of which comprised Julius Caesar, Pompeius Magnus, and Marcus Crassus. After the death of Crassus in 53 BC, Caesar and Pompey fought another bitter Civil War, in which Pompey was killed and Caesar set himself up as a perpetual dictator. The Second Triumvirate was formed between Octavian (Caesar's adopted heir), Mark Antony, and Marcus Aemilius Lepidus as something as an afterthought. Octavian was victorious at the decisive Battle of Actium, and established the Roman Empire from the detritus of the Republic. It was only at this point that the seven-hundred-year-long Roman predeliction for belligerence and confrontation came to anything resembling an end.

Augustus's rule was marked by a tendency to secure frontiers and preserve what the Romans already had. There were, of course, battles and wars still to fight in the early years of the Empire—not least against the Germans, culminating in the catastrophe in the Teutoburg Wald—but, by and large, Augustus was happy to pursue a diplomatic foreign policy of containment. In any event, there was now little out there beyond the existing borders, in terms of mineral resources or opportunity for booty, that the Romans considered worth the expense or bother of conquering.

From its very earliest days, the Romans had stepped onto a roller-coaster of war from which it proved impossible to get off. The constant harrying of Latin neighbours meant that Rome had to defend her borders, expanding them to snuff out or prevent further incursions. In turn, this led to a constant need to resupply the war machine with ever-more recruits and matériel. The Gallic invasion and the sack of Rome shook the Romans out of their complacency, and, as we have seen, led to significant changes in the way Rome defended herself. Positive and constructive military soul-searching brought more reform after the wars with Pyrrhus and the catastrophies against Hannibal and his Carthaginian armies at Trebia, Trasimene, and Cannae. The Punic Wars compelled Rome to build a credible fleet, the success of which contributed enormously to their victory. Rome's willingness to learn from errors, and to know her enemy, equipped her to deal with threats from Iberia, Macedonia, the Galatians, Ligures, Jugurtha, and the Celtic Northmen. Over the years, Rome proved flexible, versatile, and eager to learn from its military disasters; the Romans could also be diplomatic and inclusive when it was required. It was this long-term, mature attitude that goes far to explaining Rome's success on the battlefield for six centuries of serial conflict and expansionism.

A chromolithographic mosaic depicting the stables of twice-consul Tiberius Claudius Pompeianus Quintianus (AD 170-217), in charge of the army under Caracella. Horses remained vital in military and agriculture throughout the Roman period, and were often a sign of wealth. Pompeianus appears to have been murdered by rebels.

The so-called Sword of Tiberius. Sword, scabbard, and spears excavated from Roman battlefields. The legionary sword was found near Mainz; the blade is 21 inches long and 2.5 inches wide at the base. The scabbard is made from wood, with silver gilt sheathing and bronze relief (enlarged, centre). The relief on the hilt shows Tiberius receiving Germanicus in AD 17.

Brand Roman Army: A striking advertisement published by the Bridgeport Brass Co., Bridgeport CT, in 1944. It is taken from a mural by L. Lambdin, entitled '*Brass Through the Ages*'. The text describes the development of metals used for military, domestic, and fashion purposes in ancient Rome.

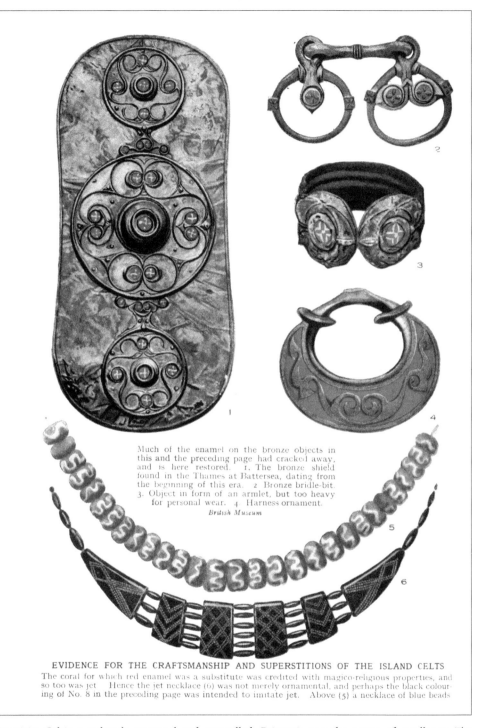

Much of the enamel on the bronze objects in this and the preceding page had cracked away, and is here restored. 1. The bronze shield found in the Thames at Battersea, dating from the beginning of this era. 2 Bronze bridle-bit. 3. Object in form of an armlet, but too heavy for personal wear. 4 Harness ornament.
British Museum

EVIDENCE FOR THE CRAFTSMANSHIP AND SUPERSTITIONS OF THE ISLAND CELTS
The coral for which red enamel was a substitute was credited with magico-religious properties, and so too was jet Hence the jet necklace (6) was not merely ornamental, and perhaps the black colouring of No. 8 in the preceding page was intended to imitate jet. Above (5) a necklace of blue beads

Exquisite Celtic metalwork, engraved and enamelled. Britannia was the centre of excellence. The bronze shield was found in the Thames near Battersea, and dates from around 1 BC. Also depicted is a bridle bit and armlet, and a harnass ornament.

This stunning collection shows two scabbards, as well as a mirror back, pins, and horse trappings.

Endnotes

Chapter 1

1. G. Williamson (tr.), Josephus, *The Jewish War*, 1959, p. 378, and Adcock, *The Roman Art of War*, pp.4-5.
2. Ovid, *Metamorphoses* 1, 89-100.
3. Genesis 4, 1-8. For an excellent history of warfare from its earliest manifestations see Keegan, *A History of Warfare*.
4. The Narmer Palette, or the Great Hierakonpolis Palette features some of the earliest hieroglyphics. Robert Brier refers to the Narmer Palette as 'the first historical document in the world'. *Daily Life of the Ancient Egyptians*, p. 202. See also Spalinger, *War in Ancient Egypt*.
5. See Copper, *The Curse of Agade,* p. 52; J. Klein, *The Royal Hymns of Shulgi*, p. 131; Hamblin, *Warfare in the Ancient Near East*.
6. See Saggs, *Civilisation Before Greece and Rome* p. 177ff.
7. Exodus 17, 14, 16. 1 Samuel, 15, 3.
8. See Luckenbill, *Ancient Records of Assyria and Babylonia II*, p. 314.
9. 2 Kings 8, 12; 15, 16.
10. Zechariah 14:2 and Isaiah 13:16; Lamentations 5, 11. All King James Version.
11. Finley, *Ancient History*, p. 67. Thucydides 1, 15, 3-5.
12. See Bagnall, *The Peloponnesian War*; Grainger, *Hellenistic and Roman Naval Wars*.
13. See Adcock, *The Greek and Macedonian Art of War*; Pritchett, *The Greek State at War*.
14. See Low, *War, Death and Burial in Classical Sparta*, in which she cautions against taking the overtly militaristic view of Sparta at face value. Palatine Anthology 7,11,2.
15. See Xenophon, *Constitution of the Lacedaemonians*, 3, 16. For Cynisca: idem, *Minor Works*, Agesilaus 9.1, 6; Pausanias, *Description of Greece*, 3, 5, 1.
16. See Connolly, *Greece and Rome at War*; Lazenby, *The Spartan Army*; Sekunda, *The Spartan Army*; Warry, *Warfare in the Classical World*.
17. See Jameson, *Sacrifice Before Battle*.

Chapter 2

1. Livy 1, 19, 2-3. For a description of the gates, the *geminae Belli portae*, and the procedure see Virgil, *Aeneid* 7, 601-15. See Fordyce, *Virgil Aeneid VII–VIII ad loc.*
2. For the association of the land with the army and Roman agronomy, see the detailed treatment by Nathan Rosenstein in his *Rome at War.*
3. See Cornell, *The Beginnings of Rome* pp. 179-197; Ogilvie, *Early Rome and the Etruscans* p. 45ff. Livy 1, 43; Dionysius of Halicarnassus 4, 16; Cicero, *De Re Publica* 1, 39, all of which are anachronistic.
4. Polybius 6, 39, 1-11; Aulus Gellius 5, 6-5, 26; Caesar, *Civil War* 3, 56.
5. Polybius 6, 15, 8; Zonaras 7, 21.
6. Brunt (1971), 44-60.
7. See G. Colin, *Rome et la Grece*; J. Griffin *Augustan Poetry p.* 88ff and the Appendix, *Some Imperial Servants.* Various suggestions for the start and or cause of the decline have been made: Polybius, 31, 25, ascribes it to the victory over Macedonia; L. Calpurnius Piso (Pliny *NH* 17, 38, 244) goes with 154 BC; Appian, *Bellum Civili* 1, 7, goes for the end of the war in Italy; Livy 39, 6, 7, prefers 186 BC; Velleius Paterculus, *Historiae Romanae*, and Sallust, *Catilina* 10, 1, and *Jugurtha* 41, 1, opt for the end of the Third Punic War. See also Catullus 51.
8. See Goldsworthy. *The Complete Roman Army.*
9. See Chrystal, *Differences.*

Chapter 3

1. For a detailed description of the ceremony performed by the fetiales, see Livy, 1, 32, 5-14; 24, 8. See also Garlan, *War in the Ancient World*, pp. 45-77. Cicero, *De Officiis* 1, 34-36, translated by W. Miller, Loeb Classical edition (Harvard, 1913).
2. Virgil, *Aeneid*, 6, 850-3. Horace, *Carmen Saeculare* 49ff. Polybius, 18, 37; trans. E. S. Shuckburgh, London, 1889. See also Livy 9. 1. 10; 30, 42, 17 and 37, 45, 8ff. Cicero, *Divinatio in Caecilium* 63; *De Provinciis Consularibus* 4; *Ad Atticum* 7, 14, 3; 9, 19, 1; *Pro Rege Deiotauro* 13; *Philippicae* 11, 37; 13, 35. See Askin, *War Crimes Against Women: Prosecution in International War Crimes Tribunals* pp. 10-21; Brownmiller, *Against Our Will: Men, Women and Rape*, pp 31-139;   Vikman, *Ancient Origins: Sexual Violence in Warfare*, Part I pp 21-31. Andromache: Homer, *Iliad* 6, 504ff.
3. Cicero, *In Verrem* 4, 116. Capsa: Sallust, *Jugurtha* 91.
4. Andromanche: Homer, *Iliad* 6, p. 504 ff.
5. Lewis & Short, *ad loc.* See Chrystal, *Women in Ancient Rome.* See also Cicero: *Fam* 14.11 and *Att.* 10.8; *Fam* 14.1. Also McDonnell, *Roman Manliness* (Cambridge 2006).
6. For a litany of anti-Carthaginian and anti-Greek vitriol see Sidebottom, *Ancient Warfare* pp. 8-14.
7. Tacitus, Histories 3, 47; Lucan, *De Bello Civile* 7, 400-10.
8. Juvenal 6, p. 434ff; especially pp. 445-447.
9. Polybius 6, 19-42.
10. Onasander 38.
11. Zosimus 1, 69.

12. Frontinus, Strategemata 2, 9, 2-5; Tacitus, *Agricola* 20.
13. Frontinus, *op. cit*, 2, 9, 3. Appian, *Bellum Civili* 1, 93-4.
14. Frontinus, *op. cit.* 2, 9, 5.
15. Frontinus, *op. cit*, 2, 9, 4.
16. Livy 2, 17, 2; 37, 2.
17. Polybius 10, 15.
18. Livy, 23, 7.
19. Caesar, *De Bello Gallico* 8, 44.
20. Tacitus, *op. cit* 18.

Chapter 4

1. See Ogilvie, *The Etruscans*; Cornell, *The Beginnings of Rome,* for details of these early days.
2. Livy 1, 2-3.
3. Livy 1, 14-15.
4. Livy 1, 27.
5. Livy, 1, 22-23. Peddling misinformation to one's troops to instill confidence was an old device well established by Tullus' day; see Polyaenus, *Stratagems in War 1*, 33, 1; 1, 35, 1.
6. Livy, 1, 23-8.
7. Livy, 1, 30-1.
8. Livy, 1, 42.
9. Livy, 2, 6-7; *Fasti Triumphales*; Plutarch, *Life of Poplicola*.
10. See Chrystal, *Roman Women*.
11. Livy 2, 10. Pliny, *Natural History* 24, 11. Dionysius of Halicarnassus 5, 25.
12. Livy 2, 12-13.
13. Livy 1, 9.
14. Livy 1, 13. Translation by B.O. Foster, Loeb edition 1919.
15. Livy 1, 30.
16. Polybius 3, 22.
17. Livy 1, 32ff. See Cary, *A History of Rome* p. 40 for details.
18. Livy 1, 53-55; 60. Dionysius of Halicarnassus, *Roman Antiquities*, 4, 58.
19. Livy 1, 36-7.
20. Livy 2, 16; Dionysius, *op. cit.* 5, 40-43.
21. Livy 2, 18.
22. Livy 2, 26.
23. See Lintott, *The Constitution of the Roman Republic*, p. 110. Livy 22, 8, 5-6.
24. Festus 100; Livy 4, 34, 6.

Chapter 5

1. See Hermann, *Historicorum Romanorum Reliquiae*.
2. See Pausanias, *Description of Greece*, 2, 27, 4.

3. Livy, 2.14; Dionysius of Halicarnassus, *Roman Antiquities* 7.5-6.

4. Livy, 2, 26; Dionysius *op. cit.* 6, 32-33.

5. Livy 2, 19-22; Dionysius *op. cit.* 6, 4-12; Florus 1, 5, 1-4.

6. Cicero, *Pro Balbo* 53. Dionysius summarizes its contents at 6, 95. Around this time it seems likely that the twelve towns in the League were: Arretium, Caere, Clusium, Cortona, Perusia, Rusellae, Tarquinii, Veii, Vetulonia, Volsinii, and Vulci.

7. Livy 2, 33, 9; Dionysius, *op. cit.* 5, 75; 6, 20.

8. See Cicero, *De Natura Deorum* 2, 6; Dionysius *op. cit.* 6, 13; Plutarch, *Life of Coriolanus* 3, 4; cf Livy 2, 20, 12.

9. Thomas Babbington Macaulay: *The Battle of The Lake Regillus* 3, 13ff; Homer, *Iliad* 3, 15ff cf Livy 2, 20, 1-3.

10. Livy 4, 27ff.

11. Livy 2, 22.

12. Livy 2, 22-33.

13. Dionysius 8, 83-85.

14. Dionysius 9, 57-8; Livy 2, 64-5.

15. Dionysius 9, 5-13.

16. Plutarch, *Life of Romulus*.

17. Livy 3, 26-9; See Ward Fowler, *Passing Under the Yoke*.

18. Livy, 4, 28-30. Plutarch, *Life of Metellus* 8, 1-3.

19. Livy 4, 30-34; 51. See Ogilvie, *Commentary ad. loc.*

20. Livy 4, 21-2; 4, 31-33.

21. Livy 5, 10; 6, 4; 5, 15; Plutarch, *Life of Camillus*.

22. Cary, *A History of Rome*, p. 72.

23. Livy 4, 59; 11, 60, 6; Polybius 6, 39, 12-15; Varro, *De Lingua Latina* 5, 86; Dionysius 4, 19, 1-4.

Chapter 6

1. Livy 5, 37-38; Diodorus Siculus 14, 114-5; Plutarch, *Life of Camillus*, 18-19. Ogilvie, *Commentary* (1997) pp. 716-7 sees this as 'baseless', arguing that it was 'a moral and psychological pretext for the impending disaster at the Allia'.

2. Strabo 4, 4, 2-5.

3. Diodorus 5, 30, 2-4.

4. See Gardiner, *The Blitz*, pp. 126-7; 184-5.

5. Livy 5, 40. Translation by Rev. Canon Roberts, J. M. Dent & Sons, Ltd., London, 1905.

6. Plutarch, *op. cit.* 22, 4; Servius, *On Virgil* 1, 720.

7. Polybius 2, 18, 3; Livy 5, 48; Diodorus 14, 116-17.

8. See Withington, *Britain's 20 Worst Military Disasters*, pp. 203-220.

9. Livy 5, 47; Plutarch, *op. cit.* 27.

10. Livy 5, 49; 5, 51-4; 10, 16; Plutarch, *op. cit.* 22-9. The quotation is by Ogilvie, *op. cit.* p. 727.

11. The wall, made from tufa, was up to 10 metres high in places, 3.6 metres wide at its base, seven miles long, and had sixteen gates. Good surviving sections can be seen outside

Termini Railway Station in Rome, including a small piece in the McDonald's at the station, and on the Aventine, where it incorporates an arch for a catapult from the late Republic.

12. See Cary, *A History of Rome* pp. 84-5.
13. Livy 42, 34, 5-11. For Spurius see Livy 42, 34, 1-11. Also Caesar, *de Bello Gallica* 2, 25, for a description of Sextius Baculus, a centurion in battle.
14. Oakley, *Roman Conquest of Italy*, p. 12, with Beloch, *Romische Geschichte*. Cf Rosenstein, in *Republican Rome*, who puts the number at 5,525 square km in 338 BC. Rosenstein has 26,805 square km for 264 BC.
15. Cornell, *Beginnings of Rome* p.351 and p. 380.

Chapter 7

1. Livy 6, 2.
2. Plutarch, *Camillus* 34. Diodorus 14, 117.
3. Oakley, *Commentary*, pp. 409-11; see Fabia, *Titii Livii loci qui sunt de praeda belli Romana*; Orlin, *Temples, Religion, and Politics in the Roman Republic*, pp. 117ff; Churchill, *Ex Qua Quod Vellent Facerent.*
4. Eg: Livy 7, 28; 10, 31; 23, 37; Cicero, *Ad Atticum* 5, 20; Tacitus, *Annals* 13, 39, 4.
5. Eg: Livy 1, 53, 3; 2, 42, 2; 26, 40, 13.
6. See Smith, William, *Dictionary of Greek and Roman Biography and Mythology*, Vol II (1867), p. 1009
7. Livy 6, 3-4.
8. Livy 6, 6-9.
9. Livy 7, 6.
10. *Livy: Rome and Italy: Books VI-X of the History of Rome from its Foundation,* trans. Betty Radice p.109, (1982)
11. Livy 7, 12; 14.
12. Livy 7, 32; 34.
13. See Pliny, *Naturalis Historia* 22, 4-5 for a description.
14. See John Rich, *War and Society in the Roman World*, (1993).
15. Livy 7, 37; 3, 28.
16. Livy 8, 11. Translation is by Rev. Canon Roberts in *The History of Rome*, Vol. 2 (London, 1905). Cicero *Tusculanae Disputationes*, 1, 89; *De Finibus Bonorum et Malorum* 2, 61. Codrus: *Lycurgus, Against Leocrates*, 84-87; Menoeceus: *Euripides, Phoenician Women*, 911ff; cf. Pausanias, *Guide to Greece*, 9, 25, 1; Hamilcar: Herodotus, *Histories* 7, 165-167.
17. Livy 8, 12; 8, 13. The exact location of the Fenectane Plain is unknown.
18. See Sherwin-White, *Roman Citizenship.*
19. Livy 8, 30.
20. Livy 9, 44.
21. Livy 10, 15; 10,30.
22. Livy 10, 26; Polybius 2, 19.
23. Diodorus 21, 6, 1. Orosius 3, 21.

24. Livy 10, 31.
25. See Cowan, *Roman Battle Tactics 109BC–AD313*. Plutarch, *Antony*, 45; *Dio Cassius*, 49, 30; translation by E. Cary (Loeb 1917). Livy 9, 21; Diodorus Siculus, *Library of History* 19, 72; 19, 76; Livy 9, 22-3.
26. Livy 10, 35.
27. Livy 10, 38-43.

Chapter 8

1. See Qviller, B. (1996) *Reconstructing the Spartan Partheniai*.
2. Chakravarti, P. *The Art of War in Ancient India*, pp. 48-9.
3. See Scullard, H. H. *The Elephant in the Greek and Roman World*.
4. Dio Cassius 9; Zonaras 8, 2; *Orosius Historiarum Adversum Paganos Libri*, 4, 1; Livy, *Epitome* 12.
5. Plutarch, *Pyrrhus* 16-17; Zonaras 8, 3; Orosius, *op. cit.*; Livy, *Epitome* 13.
6. Plutarch, *op. cit.* 21. Translation is by John Dryden.
7. Orosius, *op. cit.* Thucydides 7, 44. Translation by Warner, *Thucydides: History of the Peloponnesian War*.
8. Plutarch, *op. cit.* 21; Dionysius of Halicarnassus, *Roman Antiquities* 20, 1-3; Zonaras 8, 5; Orosius, *op. cit.*; Livy *op. cit.*
9. Garouphalias, *Pyrrhus: King of Epirus*.
10. Plutarch, *op. cit.* 24; Orosius 4, 2; Dionysius, *op. cit.* 20, 10-11; Livy, *Epitome* 14.

Chapter 9

1. Polybius 2, 24; 6,19ff.
2. Livy, 1, 11.
3. See Polybius 6, 27ff.
4. Josephus, *The Jewish War* 3, 5, 1.
5. Polybius, 6, 52.
6. Appian, *The Foreign Wars*; Libyca, 80.
7. Diodorus, *Historical Library* 16, 80, 4-5.
8. Ennius *Annales* 216, Skutsch 89; quoted by Cicero, *De Inventione Rhetorica* 1, 27. Polybius 1, 11, 9-15; 1, 12, 1-4; Zonaras 8, 9.
9. Polybius 1, 63, 4-5.
10. Polybius 1, 11; Zonaras 8, 9.
11. Polybius 1, 12.
12. Polybius 1, 19. Zonaras 8, 10.
13. Cary, *A History of Rome*, p. 118.
14. Polybius 1, 21; Zonaras *op. cit.*; Livy *Epitome* 17.
15. Polybius 1, 22-3; Zonaras 8, 11; Diodorus 23, 1; Livy, *op. cit.* For the inscription see Warmington, *Remains of Old Latin*, 4, 128-31. Columna Rostrata C. Duilii: the second

and more famous of these two columns (Servius *ad Georgics* 3, 2; Pliny *NH* 34, 20; Quintilian. I, 7, 12) stood either on or near the rostra, and with its inscription was restored in around 150 B.C. (*CP* 1919, 74-82; 1920, 176-183), and again later by Augustus (*CIL* I225). To show the importance of Duilius in Italian naval history, four battleships have been named after him: the battleship *Duilio*, in the nineteenth century; the First and Second World War battleship *Caio Duilio*; the missile cruiser *Caio Duilio*, launched in 1962; and the destroyer *Caio Duilio*, commissioned in 2009.

16. Zonaras 8, 12; Livy, *op. cit.*; Orosius 4, 8. For the Grass Crown see Pliny, NH 22, 6. Translation from *The Natural History Pliny the Elder* by John Bostock (London, 1855). Strabo's story is repeated by Carl Sagan in his *Pale Blue Dot* as a lesson; namely, that action governed by fear and ignorance often intensifies the problems it seeks to resolve.
17. Polybius 1, 25; cf. Zonaras, *op. cit.*
18. Polybius 1, 25-8.
19. Polybius 1, 30.
20. Polybius 1, 36; Zonaras 8, 14; Diodorus 23, 18.
21. Panormus: Polybius 1, 36; Zonaras 8, 14; Diodorus 23, 18. See Kistler, *War Elephants*, p.100.
22. Polybius 1, 49-51; Diodorus 24, 1; Livy, *Epitome* 19.
23. Polybius 1, 59-61; Diodorus 24, 11; Livy, *op. cit.*

Chapter 10

1. Polybius 2, 25-6.
2. Diodorus Siculus, *Historical Library* 5, 30.
3. For *spolia opima* see above. Polybius 2, 34; Plutarch, *Marcellus* 6; Livy, *Epitome* 20.
4. Polybius 2, 34.
5. See Wilkes, *The Illyrians*, p. 120.
6. Polybius 3, 18-19.

Chapter 11

1. Livy 21, 16; translation by Rev. Canon Roberts, *Livy History of Rome Vol. 3* (London 1905)
2. Livy 21, 18; translation as above.
3. Polybius, 3, 42-5; Livy 21, 26; 27-9.
4. Polybius 3, 65; Livy 21, 45-6.
5. Ennius *Annales* 363. See Elliott, Ennius' *Fabius Maximus Cunctator*. See its use in Cicero, *de Officiis* 1.84; *de Senectute* 10; *ad Atticum* 2.19.2; Virgil, *Aeneid* 6, 846; Ovid, *Fasti* 2, 240; Suetonius, *Tiberius* 21; Livy 22, 14, 14; 22, 24, 10; 22, 53, 7; 25, 23, 15; Sallust *Histories*, fr. 1, 55, 7, 77, 17; 2, 98, 2; 4, 69, 20-21. The name of Fabius also lives on in the Fabian Society, the British socialist organisation which promotes socialism through reform.
6. Livy 23, 44-6; Plutarch, *Marcellus* 12; Polybius 15, 16.
7. Livy 23, 40-41; 28-9; 49;
8. Livy 24, 14-16.

9. Plutarch, *Marcellus*; Livy 21, 49–51; 22, 37; 23, 2

10. Livy 25, 40-1.

11. Livy 25, 32-3; 35-6; see Pliny, *NH* 3, 9 for Ilorci.

12 Livy 25, 5-6.

13. Livy 26, 10.

14. Livy 26, 39. Cartagena: Polybius 10, 15. Translation by Ian Scott-Kilvert: *Polybius: The Rise of the Roman Empire*, p. 415.

15. Appian, *Spanish Wars 25-7*.

16. Appian may have confused the details of this battle with the Battle of Ilipa.

17. Livy 27, 41-2; cf. Polybius 15, 16.

18. Livy 27, 43-9; Polybius 11, 1-3; Zonaras 9, 9.

19. Livy 28, 12; Polybius 11, 20-24.

20. Livy 28, 22.

21. Livy 29, 24; Appian, *Punic Wars* 14.

22. The most famous are probably *Africa* by Petrarch (1396) and *Sophinisbe* by Corneille (1663).

23. Livy 30, 3-6; Polybius 14, 4-5; Appian, *op. cit.* 21-3. *Great Plains: Polybius* 14, 7-9; Livy 30, 8. *Ampsagar*: Livy 30, 11; Appian, *op. cit.* 26. Utica: Livy, 30, 10.

24. Livy 30, 32-5; Polybius 15, 9-14; Appian, *op. cit.* 40-47.

25. Polybius 7, 9.

Chapter 12

1. Livy 31, 10; 21; 32, 30; 33, 36.

2. Livy 34, 46; 35, 4-5.

3. Livy 31, 34-36; 31, 36-7.

4. Livy 32, 5-6, 10-12; Plutarch, *Flamininus* 3-5.

5. Livy 33, 6-10; Plutarch, *op. cit.* 7-8; Polybius 18, 19-26.

6. Isthmian Games: Appian, *History of the Macedonian Wars* 13; translation by Horace White in *Appian, The Foreign Wars* (New York, 1899).

7. Livy 33, 34; 34, 10; 34, 11-16; Appian, *Spanish Wars* 40.

8. Livy 35, 1; 7; 22.

9. Livy 36, 15-19; Appian, *Syrian Wars* 17-20; Plutarch, *Cato Maior* 13-14.

10. Livy 36, 44-5; Appian, *op. cit.* 22; Livy 37, 10-11; Appian, *op. cit.* 24.

11. Livy 37, 28-30; Appian, *op.cit.* 27.

12. Livy 37, 37-44; Appian, *op. cit.* 30-36.

13. Livy 38, 18; 38, 20-23; Appian, *op. cit.* 42; Florus 1, 27; Livy 38, 25; Polybius 21, 39; Livy 38, 26-7.

14. Livy 39, 21; 39, 30.

15. Livy 40, 30-32; 40, 33.

16. Livy 40, 39-40. Appian, *Spanish Wars* 43; Livy 40, 48; 40, 50. For Fulvius see Mueller, *Roman Religion in Valerius Maximus*, p. 35ff.

17. Livy 41, 2-4.

18. Livy 35, 21; 41, 12; 41, 17; 42, 7.

19. Livy 42, 57-60; Plutarch, *Aemilius Paulus* 9; Livy 42, 65-66.
20. Livy 43, 10.
21. Livy 44, 31; 44, 35; Plutarch, *op. cit.* 15-16.
22. Plutarch, *op. cit.* 16-22; Livy 44, 40-42.
23. Appian, *op. cit.* 51.
24. Appian, *op. cit.* 53; Livy, *Epitome* 48.
25. Cary, *History of Rome* p. 143.
26. Florus 1, 32.
27. Pausanias, *Description of Greece* 7, 15; Livy, *op. cit.*
28. Pausanias, *op. cit.* 7, 16; Florus, *op. cit;* Livy, *op. cit.*
29. Cicero in *Tusculanae Quaestiones* 3, 53 and Dio 21 suggest that Corinth was not totally destroyed.

Chapter 13

1. Appian, *Punica* 102-3; Livy, *Epitome* 49.
2. Plutarch, *Cato Maior* 17.
3. Appian, *op. cit.* 102-105
4. Appian, *op. cit.* 120-3. See Beevor, *Stalingrad*.
5. Appian, *op. cit.* 118.
6. Polybius 38, *Excidium Carthaginis,* 5, 7-8 and 20-22. Translation by W. R. Patton. Loeb (1927). Diodorus Siculus 32, 24. Homer, *Iliad* 6, 448-9 (spoken by Hector), and 4, 164-5 (spoken by Agamemnon).
7. See Ridley, *To Be Taken with a Pinch of Salt*.

Chapter 14

1. Strabo 4, 1, 38; Orosius 5, 10; Livy, *Epitome* 59; Eutropius 4, 20.
2. Sallust, *Jugurthine War* 35, 10.
3. Sallust, *op. cit.* 37-8.
4. Sallust, *op. cit.* 48-53.
5. Sallust, *op. cit.* 101; Orosius 5, 15.
6. Polybius 10, 16, 1-17, 3.

Chapter 15

1. Appian, *Gallic Wars fr.* 13; Livy, *Epitome* 63; Strabo 5, 1, 8.
2. Cicero, *Ad Familiares* 9, 21; Livy, *op. cit.*
3. Strabo 4, 1.
4. Livy, *Epitome* 67; Orosius 5, 16; Dio 27 *fr.* 91; Eutropius 5, 1.
5. Jerome, *Letter* 123, 8.
6. Plutarch, *op. cit* 24-27; Livy, *op. cit.*; Orosius, *op. cit.*; Florus, *op. cit.*; Eutropius 5, 2.

Maps

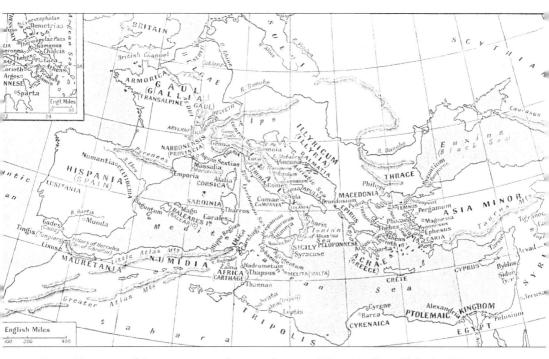

Above: The extent of Roman power in the second century BC; originally published in Hammerton, J. A., (ed.), *Universal History of the World Vol. 3*, (London, 1930), p. 1688.

Opposite above: Hannibal's Seventeen Year-Long March; originally published in Hammerton, *op. cit.*, p. 1660

Opposite below: Distribution and Wanderings of the Celtic peoples in the fourth century BC; originally published in Hammerton, *op. cit.*, p. 1508.

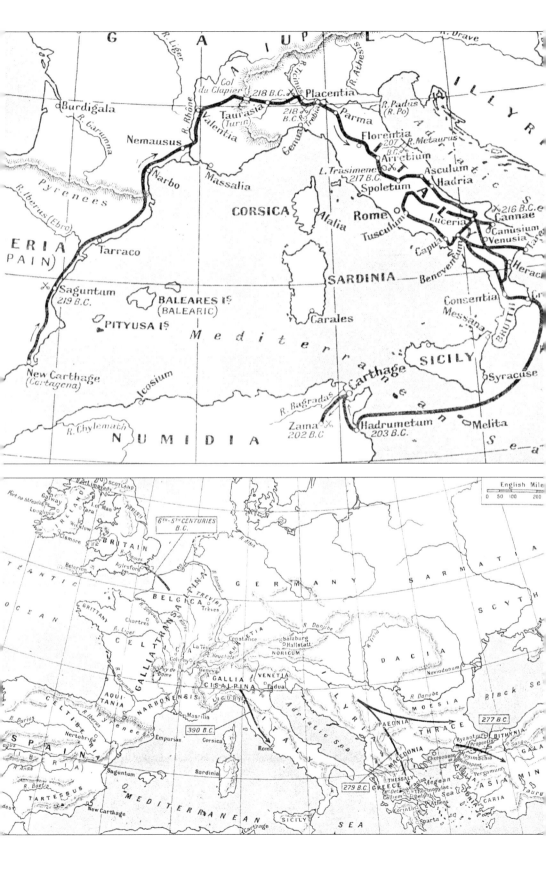

The Italian Peninsula at the time of the Punic Wars; originally published in Hammerton, *op. cit.*, p. 1592

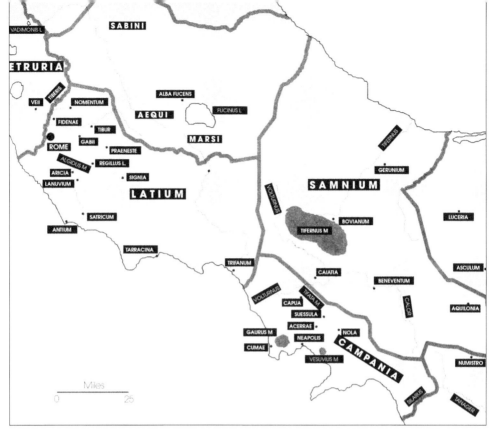

Above: Rome, Latium and Campania

Below: Northern Italy

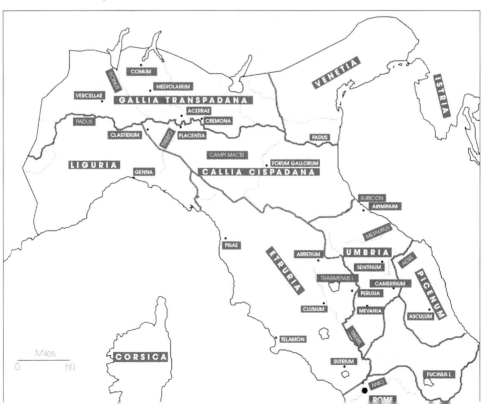

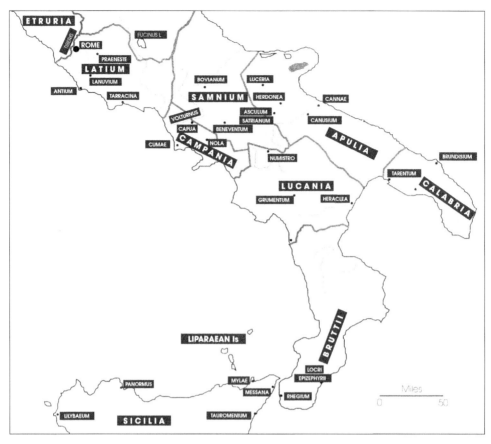

Above: Southern Italy

Below: Sicily

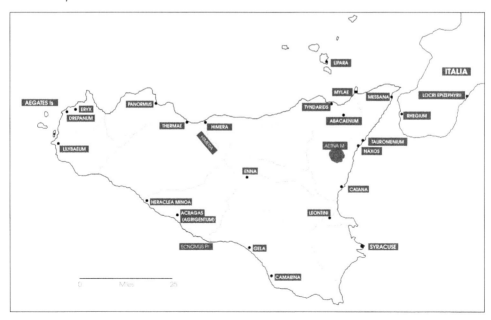

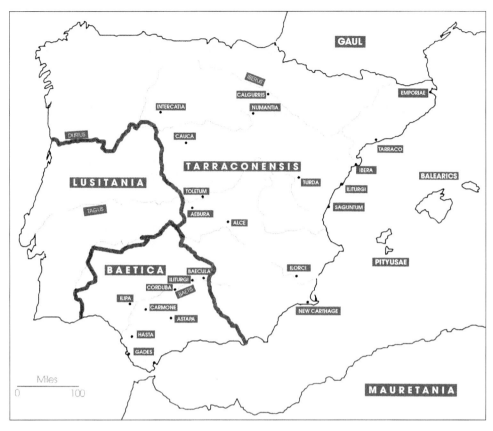

Above: Spain

Below: Northern Greece

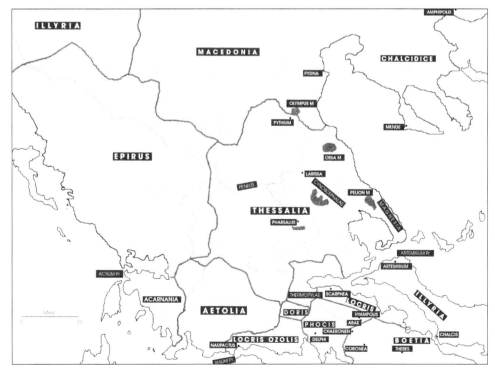

Chronological List of
Wars & Battles

1649 BC	Battle of Megiddo: The world's first battle for which we have a date and place.
509 BC	Battle of Silvia Arsia: The Romans defeat the Tarquinii and Veii under deposed king Lucius Tarquinius Superbus.
506 BC	Battle of Aricia: Latins defeat the Etruscans under Lars Porsena.
501 BC	The Bloodless War
497 BC	Battle of Lake Regillus: Aulus Postumius Albus Regillensis defeats the Tarquinii, commanded by Tarquinius Superbus.
495 BC	Battle of Aricia: Romans defeat the Aurunci. The inconclusive One Day War.
480 BC	Battle of Veii: Romans win against the Veii and their Etruscan allies.
458 BC	Battle of Mons Algidus: Cincinnatus is victorious over the Aequi.
426 BC	Battle of Fidenae: Mam. Aemilius Mamercus wins over the Fidenates and the Veii.
396 BC	Battle of Veii: Romans subdue the Etruscans.
390 BC	Battle of Allia River: Gauls defeat the Romans—the Sack of Rome.
389 BC	Battle of Lanuvium: Romans defeat the Volscii
389 BC	Battle of Sutrium
386 BC	Battle of Satricum: M. Furius Camillus defeats the Volsci, Latini,n and Hernici.
362 BC	Battle of Signia: Ap. Claudius Inregillensis victorious over the Hernici.
361 BC	Battle of Anio River: Gauls defeated.
358 BC	Battle of Pedum: Gauls defeated again.
342 BC	Battle of Mount Gaurus: Marcus Valerius Corvus defeats the Samnites.
341 BC	Battle of Suessula: Marcus Valerius Corvus defeats the Samnites again.
339 BC	Battle of Mt Vesuvius: P. Decius Mus and T. Manlius Imperiosus Torquatus defeat the Latins.
338 BC	Battle of Trifanum: Torquatus defeats the Latins.
338 BC	Battle of Pedum: L. Furius Camillus is victorious over the Pedani.
338 BC	Battle of Antium
325 BC	Battle of Imbrimium: Samnites vanquished.
321 BC	Battle of the Caudine Forks: Romans, under Spurius Postumius Albinus and T. Verturius Calvinus, are beaten by the Samnites, under Gaius Pontius.

316 BC	Battle of Lautulae: Romans defeated by the Samnites.
305 BC	Battle of Bovianum: Roman consuls M. Fulvius and L. Postumius defeat the Samnites to end the Second Samnite War.
298 BC	Battle of Camerinum: Samnites beat the Romans, under Lucius Cornelius Scipio Barbatus, in the opening battle of the Third Samnite War.
295 BC	Battle of Sentinum: Romans, under Fabius Rullianus and Publius Decimus Mus, defeat the Samnites and their Etruscan and Gallic allies.
294 BC	Battle of Luceria: M. Atilius Regulus defeats the Samnites.
293 BC	Battle of Aquilonia: Romans defeat the Samnites.
284 BC	Battle of Arretium: Lucius Caecilius' army is destroyed by the Gauls.
282 BC	Battle of Tarentum
280 BC	Battle of Heraclea: First conflict between Roman and Greek armies. The Greeks are led by Pyrrhus, who wins, but at devastating cost—a Pyrrhic victory.
279 BC	Battle of Asculum: Pyrrhus wins again but again—another Pyrrhic victory.
277 BC	Battle of Mt Eryx
275 BC	Battle of Beneventum: inconclusive encounter between Pyrrhus and the Romans, under Manius Curius.
264 BC	Battle of Messana: The opening shots of the First Punic War.
264 BC	Battle of Heraclea Minoa
261 BC	Battle of Agrigentum: Carthaginian armies, under Hannibal Gisco and Hanno, are defeated by the Romans, who take control of most of Sicily.
260 BC	Battle of Lipara: The Roman navy is defeated by the Carthaginians
260 BC	Battle of Mylae: A Roman naval force under C. Duilius defeats the Carthaginian fleet, giving Rome control of the western Mediterranean.
258 BC	Battle of Camerina: Roman naval victory against the Carthaginians off Sardinia.
257 BC	Battle of Tyndaris: Naval victory over Carthage.
256 BC	Battle of Cape Ecnomus: A Carthaginian fleet, under Hamilcar and Hanno, is beaten.
256 BC	Battle of Adys: Romans, under Regulus, defeat the Carthaginians.
255 BC	Battle of Tunis: Carthaginians, under Xanthippus, defeat the Romans, under Regulus—who is captured.
251 BC	Battle of Panormus: Carthaginian forces, under Hasdrubal, are defeated by the Romans, under L. Caecilius Metellus.
249 BC	Battle of Drepana: Carthaginians, under Adherbal, defeat the Roman fleet of Publius Claudius Pulcher.
242 BC	Battle of the Aegates Islands: Roman naval victory over the Carthaginians, ending the First Punic War.
225 BC	Battle of Clusium: Romans are defeated by the Gauls in Northern Italy.
224 BC	Battle of Telamon: Romans defeat the Gauls.
222 BC	Battle of Clastidium: Romans, under Marcus Claudius Marcellus, defeat the Gauls.
222 BC	Battle of Mediolanum

219 BC	Battle of Pharos
218 BC	Battle of the Rhodanus
218 BC	Battle of the Ticinus: Hannibal defeats the Romans, under Publius Cornelius Scipio the Elder.
218 BC	Battle of the Trebia: Hannibal ambushes the Romans, under Tiberius Sempronius Longus. Massacre.
217 BC	Battle of Lake Trasimene: Hannibal destroys the Roman army of Gaius Flaminius.
216 BC	Battle of Gerunium
216 BC	Battle of Cannae: Hannibal destroys the Roman army of Lucius Aemilius Paulus and Publius Terentius Varro, in what was one of the greatest-ever tactical masterpieces.
216 BC	Battle of Nola: Marcus Claudius Marcellus resists an attack by Hannibal.
214 BC	Battle of Beneventum
213-211 BC	Siege of Syracuse.
212 BC	Battle of Herdonia: Hannibal destroys the Roman army of Gnaeus Fulvius.
211 BC	Battle of Himera.
211 BC	Battle of the Baetis
211 BC	Battle of Capua: Hannibal fails to break the Roman siege of the city.
211 BC	Battle of Colline Gate
210 BC	Battle of Saproportis
209 BC	Battle of Cartagena
207 BC	Battle of Carmona: Romans, under Publius Cornelius Scipio, besiege the city and take it from Hasdrubal Gisco.
207 BC	Battle of the Metauru
206 BC	Battle of Ilipa: Scipio decisively defeats the remaining Carthaginian forces in Hispania.
206 BC	Battle of Astapa
203 BC	Battle of Utica
202 BC	Battle of Zama: Scipio Africanus Major defeats Hannibal, ending the Second Punic War.
200 BC	Battle of Cremona: Romans defeat the Gauls of Cisalpine Gaul.
198 BC	Battle of the Aous: Titus Quinctius Flamininus defeats the Macedonians, under Philip V.
197 BC	Battle of Cynoscephalae: Romans, under Flamininus, decisively defeat Philip in Thessaly.
195 BC	Battle of Emporia
191 BC	Battle of Thermopylae: The Romans, under Manius Acilius Glabrio, defeat Antiochus III the Great and expel him from Greece.
191 BC	Battle of Corcyra
190 BC	Battle of Panormus
190 BC	Battle of Myonessus

190 BC	Battle of Magnesia: The Romans, under Lucius Cornelius Scipio and his brother Scipio Africanus Maior, defeat Antiochus to end the war.
189 BC	The Four Battles of the Galatean Expedition
185 BC	Battle of the Tagus
181 BC	Battle of Aebura
181 BC	Battle of Manlian Pass: The Romans defeat the Celtiberians.
178 BC	The Istrian and Ligurian Wars begin
171 BC	Battle of Callicinus: Perseus of Macedon defeats the Romans, under Publius Licinius Crassus.
171 BC	Battle of Phalanna
170 BC	Battle of Uscana
170 BC	Battle of Scodra
168 BC	Battle of Pythium
168 BC	Battle of Pydna: Romans defeat and capture Perseus, ending the Third Macedonian War.
153 BC	Battle of Numantia
151 BC	Battle of Cauca
151 BC	Battle of Intercauta
149 BC	Battle of Neferis: Scipio Aemilianus wins a decisive victory against Carthage.
147 BC	Battle of Carthage: Scipio Africanus Minor captures and destroys Carthage, ending the Third Punic War.
147 BC	Battle of Tribola
146 BC	Battle of Alpheus
146 BC	Battle of Scarphea
146 BC	Battle of Chaeronea
146 BC	Battle of Corinth: Rome defeats the Achaean League forces. Corinth is destroyed and Greece falls under Roman rule.
141 BC	Battle of Numanti
121 BC	Battle of the Isara River
109 BC	Battle of Suthul
108 BC	Battle of the Muthul: Rome faces the forces of Jugurtha.
107 BC	Battle of Burdigala: Roman forces are defeated by the Helvetii.
105 BC	Battle of Arausio: The Cimbri inflict a major defeat on the Roman army of Gnaeus Mallius Maximus.
102 BC	Battle of Aquae Sextiae: Gaius Marius defeats the Teutones, with mass suicides among the captured women.
101 BC	Battle of Vercellae: Gaius Marius annihilates the Cimbri.

Glossary of Greek and Latin Terms

aedile	public officer responsible for public works, entertainment, and the distribution of grain, markets etc.
aerarium	the public treasury
ager publicus	Roman land in Italy; public land belonging to the Roman people
ager Romanus	Roman territory comprising *ager publicus* and *ager privatus*
ala (pl. alae)	wing of an army; usually a contingent of allies, about the size of a legion
amicitia	friendship without any further obligations; it could be concluded by a treaty, but also without
aristeia	epic poetry convention in which a hero in battle has his or her finest hour. An aristeia can result in the death of the hero
auctoritas	influence, prestige—especially in the early Empire
auxilia	troops provided by Rome's allies (*socii*)
candidati	imperial bodyguards
capite censi	the head–count of *proletarii* of Roman citizens, who did not have sufficient property to qualify for military service and featured as numbers in the census. Marius changed all that and included the *proletarii* in his armies
Capitol	one of the seven hills—the religious and symbolic centre of Rome
castra	military camp
centuria	a unit of the Roman legion; of varying size, around 80-100. A voting unit in the *comitia centuriata*. See Appendix 2
centurio	commander of a century
civitas sine suffragio	citizenship without suffrage—a form of citizenship granted to towns (eg Capua in 338 BC) who were subject to Roman taxation and military service, but were denied the right to vote or hold political office
classis	fleet; also the Roman soldiers who made up the bulk of the armies. The *infra classem* were less wealthy, lightly-armed skirmishers
cognomen	a man's third name; a woman's second. The name of a legion
cohors	one of ten sub-units of a legion
colonia	a town founded at a strategic place (eg a river crossing), populated with Romans and/or Latins
comes domesticorum	imperial household troops

Comitia Centuriata	the assembly of citizens which legislated, elected magistrates, declared war, ratified treaties, and judged capital offences
consul	the highest political office on the *cursus honorum*; two elected annually (usually). Consuls held *imperium*
corvus	bridge-shaped grappling/boarding device on warships. 'The raven'
cursus honorum	the sequence of public offices held by men of senatorial class
damnatio memoriae	the erasing of records, statuary, and the memory of *persona non grata* after their death
decimation	the execution of every tenth man, chosen by lot from the ranks
deditio	surrender, with the assumption that the victor would extend *fides* and spare the lives of the defeated
delator	informer, particularly prevalent and successful in the early Empire
devotio	an extreme act of bravery, in which a Roman gave himself up in battle in what was a suicidal attack against the enemy
dictator	temporary absolute leader, appointed for a limited period to resolve a crisis
dies nefasti	inauspicious days
dignitas	political dignity, related to tenure of offices in the cursus honorum
dilectus	the annual military levy
dominae	the domineering mistresses of Catullus and the love poets
dona militaria	military decorations
dux	leader
equites	the equestrian order ranked below senators; the *equites* were middle class businessmen and farmers; cavalry
exclusus amator	the love poet locked out by his mistress
exercitus	army
fetialis	war priest responsible for ensuring that Rome's wars were just in the eyes of the gods. Responsible for the rites performed for declaring war and concluding peace
fides	trustworthiness, good faith, loyalty—a quality the Romans were anxious to be seen to uphold, including respect for the law and *fides* in foreign relations
foederati	nations to which Rome provided benefits in exchange for military assistance
foedus	originally a sacred oath made by a fetial priest on behalf of the Roman people; a treaty
gens	family; clan, e.g. Claudii
gladius	short sword
glans	slingshot
haruspex	soothsayer
hasta	spear
hastati	soldiers of the second class, who stood in the front line; green, raw recruits
Hellenism	the culture of classical Greece, which percolated into Rome in the second century BC

hetaira	courtesan
hoplite	heavily-armed infantryman
imagines	portraits of ancestors
imperium	power, command, empire; power, particularly that bestowed on consuls, generals, and praetors
incestum	unchastity, particularly in Vestal Virgins; incest
indutia	cease-fire
latifundia	estates in Italy
Latin League	an association of communities in Latium, who were allied militarily.
latrones	bandits; pirates
laudation	eulogy
legio	legion; a levy of troops
lex	law
magister equitum	second-in-command to the dictator; the master of the horse usually commanded the cavalry, as the dictator was forbidden to ride a horse
maiestas	power; authority; treason
manipulus	maniple; sub-unit of the legion, comprising two centuries
manubiae	the general's share of the booty
miles	soldier
miles amoris	a soldier in the war of love, as described by the Roman elegists of the first century BC
naumachia	naval warfare
novus homo	a 'new man'; a man not of the aristocracy; a self-made man
onager	stone-lobbing torsion catapult
otium	a lifestyle of ease and commercial, political, or military inactivity
patricius	patrician; the dominant political class; aristocratic families
pax	peace
phalanx	close-knit body of heavily-armed infantry
pietas	dutifulness—in all aspects of life
pilum	javelin
plebeian	non-patricians
polis	Greek city-state
pontifex maximus	chief priest
praefectus	prefect, commander of an auxiliary force
preafectus urbi	prefect of the city
praetexta	White robe with a purple border, worn by a Roman boy before he was entitled to wear the *toga virilis*, and by girls until their marriage. Also worn by magistrates and priests
praetor	public office, responsible for justice. Second-highest political and military office
Principate	the period of the Emperors, from 27 BC onwards
principes	troops in their twenties and thirties

proconsul	acting consul
proletarii	volunteer soldiers of the poorer orders, first recruited by Marius
raptus	seized, abducted, raped
Republic	the period of Republican government in 509–43 BC
res gestae	political and military achievements
rex	king
scutum	shield
secessio plebis	a general strike in which the plebeians downed tools, shut-up shop, and deserted Rome, leaving the patricians to get on with running the city on their own. All business and services ground to a halt; there were five between 494 BC and 287 BC
Sibylline Books	three sacred scrolls, kept under guard. Only consulted when decreed by the senate to give oracular advice in times of crisis, or to interpret portents and omens
signifier	standard-bearer
societas	synonymous with *amicitia*. Peace and neutrality, with an obligation to military support
socius (pl. *socii*)	ally
spolia opima	the highest award for gallantry—won when a commander defeated an enemy leader in unarmed combat
testudo	tortoise-shaped formation in which shields are interlocked above the head
toga virilis	the plain white toga worn on formal occasions by Roman men between fourteen and eighteen years of age; also worn by senators. The first wearing of the toga virilis was one of the rites of passage of reaching maturity. See *praetexta*
triarii	veteran troops
tribuni plebei	officials responsible for protecting their fellow plebeians against injustices from the patricians; had a veto and sacrosanctity
tribunus militum	military tribune
trireme	standard warship, with three banks of oars
triumphator	a general who had been awarded a triumph
triumphus	triumph: the military procession along the Via Sacra, in Rome, for victorious generals. Spoils of war, prisoners, and captured chieftains were paraded. The enemy chieftains were sometimes executed; the triumphator rode in a chariot, and was dressed as Jupiter
tumultus	crisis
vates	soothsayer; prophetess; priestess
velites	lightly-armed skirmishing troops. 1200 or so in a legion
via	road, as in Via Appia
virtus	manliness; courage; virtue
vis	force; rape; military strength

Typical *Cursus Honorum* in the Second Century BC

Required ten years of military service in cavalry or on the political staff of a relative or friend.

Minimum Age	Office
30	*quaestor* (8–12 in number): Financial admin in Rome, or in a province, as 2-ic to the Governor. '*tribune of the plebs*' (10): preside over the *concilium plebis*.
36	*aedile* (4, two curule and two plebeian): Admin role in Rome; responsible for the corn supply, festivals etc.; optional.
39	*praetor* (6): judicial role in Rome; in charge of provinces not allocated to consuls; commanded one legion and allies.
40	*consul* (2): governed larger provinces and held major commands in all wars; led two legions and two allied *alae*. Other roles: to preside over the Senate and assemblies. *censor*: magistracy held by most distinguished ex-consuls. Two in office for five years; function: to carry out the census.

Roman Assemblies

Senate

300 members regulated by the censors. Members were from the eighteen senior centuries, i.e. they had property worth > 400,000 HS. Role was to advise magistrates, especially the consuls.

Concilium Plebis

Made up of plebeians; divided into thirty-five tribes; membership based on ancestry; role was to elect the tribune and the *aedile*; passed laws.

Comitia Tributa

Made up of citizens, including patricians; role as above, but elected *curule aediles* and *quaestors*.

Comitia Centuriata

Comprised citizens divided into 193 voting centuries; originally formed from citizen militia, with membership based on possession of military equipment. Presided over by a consul or praetor. Function: election of consuls, praetors, and censors; declarations of war and ratification of peace treaties.

The Seven Kings of Rome

Romulus (753–715 BC), the fabled founder of Rome.

Numa Pompilius (715–673 BC), unusually peaceful Roman king.

Tullius Hostilius (673–642 BC), responsible for the destruction of Alba Longa and the migration of its inhabitants to Rome.

Ancus Marcius (642–617 BC), extended the city, built the first bridge across the Tiberk, and founded Ostia to give Rome a seaport.

Tarquinius Priscus (617–579 BC), was an Etruscan who built Rome's first sewer, the Cloaca Maxima (laid out the Circus Maximus), and started work on a temple to Jupiter on the Capitoline Hill.

Servius Tullius (579–535 BC), divided the Romans into tribes and classes, and so established a constitution in which wealth was the main factor. Built the city walls: five miles in circumference, with nineteen gates, embracing all the Seven Hills of Rome. He transferred the regional festival of Diana from Aricia to the Aventine Hill.

Tarquinius Superbus (534–510 BC), Rome's last king. His son Sextus raped Lucretia, a virtuous *matrona*, with the consequence that Tarquinius was exiled, and the monarchy gave way to the Roman republic.

Illustrations and Credits

As with my earlier books I have tried to be original and refreshing with the illustrations. Most books published on the subject rightly feature instructive and interesting photographs and diagrams; however, many of these are now overly familiar and somewhat predictable. I have illustrated this book with less well-known images, using pictures taken from trade cards, advertisements, and from books published in the late nineteenth and early twentieth century. These will, I hope, provide an original take on Roman battles and the Roman war machine while still being educational and stimulating.

My thanks to the publishers of:

Universal History of the World Volume 3: Hellenistic Age to Roman Empire, edited by J. A. Hammerton (London, 1930)
Roman History, Literature, and Antiquities, by A. Petrie (London, 1926)
The Comic History of Rome by Gilbert Abbot a Beckett (London, 1852)
The Harmsworth Encyclopedia, 1921; this was edited by John Hammerton, published as a fortnightly part-work, and sold twelve million copies throughout the English-speaking world,
A Brief History of Rome, by J. D. Steele (New York, 1885)
Aunt Charlotte's Stories of Roman History for the Little Ones, by Charlotte M. Yonge (London, 1884)
Stories from Livy, by A. J. Church (London, 1902)
Hannibal: Heroes of the Nations, by W. O'Connor Morris (London, 1897)
A Guide to the Exhibition Illustrating Greek and Roman Life, (British Museum, London 1908)
The Grandeur That Was Rome, by J. C. Stobart (London, 1920)
Das Wissen des 20 Jahrhunderts, Bildungslexicon, Rheda (1931)
Histoire de Romains T. VII (Paris, 1890)

And to:

Liebig Company, Antwerp
The Wyland Stanley Collection, San Francisco

Bridgeport Brass Company, Bridgeport CT
New Yorker Magazine

Thomas Fisher Rare Book Library, University of Toronto: www.fisher.library.utoronto.ca

Professor Robin Osborne, editor of *Omnibus,* for kind permission to reproduce the *lorica* in plate; it was originally published in *Omnibus* 62: 'Ancient Military Technology', by Tracey Rihll. *Omnibus* is published by JACT—The Joint Association of Classical Teachers.

Bibliography

Abbreviations

BStudLat Bollettino di Studi Latini
CJ   Classical Journal
CPh   Classical Philology
CQ   Classical Quarterly
CW   Classical World
G&R   Greece and Rome
HSCPh   Harvard Studies in Classical Philology
JRS   Journal of Roman Studies
RBPH   Revue Belge de Philologie et d'Histoire
SO   Symbolae Osloensis
TAPhA   Transactions of the Proceedings of the American Philological Asscn
ZPE   Zeitschrift fur Papyrologie und Epigraphik

Bibliography

Achaud, G., *Bellum iustum, bellum sceleratum* Sous les Rois et Sous la Republique, *BStudLat* 24, pp. 474-86, (1994)

Adams, J. P., *Logistics of the Roman Army*, (London, 1976)

Adcock, F. E., *The Greek and Macedonian Art of War*, (Berkeley, 1957); *Delenda est Carthago, Cambridge Historical Jnl* 8, 117f, (1946); *The Roman Art of War Under the Republic*, (Cambridge MA, 1940)

Afflerbach, H., (ed.), *How Fighting Ends: A History Of Surrender*, (Oxford, 2012)

Alfoldi, A., *Early Rome and the Latins*, (Ann Arbor, 1965)

Anglim, S., *Fighting Techniques of the Ancient World 3000 BC–AD 500*, (London, 2002)

Arieti, J. A., *Rape and Livy´s View of Roman History* in Deacy, *Rape in Antiquity,* pp. 209-229, (1997)

Astin, A. E., *Scipio Aemilianus,* (Oxford, 1967); Saguntum and the Origins of the Second Punic War, *Latomus* 26, pp. 577-96, (1967)

Austin, N. J. E., 'Ammianus on Warfare', *Latomus* 165, (1979)

Badian, E., *Roman Imperialism in the Late Republic*, (Oxford, 1968); *The Early Historians* in Dorey, *Latin Historians* 1-38, (1966); *Foreign* Clientelae, (London, 1958); *The Punic Wars: Rome, Carthage and the Struggle for the Mediterranean*, (London, 1999)

Balsdon, J. P. V. D., *Romans and Aliens*, (London, 1979)

Barnes, J., 'Ciceron et la Guerre Juste', *Bulletin de la Societe Francaise de Philosophie* 80, pp. 41-81, (1986)

Baronowski, D. W., *Polybius and Roman Imperialism*, (London, 2013); Roman Military Forces in 225 BC, (Polybius 2, 23-4) *Historia* 42, 181-201, (1993)

Beard, M., *The Roman Triumph*, (Harvard MA, 2009)

Bell, M. J. V., 'Tactical Reform in the Roman Republican Army', *Historia* 14, 404-22, (1965)

Beloch, K. J., *Romische Geschichte bis zum Beginn der Punische Kriege*, (Berlin, 1926)

Bloch R., *Combats Singuliers Entre Gaulois et Romans*, (Paris, 1968)

Boardman, J., *The Greeks Overseas*, (Harmondsworth, 1964)

Bonfante, W. L., 'Roman Triumphs and Etruscan Kings', *JRS* 60, 49-66, (1980)

Boot, M. *Invisible Armies: An Epic History of Guerilla Warfare from Ancient Times to the Present,* (London, 2014)

Brown, J. E. T., 'Hannibal's Route Across the Alps', *G&R* 10, 38-46, (1963)

Brown, R. D., 'Livy's Sabine Women and the Ideal of *concordia*', *TAPhA* 125, 291-319, (1995)

Brunt, P. A., 'Conscription and Volunteering in the Roman Army', *Scripta Classica Israelica* 1, 90-115, (1974), *Italian Manpower*, (Oxford, 1971), The Army and the Land in the Roman Revolution, *JRS* 52, 69-86, (1962)

Bruun, P., *Studies in the Romanization of Etruria*, (Rome, 1975)

Burns, T. S., *Rome and the Barbarians, 100 BC–AD 400*, (Baltimore MD, 2009), *Barbarians Within the Gates of Rome,* (Bloomington IN, 1995)

Cagniart, P., *The Late Republican Army, (146-30 BC)* in Erdkamp, *A Companion to the Roman Army*, (Chichester, 2007)

Campbell, B., (ed.), *Oxford Handbook of Warfare in the Classical World*, (Oxford, 2013)**,** *Greek & Roman Military Writers*, (London, 2004), *The Roman Army, 31 BC–AD 337: A Sourcebook*, (London, 1984), 'The Marriage of Roman Soldiers Under the Empire', *JRS* 68, 153-66, (1978)

Campbell, D. B., *Besieged: Siege Warfare Ancient World*, (Oxford, 2006), *Ancient Siege Warfare: Persians, Greeks, Carthaginians*, (Oxford, 2005)

Carter, J., *The Battle of Actium: The Rise and Triumph of Augustus Caesar*, (London, 1970)

Cary, M., *A History of Rome 3/e, (London, 1975)

Chakravarti, P., *The Art of War in Ancient India*, (2003 repr.)

Chaplin, D., (ed.), *Livy: Oxford Readings in Classical Studies,* (Oxford, 2009), *Livy's Exemplary History*, (Oxford, 2000)

Charles, M. B., *Magister Elephantorum*: A Reappraisal of Hannibal's Use of Elephants *CW*100, 363-89, (2007)

Chrystal, P., *Roman Military Disasters,* (Barnsley, in press 2015); *Roman Women: The Women Who Influenced the History of Rome*, (Stroud, in press 2015); *In Bed with the Romans*, (Stroud, in press 2015); 'A Powerful Body of Women', *Minerva,* January-February 2014, 10-13; 'Roman Women Go to War', *Omnibus* 68, October 2014; *Women in Ancient Rome,* (Stroud 2013); *Differences in Attitude to Women as Reflected in the Work of Catullus, Propertius, the Corpus Tibullianum, Horace and Ovid,* (diss, University of Southampton, 1982)

Colin, G., *Rome et la Grece de 200 a 146 BC avant JC,* (Paris, 1905), *Luxe Oriental et Parfums Masculins dans la Rome Alexandrine, RBPH 33, p. 5-19*, (1935)

Copper J. S., *The Curse of Agade*, (Baltimore, 1983)

Corbett, J. H., 'Rome and the Gauls 285–280 BC', *Historia* 20, 656-64, (1971)

Cornell, T. J., *Gender and Ethnicity in Ancient Italy*, (London, 1997), (ed.) *The Second Punic War: A Reappraisal*, (London, 1996); *The Beginnings of Rome*, (London, 1995)

Cottrell, L., *The Battle of Trebbia*, in *Hannibal: Enemy of Rome*, (London, 1992)

Cowan, R., *The Roman Conquests: Italy,* (Barnsley, 2009); *Roman Battle Tactics 109 BC–AD 313,* (Oxford, 2007)

Crawford, H., *Sumer and Sumerians,* (Cambridge, 2004)

Crump, G., *Ammianus Marcellinus as Military Historian*, (Wiesbaden, 1975)

Curto, S., *The Military Art of the Ancient Egyptians*, (Milan, 1971)

David, J. M., *The Roman Conquest of Italy*, (Oxford, 1997)

Davies, G., *Roman Siege Works*, (Stroud, 2006)

Deacy, S., (ed.), *Rape in Antiquity*, (London, 1997)

Dixon K., *The Roman Cavalry*, (London, 1992)

Dorey, T. A., *Rome Against Carthage*, (London, 1971); (ed.) *Livy*, (London, 1971); (ed.) *The Latin Historians*, (London, 1966); 'Hannibal's Route Across the Alps', *Romanitas* 3, 325-30, (1961); 'The Treaty with Saguntum', *Humanitas*, 1-10, (1959)

Evans, J. K., *War, Women and Children in Ancient Rome*, (London, 1991)

Feldherr, A., (ed.), *Cambridge Companion to the Roman Historians*, (Cambridge, 2009)

Flory, M. B., 'The Integration of Women into the Roman Triumph', *Historia* 47, 489-94, (1998)

Gabba, E., 'True History and False History in Classical Antiquity', *JRS* 61, 50-62, (1981)

Garlan, Y., *War in the Ancient World*, (London, 1975)

Garouphalias, P., *Pyrrhus: King of Epirus*, (London, 1979)

Goldsworthy, A., *Cannae: Hannibal's Greatest Victory*, (London, 2007)

Grant, M., *Greek and Roman Historians: Information and Misinformation*, (1995)

Griffin, J., 'Augustan Poetry and the Life of Luxury', *JRS* 66, 87-105, (1976)

Grundy, G. B., 'The Trebbia and Lake Trasimene', *Journal of Philology* 24: 83-118, (1896)

Halliday, W. R., 'Passing under the Yoke', *Folklore* 35, 93-95, (1924)

Hermann, P., *Historicorum Romanorum Reliquae*, (Leipzig, 1870)

Herzog, C., *Battles of the Bible*, (London, 1978)

Hoyos, B. D., *Roman Imperialism*, (London, 2013); *Hannibal: Rome's Greatest Enemy*, (Bristol, 2005); *Unplanned Wars: The Origins of the First and Second Punic Wars*, (Berlin, 1998)

Hunt, P., *Slaves, Warfare, and Ideology in the Greek Historians*, (Cambridge, 1998)

Hyland, A., *Equus: The Horse in the Roman World*, (London, 1990)

Jameson, M., *Sacrifice Before Battle*, in Hanson, V., (ed) *Hoplites* p. 220, (1991)

Janssen, L. F., 'Some Unexplored Aspects of *devotio* Deciana', *Mnemosyne* 357-381, (1981)

Keaveney, A., *Rome and the Unification of Italy*, (Liverpool, 1987)

Keegan, J., *A History of Warfare*, (London, 1993)

Keeley, L. H., *War Before Civilisation: The Myth of the Peaceful Savage*, (Oxford, 1996)

Klein, J., *The Royal Hymns of Shulgi, King of Ur*, (Philadelphia, 1981)

Knapp, R., *The Invisible Romans*, (London, 2011)

Last, H., 'The Servian Reforms', *JRS* 35. 30-48, (1945)

Lazenby, J. F., *The Spartan Army*, (Barnsley, 2011)

Litchfield, H. W., 'National Examples of *virtus* in Roman Literature', *HSCPh* 25, 1-71, (1914)

Matyszak, P., *Sertorius and the Struggle for Spain*, (Barnsley, 2013), *Mithridates the Great*, (Barnsley, 2008), *The Enemies of Rome: From Hannibal to Attila the Hun*, (London, 2004)

McDonald, A. H., 'Hannibal's Passage of the Alps', *Alpine Jnl* 61, 93-101, (1956)

McDonnell, M., *Roman Manliness*: Virtus *and the Roman Republic*, (Cambridge, 2006)

Miles, G. B., *Livy: Reconstructing Early Rome*, (New York, 1997)

Millar, F., *Rome the Greek World and the East Vol. 1*: *The Roman Republic and the Augustan Revolution*, (Chapel Hill NC, 2001)

Mommsen, T., *History of Rome*, (London, 2014 repr.)

Moses, D., *Livy's Lucretia and the Validity of Coerced Consent in Roman Law*

Murgatroyd, P., *Militia amoris* and the Roman Elegists, *Latomus* 34, 59-79, (1975)

Nilsson, M. P., 'The Introduction of Hoplite Tactics in Rome', *JRS* 19, 1-11, (1929)

Oakley, S. P., *A Commentary on Livy Books VI-X, Volume 1 Introduction and Book VI* (Oxford, 1997); *A Commentary on Livy Books VI-X, Volume II: Books VII-VII*, (Oxford, 1998); *The Roman Conquest of Italy* in Rich, J., (ed.) in *War and Society in the Ancient World*, 9-37, (1993); 'Single Combat and the Roman Republic', *CQ* 35, 39-410, (1985)

O'Connor Morris, W., *Hannibal: Soldier, Statesman, Patriot*, (London, 1927)

Ogilvie, R. M., *Early Rome and the Etruscans*, (Glasgow, 1976); *A Commentary on Livy Books 1-5*, (Oxford, 1965)

Peddie, J., *The Roman War Machine*, (Gloucester, 1994)

Pitassi, M. P., *The Roman Navy: Ships, Men & Warfare 350 BC–AD 475*, (Barnsley, 2012); *The Navies of*

Rome, (London, 2012); *Roman Warships*, (London, 2011)

Qviller, B., 'Reconstructing the Spartan Partheniai: Many Guesses and a Few Facts', *SO* 71, 34-41, (1996)

Raaflaub, K. A., (ed.) *War and Peace in the Ancient World*, (Chichester, 2007)

Rankin, H. D., *The Celts and the Classical World*, (London, 1987)

Regan, G., *Backfire: A History of Friendly Fire from Ancient Warfare to the 21st Century, (*London, 2002)

Rodgers, W., *Greek and Roman Naval Warfare*, (Annapolis, 1937); *The Consul(ar) as* exemplum*: Fabius Cunctator's Paradoxical Glory* in Beck, *Consuls and* Res Publica*: Holding High Office in the Roman Republic, (*2008); 'Exemplarity in Roman Culture: The Case of Horaius Cocles and Cloelia', *CPh* 99, 1-56, (2004)

Sabin, P., *Lost Battles: Reconstructing the Great Clashes of the Ancient World,* (2008); (ed.) *The Cambridge History of Greek and Roman Warfare,* (Cambridge, 2007)

Sagan, C., *Pale Blue Dot: A Vision of the Human Future in Space*, (New York, 1994)

Saggs, H. W. F., *Civilisation Before Greece and Rome*, (London, 1989)

Salmon, E. T., *The Making of Roman Italy*, (London, 1982); *Roman Colonization under the Republic*, (London, 1969); *Samnium and the Samnites*, (Cambridge, 1967); Rome and the Latins, *Phoenix* 7, 93-104; 123-55, (1953)

Samuels, M., 'The Reality of Cannae', *Militargeschichlichte Miteillungen* 47, 7-29, (1990); *Persia* in A. Cameron, *Images of Women in Antiquity*, 20-33, (London)

Schatzmann, I., 'The Roman General's Authority over the Distribution of Booty', *Historia* 21, 17-28, (1972)

Scullard, H. H., *Roman Politics : 220-150 BC*, (Westport, CT, 1981); *The Elephant in the Greek and Roman World*, (London, 1974); *Scipio Africanus: Soldier and Politician*, (London, 1970); *The Etruscan Cities and Rome*, (London, 1967), *Scipio Africanus in the Second Punic War*, (London, 1930)

Sheldon, R. M., *Rome's Wars in Parthia: Blood in the Sand*, (London, 2010); *Intelligence Activities in Ancient Rome: Trust in the Gods but Verify*, (London, 2007); *Ambush: Surprise Attack in Ancient Greek Warfare*, (London, 2001)

Sidnell, P., *Warhorse: Cavalry in Ancient Warfare*, (London, 2006)

Spaulding, O. A., 'The Ancient Military Writers', *CJ* 28, 657-669, (1933)

Speidel, M. P., *Ancient Germanic Warriors*, (London, 2004)

Thapliyal, U. P., *Warfare in Ancient India,* (New Delhi, 2010)

Thiel, J. H., *A History of Roman Sea Power Before the Second Punic War*, (1954)

Tipps, G. K., 'The Battle of Ecnomus', *Historia* 34, 432-465, (1985)

Toner, J., *Roman Disasters*, (London, 2013)

Versnel, H. S., 'Two Types of Roman *devotio*', *Mnemosyne* 29, 365-410, (1976); *Triumphus*, (Leiden, 1970)

Walbank, F. W., *A Historical Commentary on Polybius Vol. 3*, (Oxford, 1979)

Wallinga, H. T., *The Boarding-bridge of the Romans*, (Groningen, 1956)

Walsh, P. G., *Livy*, (Oxford, 1974); Masinissa, *JRS* 55, 149ff, (1965); *Livy: His Historical Aims and Methods,* (Cambridge, 1961)

Warde Fowler, W., Passing under the Yoke, *Classical Review* 27, 48-51, (1913)

Warmington, E. H., The Destruction of Carthage, A *Retratatio*, *CP*83, 308-10, (1988); *Carthage, (*New York, 1960); (ed.) *Remains of Old Latin 4 Vols, (*Cambridge MA, 1940)

Wellesley, K., *Tacitus as a Military Historian*, in Dorey, *Tacitus* 63-97, (1969)

Whitehead, D., *Aineias Tacticus: How to Survive Under Siege* 2/e, (Bristol, 2002)

Wiseman, T. P., 'Roman Republic, Year One', *G&R* 45, 19-26, (1998); 'Lying Historians—Seven Types of Mendacity', in Gill, *Lies and Fiction in the Ancient World*, (1993)

Woolliscroft, D., *Roman Military Signalling*, (Barnsley, 2001)

Ziolkowski, A., Urbs Direpta *or How the Romans Sacked Cities* in Rich, J., *War and Society in the Ancient World*, (London, 1993), 69-91*;* Credibility of Numbers of Battle Captives in Livy XXI-XXV, (1990)

Primary Sources

Aelian, *De Natura Animalium*
Aeneas Tacticus, *How to Survive under Siege*
Aeschylus, *Seven Against Thebes*
Ammianus Marcellinus, *Histories*
Appian, *Bellum Civili*
Aristophanes, *Lysistrata; Ecclesiazusae; Birds*
Aristotle, *Politics*
Athenaeus, *Deipnosophistai*
Augustine, *De Civitate Dei*
Aulus Gellius, *Noctes Atticae*
Ausonius, *Epigramata de Diversis Rebus.*
The Bible: *Genesis; Exodus; Samuel; 2 Kings; Zechariah; Isaiah; Lamentations; Numbers; Joshua; Judges,*
    The Song of Deborah; Judith; Matthew; Mark; John; Luke
Caesar, *Bellum Civile; De Bello Gallico*
Catullus
Cicero, *De Re Publica; Ad Familiares, Ad Atticum; Philippics; De Officiis; Tusculanae*
Disputationes; De Finibus Bonorum et Malorum; De Inventione Rhetorica; De Senectute; In Verrem; Pro
    Plancio.
Clement of Alexandria, *Protrepticus, Consolatio ad Liviam*
Ctesias, *Persica*
Dio Cassius, *Historia Romana*
Diodorus Siculus, *Bibliotheca Historica*
Diogenes Laertius, *Lives and Opinions of Eminent Philosophers*
Dionysius of Halicarnassus, *Roman Antiquities*
Ennius, *Annales*
Epictetus, *Discourses*
Euripides, *Phoenician Women; Bacchae*
Eutropius, *Abridgement of Roman History*
Fasti Triumphales
Florus, *Epitome of Roman History*
Frontinus, *De Aqueductibus Urbis Romae; Strategemata*
Homer, *Iliad*
Horace, *Odes, Carmen Saeculare, Satires*
Jerome, *Letters*
John Chrysostom, *The Kind of Women Who Ought To Be Taken As Wives*
Josephus, *The Jewish War*
Juvenal, *Satires*
Laudatio Turiae
Livy, *Ab Urbe Condita*
Lucan, *De Bello Civili*
Lycurgus, *Against Leocrates*
Martial, *Epigrams*
The Narmer Palette
Onasander, *Strategikos* (Στρατηγικός)
Orosius, *Historiae Adversus Paganos*
Ovid, *Metamorphoses, Fasti*
The Palatine Anthology or *Anthologia Palatina*
Pausanias, *Description of Greece*
Pindar, *Pythian Ode*

Plato, Republic, Laws
Pliny the Elder, *Naturalis Historia*
Pliny the Younger, *Epistles*
Plutarch, *Alexander; Galba; Lacaenarum Apophthegmata; Antony; De Virtutibus Muliebrum; Pyrrhus; Marius; Poplicola; Marcellus; Flaminius; Cato Maior; Aemilius Paullus; Alcibiades*
Polyaenus, *Stratagems*
Polybius, *Histories*
Propertius, *Elegies*
Quintilian, *Institutio Oratoria*
Quintus Curtius Rufus, *Historiae Alexandri Magni*
Sallust, *Catalina; Jugurtha; Histories*
Seneca the Elder, *Controversiae*
Seneca the Younger, *Consolatio ad Marciam*
Servius, *On Virgil; On Georgics*
Sophocles, *Oedipus at Colonus*
Statius, *Silvae*
Strabo, *Geography*
Suetonius, *Augustus; Tiberius*
Tacitus, *Agricola, Germania, Annales, Histories*
Thucydides, *History of the Peloponnesian War*
The Anonymous *Tractatus De Mulieribus*
Valerius Maximus, *Factorum et Dictorum Memorabilium*
Varro, *De Lingua Latina*
Velleius Paterculus, *Historiae Romanae*
Virgil, *Aeneid*
Xenophon, *Constitution of the Lacedaemonians; Cyropaedia; Anabasis; Minor Works, Agesilaus.*

Websites

www.perseus.org—a fathomless source of Greek and Latin texts
www.romanarmy.net—the website of the *Roman Military Research Society*
www.roman-empire.net/army/army/html
www.vindolanda.com
oxbow@oxbowbooks.com—booksellers/publishers specializing in classics and archaeology
www.jrmes.org.uk—website of the Jnl of Roman Medical Equipment Studies
www.hellenicbookservice.com
www.classicsbookshop.co.uk
www.fisher.library.utoronto.ca—has some superb classical prints
www.jact.org—Joint Association of Classical Teachers, publishers of *Omnibus*
www.friends-classics.demon.co.uk—publishers of *Ad Familiares*
www.yayas.free-online.co.uk—Yorkshire Architectural and York Archaeological Society
www.scholar.lib.vt.edu/stats/ejournals/ElAnt-current.html—the website for Virginia Tech's *Electronic Antiquity*
www.womenforwomen.org.uk—helping female survivors of war rebuild their lives

Index

Illustrations are in italics; wars and battles in bold

Abydus, 111
Achaean League, 120, 122
Adherbal, 79, 80
Adys, 79
Aebura, 116
Aegates Islands, 81, 87
Aemilius, Paulus, 119
Aetolian League, 113
Aequi, 36, 43
Agricola, Gnaeus Julius, 28, 29
Agrigentum, 99
Agrigentum, Battle of, 76
Akkadia, 11
Alexander the Great, 15, 67
Alpheus River, 120
Alps, crossing of by Hannibal, 89ff, *109*
Allia, River, 48-9, 92
allies, 20, 21, 22, 35, 36, 94
Anatolia, 114
Ancus Martius, 34
Anio River, 56
Antiochus III, 111, 114, 115
Antium, 42, 60 (338 BC)
Aous, River, 112
Aquae Sextiae, 132
Aquilonia, 64
archers, 11, 12, 13, 80, 115
Archimedes, 96, 99
Aricia, 40
armour and weapons, 13, 14, *22,* 51, 72, 95, 101, 119, 130, *135, 136, 137-138*
Asculum Satrianum, 70
Assyria, 11, 12
Astapa, 104
Athacus, 111

Athens, 13
Atia, mother of Augustus, 40
atrocities, 11, 12, 13, 26, 28, 29, 31, 46, 49, 90, 91, 95, 96, 100, 102, 106, 111, 113, 119, 120, 127-128

Baecula, 101, 104
Bagradas, 79-80
battering ram, 13
Beneventum, 71, 95 (214 BC)
Bloodless War, 35
booty, 24, 26, 27, 32, 46, 47, 51, 54, 55, 58, 75, 76, 77, 88, 117, 129-30, 131, 132
Bostar, 79
Bovianum, 62
Brennus, 48, 49, *52*
Britannia, 28, 49, *137*
Byron, 102

Callinicus, 117-118
Camarina, 78
Camillus, Marcus Furius, 46, 51, 54-55
Cannae, 91-92, *93,* 101, 104
Canusium, 101
Cape Ecnomus, 79
Cape Hermaeum, 79-80
Capua, 57, 58, 94, 100
Cape Myonnesus, 114
Carales, 95
Cartagena, 100, 101
Carthage, 20-21, 27, 58, 70-1, 73ff, 87ff, *107,* 123
Carthage, Battle of, 125
Carthage, siege of, 79
Carmone, 101
Cato, Marcus Porcius, 113, 114, 123, 124
Catulus, Gaius Lutatius, 81

Catulus, Quintus Lutatius, 132
Cauca, 119
Caudine Forks, 64
cavalry, 19
centurions, 52, 130
chariots, 12, 13, 49
Chaeronea, 121-122
Cicero, 25, 26, 81, 96, 126
Cimbri, 131, 132
Cincinnatus, Lucius Quinctius, 43
Cirta, 129
civitas sine suffragio, 61
Clastidium, 85
Colcles, Publius Horatius, 32, *39*
Colline Gate, 56, 100 (211 BC)
Conflict of the Orders, 18, 43
Corinth, 86, 112, 122, *122*
Corinth, Battle of, 122
Coriolanus, 42
Cornus, 95
corona graminea, 57, 78
Corsica, 82, 117
Corycus, 114
corvus, 77
Cremona, 110
Crete, 13
Cunctator, Quintus Fabius Verrucosus
    Maximus, 90, 94
Cursor, L. Papirius, 64
cursus honorum, 28, 52, 101
Cynoscephalae, 112
Cynisca, daughter of the King of Sparta, 15

damnatio memoriae, 11
deserters, 96
devastation of the land, 11, 13
devotio, 59, 59-60, 63, 102
dictator, 36, 44, 56, 61, 78, 90, 94
divine approval for war, *hubris,* 12, 16, 25, 30,
    31, 46, 47, 56, 59-60, 65, 81, 90
Drepana, 80
Duilius, Gaius, 77

Egypt, 12, 13, 21
elephants, 67, *68,* 69, 70, 71, 74, 80, 100, 101, 105,
    109, 112, 114, 115, 128
Emporiae, 113
Ennius, 75, 91
Eryx, 70, 81
ethnic cleansing, 13, 120
Etruscans, *17,* 19, 30, *39,* 40, 55, 62, 63

fetiales, 25
Fidenae, 46
fides, 11, 25, 33, 87-88
finance, economics and the soldier, 16, 18, 19,
    21, 36-7, 51
Flamininus, Titus Quinctius, 26
foedus Cassianum, 41
friendly fire, 58, 69-70, 74, 80, 101, 105
Frontinus, 28

Gabii, 34-5
Galatean Expedition, 115
Gauls, 48ff, 56, 63, 84ff, 110, 115
Greece, 13, 16, 27, 85, 112, 120
Grumentum, 102
guerrilla warfare, 81, 90, 94, 120

Hamilcar, 77
Hamilcar Barca, 81, 82, 87, 95
Hannibal, 80, 87ff, 100, *103,* 105, 114, 123
Hannibal Gisco, 77
Hanno, 76, 81, 89, 95
Hasdrubal, 79, 80, 87
Hasdrubal the Boeotarch, 124
Himera, 99
Horace, 26

Iberia, 87, 113ff, 116
Iliad, The, 27, 42, 125
Ilipa, 101-102
Ilorci, 99
Illyria, 85-6, 111
Imbrimium, 61
incendiaries, 46, 54, 105, 114
infanticide, 12, 104, 111, 125, 132
Intercatia, 119
intelligence, military, 15
Isthmus, 122
Istrian War, 117

Jerome, 132
Josephus, 73
Jugurtha, 26, 127-128
Julius Caesar, 28, 29, 36, 49
Juvenal, 27

Lake Regillus, 41
Lake Trasimene, 90, 91-2
Lanuvium, 54
Lars Porsenna, 32, 40
Latins and Latin League, 34, 41, 58, 61, 101

Latin War, Second, 41
legions, 19, 36, 43, 72, 94, 130
Ligurian War, 117
Lilybaeum, siege of, 71, 80
Linen Legion, 64-5
Livy, 31
logistics, 11
looting, 49
Luceria, 64
Lucius Tarquinius Priscus, 35
Lucretia, 32
Lucius Tarquinius Superbus, 32
Lusitania, 113, 119

Macedonian Wars, 111ff, 119
Maenius Antiaticus, Gaius, 59-60
Magna Graecia, 66
Magnesia ad Sipylum, 115
Manlian Orders, 58
Manlian Pass, 116
Marcellus, Marcus Claudius, 85, 94
Marius, 21, 26, 92, 128, 129, 130, 132
Masinissa, 104, 105, 106, 112, 123, 124
Mediolanum, 85
Megiddo, Battle of, 12
Mesopotamia, 10
Messana, 75
Metaurus River, 102
Metellus, Lucius Caecilius, 80
Mons Algidus, 44, 46
Mons Gaurus, 57
Mons Tifernum, 62
Mons Vesuvius, 59, 59
Mus, Publius Decius, 57, 58, *59*, 60
Mus, Publius Decius, (son of the above), 62-63
Muthul River, 128
mutiny, 58, 64, 72, 82
Mylae, 76

Narmer Palette, 10
naval warfare, 11, 13, 14, 21, *23*, 60-61, 69, 75,
    76-77, 105, 106, 114, 125
Nepheris, 124
Nola, 94
Numantia, 120
Numidia, 74, 99-100, 101-102, 123-124, 129

Onasander, 28
One Day War, 36
Orosius, 63
Ovid, 9

Panormus, 80, 114 (190 BC)
Partheniae, 66
pay, army, 20, 22, 37, 47, 51
Pedum, 56, 60 (338 BC)
Peloponnesian Wars, 14, 16
Persians and **Persian Wars, 14, 15, 16**
Perseus of Macedon, 118
Phalanna, 117
phalanx, 14, 51, 75, 92
Pharos, 86
Philip II of Macedon, 15
Philip V, 111, 117
Phthia, 67
pietas, 33, 43, 50
polis, 13, 30, 66
Polybius, 28, 75, 125-126
population of Rome and her territories, 53
proletarii, 129, 132
psychological warfare, 69-70
Punic Wars, 21, 51, 72ff, 87ff, 123ff, 130
Pydna, 119
Pyrrhus, 63, 66ff, 75
Pythium, 118

rape, 12, 13, 26, 27, 33, 35, 106, 111
Rhodanus, River, 89
Roman territory, extent of, 53, 85
Rome, sack of, 49, 51, *52*, 92
Romulus, 31
Rufus, Publius Rutilius, 128
Rullianus, Quintus Fabius Maximus, 61

Sabines, 33, 34, 35
Saguntum, 77-78
Saguntum, siege of, 88
Salaeca, 104
Sallust, 26
sambuca, *97, 99*
Samnite War, First, 57; Second, 61; Third, 62
Sardinia, 82, 95, 117
Saticula, 57
Satricum, 55
Scaevola, Gaius Mucius, 32-33
Scipio Aemilianus, P. Cornelius, 119, 120, 125
Scipio Africanus, Publius Cornelius 92, 100, 101,
    103, 106, *109*
Scipio, L. Cornelius, 114, 115
Scipio Nasica, Publius Cornelius, 113
Scipio, Publius Cornelius, father of Scipio
    Africanus 85
Scarphea, 121-122

Scodra, 118
Second Punic War, 19, 87ff
Sentinum, 62
Servius Tullius, 18-19
Sextus Tarquinius, 34
Sibylline Books, 90
Sicily, 72ff, 81, 101, 104, 126
siege warfare, 11, 28, *97-98,* 99
Signia, 55-56
Silva Arsia, Battle of, 32
single combat, 32, 56, 58, 71, 85, 119
slaves, slavery and enslavement, 46, 54, 88, 95,
    111, 117, 12, 122, 125, 129, 132
Sophinisba, 105
Sparta, 13, 14, 15, 16, 66
spolia opima, 20, 45, 85
Standard of Ur wall panel, 10
Stele of the Vultures of Lagash, 10
Strabo, 49, 131
strategy and tactics, 28, 43, 56-7, 64-5, 78, 91,
    104
Suessula, 57
Sulla, 28, 36, 129, 132
Sumerians, 10-11
Suthul, 127
Sutrium, 55
Syphax, 104, 105
Syracuse, 76, 95f
Syracuse, siege of, 96, *97*
Syria, 115

Tagus River, 116
Tarentum, 66, 69
Tarentum, Battle of, 69
Tarpeia, 33
Tarquinius Superbus, 41
Telamon, 84, 130
Temple of Janus, 18, 84
testudo, 53, 63
Teuta, Queen, 85
Teutoburg Forest, 92

Teutones, 131, 132
Thermae Himerienses, 77
Thermopylae, 113
Thucydides, 13-14, 69-70
Ticinus River, 91-2
Titus Manlius Torquatus, 56, 58, 60
tolerance of the vanquished, 11
Trajan's Column, 28
Trebia River, 91-2
tribune of the plebs, 55-56
Trifanum, 59
triumph, 20, *23,* 46, 51, 60, 77
Tullus Hostilius, 31
Tyndaris, 78

Uscana, 118
Utica, 104

Vegetius, 28
Veii, 18, 31, 32, 34, 46, 49
Veii, Battle of, 43
Vercellae, 132
Vestal Virgins, 50
Virgil, 26, 31, 90
Viriathus, 120, *121*
virtus, 27, 43
Volsci, 36, 42
Volturnus, River 62

weapons, 19
wives, 12, 13, 27, 124, 125, 132
women, 12, 15, 18, 19, 27, 28, 46, 49, 50, 75, 104,
    122, 131, 132
women, Sabine, 33-34, *37*
women chariot race victors, 15-16

yoke, under the, 44, *45,* 64, 128, 131

Zama, *68,* **105,** *109*
Zosimus, 28